MW01233731

ONE *for* ALL

THE BIBLICAL VERSION OF SALVATION

www.danielhilliard.com

Contact Information:
danielhilliard@yahoo.com
daniel@danielhilliard.com

HIAWATHA BOOKS
Durham, NC

HIAWATHA BOOKS
Durham, NC

TABLE OF CONTENT

About Scripture References and Definitions

Scriptures: Unless otherwise indicated, "Scripture taken from the NEW AMERICAN STANDARD BIBLE®, Copyright © 1960, 1962, 1963, 1968, 1971, 1972, 1973, 1975, 1977 by The Lockman Foundation. Used by permission."

Additionally, selected words in certain passages of Scripture will be bracketed; those words are enhanced or are replaced with either the definitions from the Strong's Hebrew and Greek Dictionaries of the Bible (see full description below) or modern-day language.

Definitions: The main source for Hebrew and Greek word definitions was "The Exhaustive Concordance of the Bible: Showing every word of the text of the common English version of the Canonical Books, and every occurrence of each word in regular order; together with Dictionaries of the Hebrew and Greek Words of the original, with reference to the English words: By James Strong, S.T.D., LL.D. Hendrickson Publishers, Peabody, Massachusetts 01961-3473."

Dedication

This book is dedicated to my parents:

Hiawatha B. and Minnie R. Hilliard

INTRODUCTION

The first objective of this book is to explain *how* mankind came to need salvation from the powers of Satan and Sin. The second objective is to describe *how* God began and accomplished the initial process of salvation for EVERYONE.

Neither the explanation nor the description is taken from any one particular religious denominational creed. The *Holy Bible* and the *Strong's Exhaustive Concordance [and Dictionary] of the Bible* are the main material sources for the contents of this book.

Obviously, the details or *facts* of *salvation* differ among the many Christ-centered religious denominations that have been officially and unofficially established worldwide. And, even though there tends to be agreement on *the need for salvation*, there is still division surrounding the facts of *how* and *when* salvation is accomplished.

Facts are specific details or essential pieces of information, which, when used in the proper context, reveal **TRUTH**. But, having a *few* facts does not result in seeing the complete truth of a topic, just like connecting together a *few* pieces of a jigsaw puzzle will not reveal the complete picture the puzzle is intended to convey.

Also, while working on this project, I have gained a better Scriptural understanding of the core of the Christian doctrine: **faith**. To this day, the topic of *faith* is misunderstood and misrepresented among most Christian-based denominations.

Most believers perceive faith as being difficult and fleeting. That is why *it* has been either elevated, so as to become an obsession and/or the pinnacle of major religious denominations, or it has been degraded, so that it can be conveniently side-stepped or perceived as being easily obtained.

Yes; **faith in the unseen God and in spiritual principles is very necessary to have.** But faith in God was intended to be the results of a quality decision, **based on what has been *seen* and heard from Him;** faith was not meant to be a completely blind requirement.

SECTION I

The First Adam

Note to the Reader:

There is an alternate *opening* to Chapter One. The alternate, which begins on **page 275**, is titled, *Genesis*. That version lightly touches on the concepts of space and time; specifically, as these relate to **the first three days of Creation**. It combines Scripture—verses from the Holy Bible with a widely accepted modern-day scientific theory to support the case that the Earth might actually be much older than 7,000-plus calendar years, as based on the 24/7/365-time calculations that are widely known and used in modern civilizations, today.

Chapter 1

What Is Man?

The first book in the Holy Bible is titled, **Genesis**, which means *origin* or *beginning*. Genesis Chapter One is a summary of what happened during the Six Days of Creation: **Jehovah God** stretched out this physical universe (Isaiah 45:12a) or this **one** (uni) **existence** (verse), and then created the Earth and its inhabitants.

God verbally declared what He wanted to happen and/or described how He wanted something to be arranged; then, the thing happened or He *made* and arranged the thing(s) exactly how He wanted. No details are given as to *how* the things God called for came to be; however, that pattern changed on the sixth day.

Unlike prior events, the creation of man did *not* begin with an outward command, as if God was still calling out for additional furnishings. Instead, it began with a statement that would reveal the purpose for, and the crowning achievement of, His creation.

> *Then God said, "Let Us make*[H6213] *man in Our image, according to Our likeness; and let them rule...."*
>
> *Genesis 1:26a*

Also, unlike the other aspects of Creation, Genesis chapter 2, beginning with verse 4, gives us a bit more details of *how* God created **man, for whom the Earth was made.**

> *Then the Lord God [squeezed into shape or molded into form,*[H3335] *man or A-d-a-m, out of the dust or clay from the (reddish) soil] ....*
>
> *Genesis 2:7a*

"Adam" was not just a random name given to the first human, such as Chris or Brandon. A-d-a-m[1] is the English language's version of a Hebrew language word, which has a root meaning of either *a human person* or *the whole species of humanity*. Therefore, **Adam was the first one of a new *kind* of creature**: human- or **man-*kind***.

Although Adam was to be made in God's image, the life*less* physical mass that was first formed out of clay or soil was NOT the image of God; because, **God *is* Spirit** (John 4:24a).

In the Strong's Dictionary, the root definition of the word ***spirit***[2] is ***wind, breath,*** *or a current of air*. The secondary or common rendering of the word ***spirit*** is ***courage*** or ***mind***.

So, from man*kind*'s perspective, **God Is BREATH** (Life) **and MIND** (absolute **Love** [1 John 4:16], **Truth** [Hebrews 6:18a], and **Knowledge** [Proverbs 8:14]).

I am aware that some people may object to using the word "mind" as a definition of the word *spirit*, especially when applied to Jehovah God; because, the *mind* is, now, considered finite—limited, and it is the source for bad (*i.e.,* corrupt, immoral, etc.) behavior. But the mind is spiritual: it is the portion of the *unseen self* that makes a person unique, much like physical DNA or a fingerprint. Additionally, the finite and negative attributes that are *now* associated with the mind are not applicable to God; nor was Adam originally created with a **de**generate mind, as is inherent, today.

> *[Then the Lord God] breathed into [Adam's nostrils, so as to inflate or kindle him with] the breath [wind, divine inspiration, intellect, or spirit] of life; and [the once lifeless Adam] became a living soul.*
>
> *Genesis 2:7b*

The Self-Existing God deposited Life, Eternity, and a hint of His complex awareness into a lifeless formation, and **Adam became a living soul** with a unique personality of his own.

---

[1] Strong's Exhaustive Concordance Of the Bible, Hebrew reference # 120

[2] Strong's Exhaustive Concordance Of the Bible, Hebrew reference #7307 and Greek reference # 4151

A living soul is something that is **natural to this planet**. It is a sentient (self-aware) *and* carnal (physical) life-form: **man-*kind* and beast-*kind***. Just to be clear: <u>the other creatures that God made on days five and six are *living souls*, too</u>. In the following passages, the words "life" and "creature" are the same Hebrew word (H5315) for *soul*: Genesis 1:20-21, 24, 30, 2:7, 19, 9:4, 10, 12, and 16. (KJV)

The primary definition of the word *soul* is *breathing creature*. The secondary and the more *commonly used* definitions are: *appetite, beast, body, breath, mind,* or *life*. As previously indicated, the sum total of both the primary and secondary definitions are equal to **a living soul, which is both physical *and* spiritual**.

The word **physical** describes something that relates to the *properties of matter*: **anything that occupies space**. In most cases, it is <u>something that can be physically handled</u>.

The word **Spiritual** describes something that is *non*-physical: it may be invisible (unseen) and/or intangible (undetectable). And, it can also describe something (*e.g.,* wind) that can be physically *felt*, or something (*e.g.,* light or a shadow) that can influence physical things; but, <u>it itself cannot be physically handled</u>.

Again, as previously stated and as the illustration below suggests, **a soul** consists of the physical **body** AND the spiritual **mind**. The

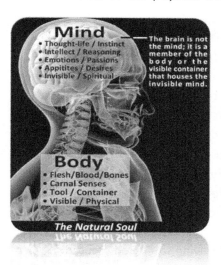

intricate blending of mind and body is like the simplistic *physical* relationship between a hand and a glove. When a *hand* is inside of a glove, <u>the two become as one</u>; but the movements or actions are governed by the hand, not the glove. That is why **the greatest potential of a soul comes from the unseen mind**. (As noted, the brain is only the physical container for the spiritual mind.)

By comparison, *all* souls or breathing creatures have a **base-animal-conscious**: the natural mind or carnal nature, which is used to process or contemplate our physical existence or **our physical experience**. As a result, a living soul (man or beast) will instinctively react to **circumstances**: what *is* physically happening, or what *has* physically happened, or what is assumed *may* happen, good or bad. Simply put, the natural mind will act only on the things that it can physically sense or, at most, reasonably predict.

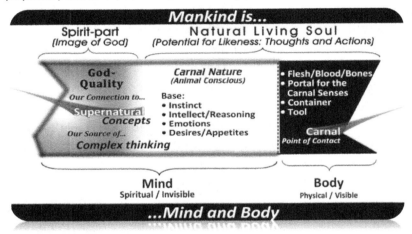

But Adam was different from the other souls. **He was an image of God** (Genesis 1:26a): **God breathed in a portion** of His Spirit-Self in a body that was designed to *primarily* experience this physical universe; and, that impartation meant **Adam had a spirit-mind-part** that could process supernatural concepts, **unlike the other souls**.

That spirit-part-of-mind also made man*kind immortal*. Immortality did *not* mean Adam could not experience physical death due to some form of physical trauma. Specifically, it meant **his mind was eternal and his physical body did not** deteriorate, or it did not decay and die, due to, what is referred to now as, *natural causes.*

The spirit-part-of-mind was also the source for complex thinking, which, when added to Adam's natural mind, made him—his overall mindset—different from the other living souls God created.

Adam was capable of complex reasoning in matters regarding his physical existence; and, more importantly, he had the ability to understand certain concepts from the spiritual universe of God. Among other things, **Adam had the God-like ability to mentally envision or see beyond *the way things physically are,* so as to be inspired by <u>the possibilities of *what can physically be*</u>**. All of which meant he was capable of more complex actions and achievements.

To further illustrate the difference between a human, which has a God-quality to enlighten his or her natural mind, and a common beast, which has only a carnal-based mind, is to describe what you, the Reader, is doing right now: reading and, hopefully, learning more about concepts that exceed the boundaries of our physical world. The abilities to have faith and to factor in unseen spiritual principles, especially about God, are higher mental qualities the other animal-souls do not possess, nor do they need to.

Also, the Holy Scripture actually gives an account of what happens to a human-soul when its higher consciousness or complex reasoning becomes *completely* inaccessible. The Old Testament's book of Daniel, Chapter 4, describes how a king, named Nebuchadnezzar, was so full of pride that he began to equate himself with Jehovah God. (See also Daniel 5:18-20.)

So, he was given a more realistic life experience without his God-part. The spirit-part of Nebuchadnezzar's mind became *inaccessible*; and, quite naturally, he began behaving like a common beast of the field (*e.g.*, an ox or deer). For seven [years] he ate grass; and, his hair grew, as if like feathers; and, his nails grew, as if like claws. After seven [years], the spirit-part of King Nebuchadnezzar's mind was again accessible and his higher reasoning was restored (4:34).

In God's Image, According to God's Likeness

> *And God [El-o-heem] created [Adam, mankind, or man (of low degree)] in His own image, in the image of God He created him;*
>
> *Genesis 1:27a*

The word image[3] has both spiritual and physical definitions.

Spiritually, **an image is a** *shade* (shadow) **or** *phantom* (mental representation). Physically, **an image is an** *idol* (statue) **or** *figure* (figurine). Both categories of definitions have the same implication: a *thing* that represents someone or something *greater* than itself.

Although Adam was an image of God and he was made to be *like* God on earth, he was *not* exactly the same as, or identical to, God.

For example, when light is present, an object is capable of casting shade or a shadow. In this case, the Light (enlightenment, brilliance, and wisdom) of God cast a mental shadow or a representation of His own Authority onto the earth, in the form of Adam—man*kind*. But again, **the shadow is only evidence of something more "real" and "greater" than itself**.

A shadow exists in fewer dimensions than its source (*i.e.*, visibly, it has width and length), whereas anything that can cast a shadow, regardless of angle or direction from which the light shines on it, is, at least, multi-dimensional (having, at least, width, length, and depth), regardless of how thin or gaseous it may be. Since a shadow exists in fewer dimensions, it will not possess the exact properties or the same intricate details of the source.

Therefore, a shadow is not an exact duplicate of the source; but, it can or will appear to mimic the source's behavior.

If the goal is to define *an image of God*, then it is *more appropriate* to apply the spiritual definition of *shade* (shadow) or *phantom* (mental representation), because **no physical form is capable of** *looking* **like God**, who is *non*-physical. Of course, the plan was for Adam to be in the *image* and the *likeness* of God.

> The *image* **part**, which referred to his higher consciousness and **connection to eternity**, was something God did. **The** *likeness* **part**, which referred to his God-like authority and power on Earth, was something **Adam had to maintain and workout to completion**.

---

[3] Strong's Exhaustive Concordance Of the Bible, Hebrew reference #6754

The word *likeness*[4] implies something identical [in composition or makeup], or something that has the same mannerism and/or purpose as the original. Since Adam was an image of God mentally, it was possible for him to **physically behave and sound *like* God**, on Earth.

Skipping ahead quite a bit chronologically, this is the same principle Jesus touched on when He said the following:

> **"[Anyone] who has seen [stared at, clearly discerned or took notice of] Me has seen [stared at or clearly discerned] the Father;"**

> *John 14:9b*

God does not look *like* Jesus' physical form.

As a man, Jesus willingly chose, not only to *know*, but He chose to also *have, the Mind of God*. As a result, He naturally behaved and sounded *like* God; and, His only purpose was to do God's Will.

Therefore, when people took notice of Jesus, in reality, they were *seeing* and *hearing* a physical version of God. *That* is the glorious **potential** the first Adam—man*kind*—had, in the beginning.

A *natural* living soul—animal or human—can mentally analyze or contemplate multiple viewpoints: past, present and, to a certain extent, the future, as it relates to projections or predictions, based on repeating patterns or cycles and estimations. But Adam was God's shadow. That meant he could see more comprehensive and complex viewpoints than the limited ones the natural mind can see by itself. For example, in accordance with his God-given authority to rule, if needed, he could have learned to declare changes in the things that already existed; and, if needed, he could have learned to call forth things into existence that did not exist.

Just to be clear: man*kind* has the *potential* to *look* and *sound like* God on earth; but it is not an entitlement or a guarantee that he will be God-like simply because he has knowledge of that truth.

---

[4] Strong's Exhaustive Concordance Of the Bible, Hebrew reference #1823

God's Breath *in* Man

The root definitions of the word **Breath**[5] are: *wind*, **divine** *inspir*ation or **intellect**. To *inspire* means to **awaken the mind**, to *cause creativity*, or to *breathe in (-to)*. The implication being: *to give, to impart, or to convey an idea, concept, courage, or other such mental qualities* that **stimulate thought or physical activity**.

In Nature, *all living souls,* including man*kind,* are **sustained** by the Earth's lower or natural atmosphere: the breathable air-pressure that exists within the space between the ground and upper atmosphere. Scripturally, it would seem **the animals**—the other living souls—**took their *first* breath from, and they were mentally awakened by, the Earth's natural atmosphere**.

But again, Adam was different. **His *first* breath or mental awakening came directly from God,** who is Spirit and supernatural.

That meant the following:

- Adam initially received divine inspiration from a universe or an existence that is above (as it relates to order and rank) this physical one; which meant...

- **ADAM DID NOT MERELY RELY ON BASIC SURVIVAL INSTINCTS AND APPETITES** that are limited to this physical world like the other animals in Nature; which meant...

- Adam's hopes or expectations were *not* initially governed merely by circumstances or by his physical senses of sight, sound, touch, taste and smell.

Adam was an interface.

An interface is a *go-between*: it connects two or more *things* that would not otherwise fit or join directly together. In this case, **Adam bridged or connected two dissimilar *universes* together**: the **spirit**ual universe of God and this physical one.

More specially, his MIND experienced and/or touched both the SPIRIT realm and the CARNAL—physical—realm.

---

[5] Strong's Exhaustive Concordance Of the Bible, Hebrew reference #5397

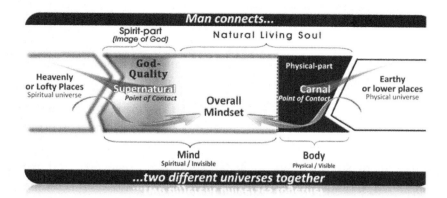

The spirit *in* Adam referred to the divine mixture of air or breath he continually breathed, which also circulated *in his blood-stream* throughout his physical body, to sustain his life. The spirit *of* Adam referred to *the eternal God-like part of his mind*, from which came a higher sense of consciousness, discernment, and thought.

Adam's Purpose

And God blessed them; and God said to them, "Be fruitful and multiply, and fill the earth, and subdue it;"

Genesis 1:28a

Physically, Adam was the first one of his *kind*. But, as the term *A d a m* implies, when God looked at what He had formed from the ground and then gave life to, He saw ALL of humanity.

That's the reason why He called the formation "them;" that's the reason why He blessed "them;" and, that's the reason why He intended for "them" to subdue and to rule.

As the first one of his *kind*, the individual called, Adam, had three primary responsibilities:

1. To stand before God and receive the blessing (verbal adoration) and the earthly authority God gave to his *kind* being, based on their uniqueness.

2. To set the tone or pattern of agreement with God's plan for his *kind*.

3. To reproduce his own *kind* and grow them up in unity, based on their unique mental abilities, and based on the blessing and Authority they received from God.

To *subdue*[6] means to tread down, **force and bring into bondage**. To *rule*[7] means to prevail against, reign or have dominion over. That meant, even though Adam was the designated ruler or first-in-rank on Earth, he still had to **establish** (and *not merely* receive) a God-like dominion or kingdom, even *within* themselves. Only then could he ensure that God's Will or His determination would be done on Earth *and* in the world, as it is in done Heaven.

Before continuing, here's an important side note:

> Although the words *Earth* and *world* seem to be the same, these words have different Biblical meanings. The word **Earth** [(H776)] **is** defined as **the firm, hard, dry ground;** in essence, **the planet.** The basic root meaning for the word **world** [(H8398)] **is moist *[top soil]*;** but, more commonly, it refers to **anything that adorns or decorates the Earth,** *such as* **vegetation, trees,** and *all living souls*—*man and animals.*
>
> The most significant use of the word **world implies** the Earth's **human inhabitants** and their overall collective behavior or character, **whether good or evil.** Therefore, the phrase **God so loved the world** does not describe God's unconditional love for the planet, **but His love for humanity** and for everything else that naturally decorates the Earth.

Adam was *never* given permission to rule over his fellowman-*kind*; neither was he given ownership of the Earth. He was only given the mandate to be the ruling authority or first-in-rank; and, even then, he was supposed to share that God-given authority with the rest of his own *kind*—those also in the image of God.

---

[6] Strong's Exhaustive Concordance Of the Bible, Hebrew reference # 3533

[7] Strong's Exhaustive Concordance Of the Bible, Hebrew reference # 7287

Adam's *Original* Virtue

To use a familiar phrase for comparison: Adam was *innocent as a newborn baby*. That's **not** to say he was naïve or had the intelligence of a newborn baby. To the contrary, by today's standards, Adam was very intelligent: he gave meaningful names to *every* species of animal (Genesis 2:19), and he could remember those names.

I have no doubt that Adam utilized his physical brain's full potential, due to his fully *active* God-consciousness or spirit-part. After all, he was an image of God.

To be *innocent is to be clean, pure or free from guilt* and, therefore, *free from any possibility of a penalty or punishment.* Adam wasn't innocent by choice; he was innocent because *he was* a new creature, as in the case of a newborn child.

But the fact that Adam was innocent and extremely intelligent did *not*, necessarily, mean he would make a dependable and righteous ruler. **He also needed to be faithful** to, and fully persuaded of, God's original purpose for his life.

To be *faithful* is to be *free of guilt, by remaining obedient* to a commandment, or by staying on course, *while being confronted with opposition.* As a result, a person is not only free of any guilt and liability, but he or she is considered to be "tried and true," due to his or her willingness to remain obedient or committed.

Therefore, **in order for Adam to be proven faithful** to God's purpose for his life, **he had to willingly submit or be obedient to a commandment that was related to his purpose.**

But first, he needed a place to live.

Chapter 2

THE GARDEN

And the Lord God planted a garden toward the East, in Eden; and there He placed the man whom He had formed.

And out of the ground the Lord God caused to grow every tree that is pleasing to the sight and good for food; the tree of life also in the midst of the garden, and the tree of [knowing by recognizing] good and evil.

Genesis 2:8-9

Alone, Adam could not possibly subdue, care for, and guard the entire Earth. Therefore, Jehovah God planted a garden or provided a smaller area for him to live in and manage.

Then the Lord God took the man and [caused him to rest or settle down in] the Garden of Eden to cultivate it and keep it.

And the Lord commanded the man, saying, "[Eating, you may eat] from any tree of the garden;

"But from the tree of the knowledge of good and evil you shall not eat, for [the day] that you eat from it [dying, you shall die or you shall die a death]."

Genesis 2:15-17

The very first commandment emphasized humanity's freedom to eat from *every* tree, except one. Although the exact number of trees that were in the Garden is unknown, there was, probably, a lot of them. Most likely, the trees numbered in the thousands; especially since there were animals in the Garden, too.

This first commandment did *not* represent some divine test to determine Adam's worthiness or loyalty to God; nor did it unfairly tempt Adam with, as if to deny him, something more pleasurable than what was already available to him in large numbers.

What Are Commandments and Why Do We Need Them?

Scripturally, commandments are a set of instructions. These instructions describe and define how the recipients of either a blessing (verbal adoration) or a gift from God should conduct themselves *before and after* the blessing or gift has become a reality in this physical world.

Jehovah God blesses people for specific reasons; and, in most cases, every gift He gives has a specific purpose. That means His commandments are *NOT* like the conditions we often place on each other: *treats for good behavior* and *punishment for bad behavior*.

There are at least two reasons why God gives commandments to those whom He has blessed or to whom He has Promised something:

1. To *prepare* (equip and *position*) people to *receive, utilize,* and *preserve* what He Promised to them.
2. To allow people—not God—to continually gauge for themselves just how much *they* honor (*i.e.,* value) Him and His Promises.

Therefore, if God does withhold or remove a Promised gift from someone, due to their disobedience, it is only because their disobedience is an indication of an impure heart towards Him. In other words, **if the intended recipients develop an unwillingness to honor God, then, eventually, they will misuse His gift**.

To further illustrate this point, imagine a father (in this time period) has just promised to give his teenage son a new car. But immediately after making the promise, the father commands or instructs his son to obtain a driver's license *before* he can receive the car. Additionally, the son must *maintain* a good driving record after receiving the car, in order to be able to keep it.

The commandment to obtain a driver's license is **not** the same kind of a *condition* where the son must faithfully mow the lawn or perform other chores, as if to earn the gift. The father loves and adores his son, and he sincerely wants to give him the car as a gift— not as a reward.

On the one hand, if the son is fully persuaded that his father has both the resources and the determination to give him the car, then that persuasion or faith becomes a sure foundation on which his father's promise will stand. More importantly, if the son is confident that his father loves him, then that confidence will support or validate the sincerity of the commandment, even though obeying it might be inconvenient or challenging for the son.

Therefore, because the son believes his father is trustworthy, he will honor his father by obeying the commandment: the son will gladly discipline himself to study and do whatever else it takes to obtain a driver's license. As a result of his faithfulness to the commandment, the son will become *legally* prepared to operate and fully enjoy the car at the appointed time.

Additionally, if the son continues to honor his father by maintaining a good driving record, then he is providing evidence of his faithfulness, which means he is proving himself to be a good steward (caretaker) of what has been given to him. The father, then, will readily give the best he has to his son, because he knows he can trust his son with the very best.

On the other hand, if the son does *not* obey his father's commandment to obtain a driver's license, then he is either revealing a lack of trust in his father's motives for giving the commandment; or he is expressing disbelief in his father's ability to give the car as promised. Either way, the son is indicating he does *not* honor (heavily value) his father.

But even if the son chooses *not* to honor and obey his father, the promise of the car will never be withdrawn; because, **the commandment** to obtain a driver's license **was *not* the foundation on which the promise was made**. The promise was based on love, alone. However, access to and enjoyment of the car will be delayed until the son chooses to truly honor his father and properly prepare himself to receive the gift.

The point is: it would be irresponsible of, and unwise for, the father to grant his son *full* access to the car; because, **it would be *illegal* for the ill prepared and unlicensed son to drive**.

In a similar way, Adam's *response* to God's commandment became the measuring stick that revealed how much honor (weightiness or value) he gave to God. And that level of honor determined Adam's ability to accurately *use* and *maintain* the authority God entrusted to him.

An examination of the big picture reveals that the first commandment was intended to do the following:

1. To express God's <u>original</u> intention for us: man*kind* should only know "good" or pleasurable things.

2. To reveal the presence of adversity (*i.e.*, Satan) or opposition to God's intention and Will for humanity.

3. To reveal man*kind*'s freedom of choice: either to see and know only what God wanted him to, or to see and know *more*. In this case, more was *not* better.

Adam's obedient or disobedient response to God determined how **accurately** he would *fill* (adorn or decorate) the Earth with the image and likeness of God. That's because his response represented how much he—man*kind*—honored God.

Of course, before there could be more of his *kind*, Adam needed someone with whom to procreate.

A Helpmate

"It is not good for the man to be alone; I will make him a helper corresponding to him."

Genesis 2:18

Before making a *mate* for the man Adam, God brought every species of animal and bird to him, in order to see what he would name each *kind of being* (Genesis 2:19). By doing so, God accomplished at least two things.

- First, God validated man*kind*'s responsibility to be the ruler or *first in rank* by having him give names to all the other breathing animals or souls.

- Second, God revealed to A-d-a-m the uniqueness of *his kind* from all the *other kinds* of breathing souls; none of them were appropriate or fitting for him (Genesis 2:20b).

God then put Adam to sleep and removed a rib^H6763 or a *side* from him (most likely, his more feminine mental expressions); and, with *that* He built^H1129 the same *kind* of life-form. But the other formation or body was slightly different, because it was fitted *for* him and designed for reproduction. And, just as He had done before, God then presented this other formation or person to Adam for him to name.

> *And [Adam] said, "This is now bone of my bones, and flesh of my flesh; [this (one of mankind)] shall be called woman [or fe-male], because [this (one)] was taken out of man [or male]."*

Genesis 2:23

Since male and female are physically compatible, Adam declared a union of marriage between him and her. He recognized that *wo*man (or man*kind* with a womb) was an expression and a characteristic that was *taken* out of man (-kind).

Adam had the godly wisdom to foresee the following: in marriage (*i.e.*, in dwelling together or (sexual) cohabitation), woman would *be separated* from her original source of identity or family name, in order to be joined to a male of man*kind*. Therefore, it is only right that the male should also *separate* himself from his father's house, in order to build his own house and increase his own family's name.

And, the man and the woman shall, again, become one unified person (Genesis 2:24), as it was in the beginning, before God separated or took *her* out of *them*.

And the man and his wife were both naked and were not ashamed.

Genesis 2:25

Chapter 3

THE LIE

The Messenger

Compared to all the other species, the serpent was the most resourceful and cunning (Genesis 3:1), but in a sneaky way. That meant its *kind* was the logical choice to be a messenger of deception: a smooth talker that was capable of hiding a lie in plain sight. The serpent was *not* the source of the lie, which he told to Adam and Eve. The source was Satan, who is the father of *all* lies (John 8:44).

It is not clear from the Scripture if Satan forcibly possessed—overtook the *will* of—the serpent and then spoke his message of deception through it, or if the serpent willingly adopted Satan's deceitful plan. I believe it was the latter: a mutual arrangement.

Satan, a *spirit*ual or nonphysical being, needed a soul that was natural to this world and recognizable to humanity, in order to deliver his spiritual plan of deception. The serpent was the likely choice, I believe, because it was easily captivated and amused by the thought of out-smarting humanity. As such, its species would enjoy the reputation of being more cunning than man*kind*—the ones chosen by God (Genesis 1:28).

The Main Opponent

Satan is not merely a name; it is a term that describes a character or nature. *S-a-t-a-n*[8] is the English language translation of a Hebrew language word, which is defined as *opponent, adversary,* or *to resist.* As will be revealed shortly, by his very nature and name, Satan is an adversary of Godliness, regarding this physical creation or world.

To be perfectly clear, **Satan is not a direct adversary or opponent of God**. He and God have NOT been at war for countless millennia.

---

[8] Strong's Exhaustive Concordance Of the Bible, Hebrew reference # 7854

Satan is not on God's level: **he is *something* created *by* God**. Satan's only avenue of opposition was to try and obscure and/or complicate the plan God had for this physical creation. Ultimately, he did so by sowing seeds of confusion and suspicion, which lead to disobedience within creation itself. That strategy was familiar to him, because *disobedience to God's plans* originated in him when he chose to reject his own original purpose.

As background, **before** this physical universe was completed (as described during the six days of creation), the individual known as Satan was originally named, Lucifer. The name Lucifer[9] means *star of the morning or son of the dawn*.

Although the Holy Bible, chronologically, begins with the creation of this physical universe, God used various passages contained in the Old Testament (OT) to describe events that happened *before* the creation of man*kind*; Isaiah 14:12-17 and Ezekiel 28:12-19 are such passages. At first glance, these passages seem to describe the downfall of two human kings.

But, in actual fact, they give us insight into the downfall and fate of Lucifer. The two kings were merely following in Lucifer's misguided footsteps: their circumstances were alike.

For example, Ezekiel Chapter 28 is about the physical and spiritual rulers of Tyre: verses 1-10 are about the man whom God, more realistically, referred to as merely *the prince* of Tyre; and, verses 11-19 are about the *king* or the actual ruling authority of Tyre, Satan.

At his creation, Lucifer was *a* work of art: he had a ***perfect balance*** of wisdom and beauty.

> *"[You were the mark, the end-product, or the sum-total of all things created—you were the fullness of wisdom and entirely beautiful.]"*
>
> *Ezekiel 28:12b (Defined)*

---

[9] Strong's Exhaustive Concordance Of the Bible, Hebrew reference # 1966

But Lucifer began to base his self-worth and his identity on his God-given beauty, instead of on his purpose. And, as with any balanced scale (*i.e.,* one used to determine value), the results of adding more weight to one side meant reducing the worth or value  of the other side. In this case, when Lucifer enlarged and added more weight to his beauty, he naturally devalued his wisdom, which was directly related to, or appraised for, his original purpose.

> *"Your heart was lifted up because of your beauty;*
> *you corrupted your wisdom [or caused it to decay,*
> *be ruined, or wasted] by reason of your splendor."*

> *Ezekiel 28:17a-b*

Lucifer's mind began to fill with self-inspired pride, which soon led to self-inspired ambition that caused him to rebel against his original purpose. As previously indicated, at his creation, he was the *pièce de résistance* [a French term describing that *the best was saved for last* (*i.e.,* the masterpiece—the most outstanding item in a series of artistic works)] among the spiritual things God made, *before* He made and arranged the physical things we see and understand, now.

For example, consider the following analogy:

> If one person was multi-talented enough to be a chief architect, a master craftsman, a renowned artist, and a professional landscaper, and he/she built a house for him/herself, naturally, this person would incorporate the best of his/her experience and creativity into its design and decoration. The land is seeded with the best grass; and, it would the most luscious fruit trees, and have multiple gardens adorned with the most vibrant-colored flowers.

> The exterior of the house is magnificently grand. Inside, each room is as exquisite as the next. And, in the center of this house is a large majestic room with a glass ceiling; and, the walls of this room are painted with living animated colors too bright and too deep to name.

The furnishings of this room are the most elegant and well-crafted pieces known to exist. And, in the center of this large room stands the most perfect and the most beautiful living piece of art that is adorned with precious jewels. Out of all the beauty that exists on the outside and on the inside of this house, this artwork was the *pièce de résistance*: the one thing or *the one piece among many that is the most difficult to resist admiring or desiring.*

When people tour this magnificent house, they are amazed at the outside—the landscape and the exterior; and they are amazed at the inside—the floors, the ceilings, the walls, and the furnishings. But, when they enter the center room and see that masterpiece, their breath is taken away by the perfect details and absolute beauty of that special, living work of art.

So, to fully appreciate it, they gaze at it for an extended period of time: they are in awe of it. But then they naturally look to, and admire, applaud, praise or glorify [speak well of], the one who had the means and creative mind to make such a remarkable *thing*.

The creation of Lucifer was similar, but on a vastly larger scale. God created a spiritual dwelling place filled with wonderful things. He also created Lucifer, an anointed cherub—angelic-like being that had outstretched wings. Lucifer had perfect beauty, so that when the angels saw him, they were in awe; but then, they would naturally—no prompting necessary—glorify God, as the Creator.

However, Lucifer's heart soon became tarnished or polluted with pride when he began to self-identify with his beauty: he sought to take full ownership of it. Meaning, when others looked upon him, he desired to receive their praises, as if praises were due him, exclusively, as the source of such beauty, instead of its vessel.

As a result of the pride or **high-mindedness that was self-generated in him**, he began to see himself as being *like* God. So, he sought to set himself above all created things—the angels—to be worshiped (adored) and revered by them (Ref. Isaiah 14:13-14).

In such instances of heart-felt rebellion, usually, there is an immediate punishment: the loss of favor and/or position. In his case, Lucifer was *weakened* or perforated, which means to pierce through [with holes, for the purpose of easily tearing, as with paper], and he was cast down from the high places of God (Ref. Luke 10:18).

That immediate punishment—being cast down—**and a future punishment yet to come are final** (Ref. Jude 6). That is to say, there is no room for debate or repentance; because, **Lucifer was neither tempted nor deceived—adversely inspired—by anyone else**.

Lucifer was the author, the originator, or the father of opposition to God's Will. As a result, he became [the] *Satan* or the Adversary.

To repeat, **Satan is not in the same class as God** in terms of wisdom, authority, and abilities. As a matter of fact, in regards to *this* physical universe and world, Satan had no authority whatsoever, until it was given to him by man, as we will soon see.

The Plan of Attack

As an agent of Satan, the serpent began with **phase-one of the plan: distort the original instructions God gave**. The point was to see if Adam and Eve knew *and* could agree upon what God said.

The serpent, apparently, spoke with Eve only, even though Adam was there *with* her (Genesis 3:6e). The serpent said to her, "*Indeed, has God said you shall* **not** *eat from* **any** *tree of the Garden?*" (Genesis 3:1)

Eve gave their response; and, since Adam remained silent, there was agreement. Of course, Eve's answer did seem to include an additional restriction to what is recorded as being God's original commandment. She seemed to have added, *they were not even supposed to* **touch** *the tree* of knowledge (Genesis 3:3).

Whether she added that part or that was how Adam relayed the instructions to her, the serpent could neither confuse the overall instructions, nor could he cause disagreement between them on what God said. Therefore, he proceeded with **phase-two: distort God's reason or motive for giving the commandment**.

The strategy behind this second phase was simple: if he could successfully cast a shadow of doubt or suspicion on God's sincerity and motive for giving the commandment, then the serpent could easily **convince Eve *not* to trust God**. And, if he could convince her not to trust God, then he could just as easily overshadow and **devalue the truth of the unseen penalty** for violating the commandment.

The serpent first **suggested**, *maybe* they would *not* die a death (Genesis 3:4). He then added, "For God knows that in the day you eat from [the tree of knowledge] your eyes will be opened, and you will be *as* God, [being able to see and, therefore, recognize both] good *and* evil" (Genesis 3:5).

The serpent implied God was withholding or hiding something from them—something *more* than the "good" He had already provided for them. This suggested God was either being selfish or He really did not have their best interest at heart, because He was keeping them from knowing or recognizing *evil*.

The lie and its implications were as follows: if you *dis*obey and eat, you do not [really] die; instead, you gain *more* knowledge or awareness than you had before, and you become [more] *like* God.

The lie distorted actual facts, for the purpose of producing a desired result: mistrust in God. It was a fact that their eyes would be opened—they would be more *aware*—if they ate; and, it was a fact that they would be [more] like God, in that they would know or recognize both good *and* evil.

But alone, those two facts did not reveal the truth: God did not open their eyes to recognize *evil* (H7451: adversity or displeasure), because He is GOOD; He is eternal Light and Life. As such, something that is created in His image will only include His Nature.

The deceptive nature of Satan convinced Eve she could be more than a just created thing. She could become *as* the Creator or *equal* to Him.

Does that line of thinking sound familiar?

Misery does love company.

Exchanging the Truth

When the woman saw that the tree was good for food, and that it was a delight to the eyes; and that the tree was desirable to make one wise, she took [of or from it] and ate;

Genesis 3:6a

Eve was deceived or she was mentally led astray (Genesis 3:13 and 1-Timothy 2:14) from what she knew to be true **when she adopted the pride of Satan,** based on the suggestion of being *self-reliant*. Because of their conversation, she looked, again, and *saw* that the tree was a good source of food and that its fruit *looked* delicious; that, then, ignited lust in her. But, more importantly, she was *inspired* to believe the tree and its fruit were **able** to make a person crafty and intelligent.

By itself, *lust* is not bad. To *lust*[10] simply means to delight in, or to set the heart—mind—upon something and long for [it]. Yes, the Tree of Knowledge was *a delight to the eyes* and it was a *source of food*. But God made *all* the trees in the Garden that way (Genesis 2:9).

The bottom line: Eve was **self-confident** that she would become *even* more like God, if she ate from *that* tree, which was forbidden.

Pride (*i.e.,* haughtiness, self-glorification) is **self-inspired-confidence**—*I have what it takes….* It is **trusting solely in one's perceived abilities to rightly *judge* a matter,** even when there is little to no understanding: self-reliant.

Humility (*i.e.,* a willingness to *bend the knee* or to honor and/or submit to someone greater than our self) in the sight of God can lead to **divinely-inspired-confidence**—*I have been given what it takes….* It is choosing to side with a Divine Cause greater than our own. The basis of *true humility* is seeing or realizing, as king Nebuchadnezzar did, *without the God-part in us, mentally, we would not differ from the other types of animals.*

---

[10] Strong's Exhaustive Concordance Of the Bible, Hebrew reference # 2530, 8378, and Greek 1937

An abundance of **pride leads to disrespect** (*i.e.*, to disesteem and, eventually, de-value others, including God). In an intimate relationship, **disrespect leads to a dissatisfied heart**, which **can more easily lead to hostility** or *adversity* and separation.

Pride is *not* necessary to legally obtain and enjoy something delightful. But pride is the main driving force when attempting to obtain and enjoy something delightful <u>and</u> forbidden.

Satan's pride influenced and deceived Eve into placing greater mental weight and, thus, giving more value to the *assumed* gratification and empowerment that was *supposed* to follow a disobedient act. At the same time, she believed the benefits of being *like* God would place them out of reach of any punishment from God for their act of disobedience.

Therefore, the desire to eat soon outweighed and devalued God's commandment. Eve did *not* trust God enough to be satisfied with the *good* or the pleasure they already knew or recognized.

Instead, she actually desired to *recognize* and become acquainted with *evil* [adversity or uselessness] without knowing its meaning. Influenced by Satan's prideful mindset, she decided that knowing something *more* was be better; so, she ate from the tree and then offered the same decision to the male, Adam.

Adam was *not* [influenced and] **deceived** [by Satan] (1 Timothy 2:14). Worse, he deliberately *exchanged* the truth of God's Word and Will *for* Eve's word and *will*. Perhaps, at that time, he really did *think* she was more *like* God. After all, she had eaten and, apparently, she did not experience any *physical* signs of a penalty. If that was the case, then **Adam conveniently considered Eve**—the other one of his *kind* with whom he probably related to more than the *unseen* God—**to be a more reliable source in determining his value or worth**.

Most likely, Adam did not want to be *only*—alone, again: he wanted to be (*i.e.*, to think and act) like the other of his kind—to have a shared social identity. This is a mental rut that was inherited by—programmed into—everyone after them.

Although Eve ate from the tree first, **their eyes** were not opened until after the male, Adam, had eaten (Genesis 3:6 & 7). This meant ALL of man*kind* had disobeyed God, because Adam and Eve were EVERYONE on Earth, at the time. In that moment, man*kind*'s awareness or perception of things changed dramatically.

They knew or could recognize evil: **they became keenly aware of the many things that** *would* **naturally obscure and hinder their God-given vision and purpose in life**, respectively. Such things included their own physical frailties and limitations, which the glory and favor of God had originally covered (over) or supplemented.

It was painfully obvious: they were *not* equal to God.

Interestingly enough, in an effort to be free from the judgment of God and become self-sufficient, they chose to present themselves to, and side with, the opposition. That chose is also an inherent one, today.

Yes, **Adam and Eve were tricked by Satan**, but they were not blameless. Yes, like newborn babes, they were **un**informed or ignorant about the meaning and nature of *adversity* or evil; but that did *not* mean God left them vulnerable to attack.

The purpose for the commandment was NOT for them to make an "informed" decision. The purpose was for them to willingly "trust" God, their Creator, Whom they personally knew.

Had they simply obeyed the Word or commandment, which instructed them *not to eat from that tree*, **they** *would* **have successfully defended themselves against Sin and Satan, based on trust alone**. Most likely, there was apprehension or concerned, during Eve's conversation with the serpent; but, apparently, they simply *chose* to ignore or devalue that internal warning.

Chapter 4

SIN CAME INTO THE WORLD

[To Sin is to go against the law].

1 John 3:4b

The Holy Bible's Old Testament (OT), as we know it today, was originally translated from an ancient Hebrew language. Almost every time the word "sin" appears, it was translated from one of two *different* Hebrew words.

The same is also true in the Holy Bible's New Testament (NT), which was, most notably, originally written in Koine Greek. Of course, in this case, the word "sin" is translated from one of two *different* Greek words. Although there is a fundamental difference in the definition and use of each word for *sin* within each set (*i.e.,* one Hebrew and one Greek set of the two words), most English versions of the Holy Bible do not make a clear distinction.

The first set of words for Sin[11] is *khat-taw-aw'* in Hebrew and *ham-ar-tee'-ah* in Greek. Both words are defined as **an offence** (the British and most common version of the word is *offense*), which suggests *the very nature or essence of being offensive or unjust.*

The second set of words for sin[12] is *khaw-taw'* in Hebrew and *ham-ar-tan'-o* in Greek. Both words are defined as **to miss**. The Greek definition also adds the implication of *not sharing in the prize, because of missing the mark* or target.

In both Hebrew and Greek, the second word, which means *to miss*, is also the root or source word. For example, the OT's book of

---

[11] Strong's Exhaustive Concordance Of the Bible, Hebrew reference # 2403, Greek reference # 266

[12] Strong's Exhaustive Concordance Of the Bible, Hebrew reference # 2398, Greek reference # 264

Judges 20:16 gives a visual interpretation of this *root* word by describing *marksmen who could sling a stone at a [very small target] and not "sin" or miss the target.*

Throughout this book, a distinction will be made between the two sets of words. A capital "S" or *Sin* will be used when I am or the Scripture is referring to either an *offense* or **the very nature of Sin itself**; and a lowercase "s" or *sin* will be used when referring to a *mark missing* **(wrongful)** *act* or *deed*.

The Nature of Sin

The true nature of Sin is: a **whole**-hearted preference to offend or dishonor the Will of God, in both thoughts and actions.

Scripturally, the *heart* is both an expression of, and is identical to, the mind, which is the invisible makeup or the unique identity and complexities of a person. The *heart* includes a person's *feelings* (emotions), *will* (determination), *intellect* (reasoning), *passion* (drive), and *understanding* (wisdom or insight).

In Lucifer's case, **his whole heart** or he himself **became the source or birthplace of Sin**: the nature of a deliberate offender. It started when he deliberately began to inspire himself with mark-missing thoughts of *ascending to Heaven, raising his throne above the stars* [presumably, the other angels] *of God*, and *making himself like the Most High* (Isaiah 14:13-14).

Such thoughts caused him to naturally offend or dishonor his *original* purpose and good-nature. Thus, he became [the] Satan or the Adversary of God-likeness, purpose, and *good nature* (Ref. Ezekiel 28:14-17).

Satan then inspired Adam and Eve to also miss the mark of God's purpose, which was for them to know or recognize only good or pleasurable things. Therefore, the first *sin* (wrongful act) gave Satan and his *Sin*ful nature legal access to the world (kosmos) or to all that adorns or decorates the earth, including its living inhabitants.

To be perfectly clear about this: man*kind* committed their first sin because of deception (Eve) and then because of poor judgment

(Adam), all **due to outside influences** from Satan. Unlike Satan, **they did *not* deliberately**—with eyes wide opened—**dishonor God's Word and Will**.

No; a deliberate *lifestyle* or preference to dishonor God takes a great deal of time to develop in a person's heart. In other words, if someone, who *intimately* knew God in spiritual truth, and not just mere religious knowledge, deliberately set his or her whole heart (mind) against the Word or Will of God, then the more offensive or Sin-filled he or she will **be**come. As a result, the more sins—mark missing acts—he or she will naturally and *deliberately* commit.

Naked and Ashamed

Since **Sin entered the world through a physical act**—eating forbidden fruit, Adam and Eve's **physical bodies became identified with Sin**. As a result, their bodies became the source of their guilt and shame.

Therefore, they sowed fig leaves together and *made themselves* loin *coverings* to hide their nakedness or shame from each other. They also tried to hide from Jehovah God when they heard His voice moving through the Garden *in the cool of the day*—as spirit or *wind* (Genesis 3:7-8).

The Lord God called out to them, asking, *"Where are you?"* The man responded, "I heard the sound of Thee in the Garden, and I was afraid because I was naked; so, I hid myself" (Genesis 3:9-10).

> **And [God] said, "Who told you that you were naked? Have you eaten from the tree of which I commanded you not to eat?"**
>
> *Genesis 3:11*

Since their creation, Adam and Eve were *naked*—without material covering for their bodies; and, since they only knew *good* or *God*, there was nothing to fear. What changed?

After Adam and Eve missed the mark of obedience to God, **their own hearts condemned them.**

> *Beloved, if our hearts [do] not condemn [or find fault with] us, we have confidence before God.*

> *1 John 3:21*

To be **condemned**[13] means *to be [declared] wrong*. Adam and Eve's own hearts did **not condemn them simply because they obeyed Satan**; they were condemned because they *disobeyed God's Word*.

For example, if Satan had asked them to climb a tree or eat some grass and they obeyed him, other than, perhaps, a mild stomachache from eating grass, *nothing bad would have happened*. There was no commandment or law forbidding those acts.

> *The power [force or ability of Sin] is the law;*

> *1 Corinthians 15:56b*

The point being: if they would have done anything else that Satan asked or led them to do (other than eating from the Tree of Knowledge), then there would have been *no* reason for *condemnation and shame* (Ref. Romans 4:15b). Even if Satan had tried to convince Adam and Eve to *feel* a sense of shame or guilt for being naked, he would not have succeeded.

Like newborn babies, they were innocent. That means they did not have the knowledge or sense of what *shame* (guilt) was, especially as it related to their nakedness.

The only way Satan could bring about any change was to tap into their free-will to disobey God; which is another way of saying **he introduced disobedience to their minds and then inspired them to commit to it**. He ultimately did so by causing them to doubt the set wage, payout, or consequence for disobedience.

Afterward, Adam and Eve **no longer felt worthy enough** to be in God's Holy presence, because of *condemnation and guilt*. So, they tried to avoid Him.

---

[13] Strong's Exhaustive Concordance Of the Bible, Hebrew reference # 7561

The Blame Game

Faced with the fearful reality of their guilt, both Adam and Eve attempted to shift or equally distribute the blame for their actions. **They quickly and erroneously adopted Satan's *prideful* trait**: *self-justification* in their desperate attempt for *self-preservation*.

Adam blamed Eve, who gave him the fruit to eat. And, he then blamed God, who gave him the woman as a helper (Genesis 3:12).

Eve blamed the serpent.

As for the serpent, since God didn't ask the serpent and it didn't blame Satan, the serpent was, most likely, a willing accomplice.

Before they sinned, Adam and Eve only knew or recognized God's love, based on their innocence.

Unfortunately, their overwhelming guilt and mental fears prevented them from seeing the truth: **God's love is unconditional, even when their own hearts condemned them**.

> *For if our hearts [do find fault with] us, God is greater than our hearts, and [knows] all things.*

1 John 3:4b (KJV)

The Consequences

Disobedience brought about **two penalties** for Adam and Eve—humanity. Both penalties had physical and spiritual consequences; the physical consequences were intentional, and the spiritual consequences were, more so, natural side effects.

A *penalty* is a disadvantage or a hindrance of some kind that is imposed or forced on a wrongdoer, usually, for a specified period of time. The disadvantage is usually **the temporary forfeiture or loss** of certain rights and privileges.

The first penalty revealed:

- 🌐 The physical part of the first penalty was *eviction* from the Garden of Eden and, thus, from God's Presence...

- 🌐 The unfortunate and eventual side effect of this penalty was a *disconnect* or discontinuation of *the inspirational-based relationship between God and mankind*; because, mankind made a choice to go against God's Will, in order to *possess* something they were not designed to have or to know.

As previously indicated, the intended Will of God was: mankind would know or recognize only *good*, continuously. **God is *good***; and, *good* was the only quality of life He designed mankind to know.

But Sin changed all of that. And, the penalty of eviction put a *temporary* hold on freely entering into God's presence, on earth.

Here's how.

The Garden of Eden was *the* specific place God made to meet with humanity. As such, it was the place where mankind was meant to be at perpetual mental REST.

In Genesis 2:15, God did not simply take Adam and *place* him in the Garden for a second time—the first time being in Genesis 2:8. Verse 15 more accurately says, *the Lord God took the man and* [14]*[caused him to rest or settle down] in the Garden of Eden, to work (or serve) it and keep it.*

In other words, mankind had **a sense of belonging,** which meant they had a sense of **purpose and permanent residency in the Garden.** Adam and Eve did not have to produce new things; they only had to work enough to maintain or keep what God had already given to them.

But, after their disobedient act, **they had to leave the Garden** or God's Presence, which meant their sense of belonging and rest was replaced with a sense of the unknown: discontentment and *restlessness.* And, as Genesis 3:17 states, *worrisome pain and sweat* were added to their labor [outside of the Garden].

And, even though paradise was lost, the big picture or the most devastating part of that penalty was being **temporarily denied access to the very place God chose to meet with mankind**, at that time. Again, that meant, mankind was **temporarily denied access to the Life and Presence intended for them**(Ref. Genesis 3:24).

---

[14] Strong's Exhaustive Concordance Of the Bible, Hebrew reference # 5117

There is a familiar saying: *you never realize or value what you have until it's gone*. This event, at the beginning of human history, embodies that proverb.

As for the other penalty associated with Sin, it will be described in the next chapter.

Chapter 5

DEATH: THE SECOND PENALTY

[God said to Adam], "...For in the day that you eat from [the tree, dying you will die]."

Genesis 2:17b

The moment Sin entered the world, the process of *dying* began for all living things. **Dying is the process** of *decay, which leads to Death.* The sting of Death is Sin (1 Corinthians 15:56a). In other words, **Sin is the *poison* that, eventually, causes death** in man*kind*.

God originally designed human-beings to be immortal; meaning, the physical bodies of Adam, Eve and everyone born after them would not have decayed or worn out. But, when Sin took up residency in, or associated itself with, **man*kind*'s flesh**, it became an impurity that, eventually, causes **physical death**.

Adam lived to be 930 years old (Genesis 5:5). When compared to today's average life-span of about 70 years, give or take, 930 years seems astonishing; but, when compared to a potential life-span of tens of thousands of years, one can see how his life was significantly shortened, because of Sin. As such, Adam and Eve did *not* enjoy the full benefits of God's blessing (adoration), which was spoken over them (Ref. Genesis 1:28).

God takes no pleasure in the death of man*kind* (Ezekiel 18:32a & 33:11); because, in Death, there is no remembrance (scent or fragrance) of Him (Psalms 6:5).

"For Sheol cannot thank Thee, death cannot praise Thee; those that go down to the pit cannot hope for Thy faithfulness.

"It is the living who gives thanks to Thee, as I do today;"

Isaiah 38:18-19a

The partners of Death are *hell* (Sheol) and the *grave* (Hades).

Hell or "the pit" is the spiritual or unseen container, reservoir, or **temporary holding place** for the eternal consciousness of man*kind* once natural breathing has stopped.

The *grave* is any place where the physical body begins to decay or decompose, as it changes back into dust. Typically, this process occurs with*in* or under the ground; because, when people die, their bodies are usually entombed, covered with, or buried in, dirt by someone else.

The wage [payout or ration] for sin is death.

Romans 6:23a

As in the case of the first penalty, the second penalty also has physical and spiritual consequences for disobedience. As before, the physical consequences were intentional, and the spiritual consequences were, more so, a natural side effect.

As may be evident by now, **physical Death** was the intended consequences of the second penalty. After all, God said that's what would happen: the process of decay would start and then end in Death—*in dying you will die*. But the least recognized effect of Sin was, inevitably, **spiritual Death**.

> ☞ Physically, Death is the absence of perpetual breathing.
>
> ☞ Spiritually, Death is **the absence of a perpetual connection to, communication with, and/or *inspir*ation from, God**, because of Sin.

A Shadow of Things to Come

And the Lord God made garments of skin for Adam and his wife, and clothed them.

Genesis 3:21

Those garments of skin came from a living animal. That meant: **the first recorded *sacrifice* or shedding of life-blood to *cover* over the guilt and shame of ALL man*kind* was carried out by God**. In doing so, He set the stage for the sacrifice of *Atonement*, which means to *cover* [over].

At that point, clothing man*kind*'s physical body was merely a symbolic gesture to cover their individual shame from one another. But the bigger picture was: that first living sacrifice *for* man*kind* became **the blueprint and standard** for a spiritual event that was to come, later.

It was necessary to immediately **establish a blueprint** for covering [over] Sin. That way, **some form of connection or relationship could exist between God and man*kind***, considering the loss of intimacy that was about to take place, because of Sin.

> **Then the Lord God said, "Behold, the man has become like one of Us, knowing good and evil; and now, lest he stretch out his hand, and take also from the tree of life, and eat, and live forever—"**
>
> **Therefore** [in order to remove any possibility of them eating from the tree of life] **the Lord God sent [them] out from the Garden of Eden....**
>
> *Genesis 3:22-23a*

At that point in time, man*kind* did NOT need to eat from *the Tree of Life*, which, apparently, would have given them long life, again. **Eating from the Tree of Life**, at that time, **would *not* have restored Adam and Eve's potential to be *first in rank*, nor would it have removed the stain of Sin from their bodies**.

The debt of Sin can only be erased or paid in full through physical death, because God said so. That meant, **the only way to completely remove the stain of Sin was to get a new body**.

If Adam and Eve would have eaten from the Tree of Life, then conceivably, they could have lived for several thousand years. But, *long life*, which was originally intended by God to be a blessing, would be a curse for them; because, they would have been condemned to spend an extended period of time in a perpetually decaying body.

How miserable and twisted would their mindset or outlook on life be?

That is to say, how dark would their mental state be after witnessing first hand and even personally experiencing bad human behavior on every level imaginable, for thousands of years? All due to the influences of Satan and Sin on the world.

As indicated, **spiritual Death—a dormant awareness—was, eventually, caused by a lack of perpetual connection to, communication with, and/or inspiration from, God**; and, as was evident in the Garden, it was due to man*kind*'s [continual] avoidance of Him: they hid themselves because they were ashamed. Even though Adam and Eve were created with a spirit-God-part, **they were, foremost, living souls or breathing life-forms** that were, first, *natural* or native to this physical universe.

> *However, the spiritual [non-carnal] is <u>not</u> first, but the natural [sensitive or animated];*

> 1 Corinthians 15:46a

> *The first man [or Adam] is from the earth [soil or ground], earthy [dusty or soil like];*

> 1 Corinthians 15:47a

The subject of Spiritual Death is not as complicated as some might think. **The progression of *spiritually dying* is quite logical.**

After Adam and Eve were evicted from the Garden, they began to have children; and, their children also began to have children: the human race began to multiply. Still, of all the people that were on Earth, **Adam and Eve were the only two who really knew** what it was like to have **a direct perpetual connection to, or fellowship and intimate communication**—walk and talk—**with God on a regular basis,** because of their (once) Sin-free condition.

Even if Adam and Eve told their children about their experiences with Jehovah God, and then their children told their children, the rift between God and humanity still existed, because of Sin's enduring presence. That meant, after Sin entered the world, **things were not**, at all, **the same for humanity outside of the Garden** as they were for Adam and Eve in the Garden—designated meeting place.

Over time, **man*kind*—the children—collectively lost their innate awareness of God**; and, because of that, they did not personally recognize or intimately know the same spiritual, mental, and supernatural concepts Adam and Eve knew in the beginning.

Such *concepts* included: **eternity** (...without end), **immortality** (without decay or weakness); also, **divine wisdom** (quick understanding or insight), **value,** and **glory** (respect and honor for self and for others as *images* of God).

Therefore, **the more man*kind*'s spirit-part or divine connection faded, the more natural it was for their minds to turn exclusively to, so as to fully embrace, their physical reality**:

- (🐦) Man*kind*'s mindset—the basis of reality—became fixated on, or fully immersed in, the physical world and the many things that decorated the Earth.

- (🐦) Man*kind* began to focus primarily or exclusively on natural **circumstances**: they could only see and accept things as they appeared to be.

🌍 Man*kind*'s **own** flesh and physical senses became his main source of inspiration and stimulation; as such, *self-regard*, *self-reliance*, and convenience became the norm.

Before continuing, it necessary to make a quick distinction:

> Man*kind*'s condition of spiritual Death is not on the same level as king Nebuchadnezzar's individual experience, wherein his spirit-part and **all the benefits thereof, specifically, complex reasoning**, were *temporarily* blocked. For all intent and purposes, he became a simple, uncomplicated *beast of the field* (Ref. Daniel 4:28-34).
>
> After Sin entered the world, people still had complex reasoning, regarding natural things; but, due to a lack of spiritual inspiration, **it became much harder to perceive and understand unseen spiritual matters above physical ones**.

Note: Scripturally, it was obvious that man*kind* was still aware of *supernatural* things; but, without God as their trusted guide and filter, they were/are more likely to be influence by opposing spiritual forces (*e.g.*, through witchcraft and demonic possession, etc.).

In *Their* Own Image and Likeness

When Adam had lived 130 years, he became the father of a son in his own likeness, according to his image….

Genesis 5:3a

Everyone that is **born by the seed or semen of a man** inherits the stain of Sin in their body from Adam. Consequently, **everyone *dies a physical death***, even though everyone did *not* commit the exact same sin or disobedient act as Adam and Eve (Ref. Romans 5:14).

The reason for this is simple: together, Adam and Eve made up **the *original* pattern, model, or mold from which *everyone* else was cut, shaped, or cast**. In the beginning, they were without Sin, and they would have naturally reproduced Sin-free children, who were not liable to Death.

But when Adam and Eve were stained with Sin, **together, they naturally reproduced others of their *kind* with the same flaw** and penalty of a limited lifespan (Ref. Romans 5:12).

In addition, all the animals, birds, and sea creatures are also subjected to physical death; because, when Satan prevailed over or subdued Adam and Eve—in that he got them to disobey God and obey him, he was also able to establish himself as first *the in rank* over the other souls, in their place. And, **whatever standard Satan put forth, naturally, it spread throughout the world**. In this case, the opposition to life is Death.

This *all*-inclusive or global predicament may not seem fair. After all, the rest of the animals, not to mention the rest of us, did not have a vote in what Adam and Eve did. But, although it may not seem fair, it was necessary to apply a global standard *for* Sin and Death, just as we will later see how beneficial it was to apply a global standard for salvation *from* Sin and Death.

Chapter 6

SERVANTS OF SIN

Do you not know that when you present yourselves to someone as slaves for obedience, you are slaves of the one whom you obey, either of [Sin] resulting in death, or of obedience [to God] resulting in righteousness?

Romans 6:16

Adam and Eve were not forced into slavery. They were convinced to submit to it, through intentional deception.

In the above passage of Scripture, to present[G3936] yourself or, as the King James version of the Holy Bible reads, to *yield* yourself to someone, means *to believe so strongly in what they're saying that you gladly give yourself over to their Cause and stand with or beside them against others; or, you eagerly recommend them to others, because the concept or path they're promoting has become the foundation of your belief system.*

That's what happened in the Garden: Satan campaigned for *distrust in*, and disobedience to, *God* and humanity presented itself to *that* cause.

True submission is to <u>willfully obey</u> a cause (or commandment), even when faced with overwhelming opposition to it.

Had they not disobeyed, Adam and Eve would have wisely returned to God the authority and freedom He gave to them. Meaning, **they would have submitted themselves to His commandment and, subsequently, to His *Cause* to know or recognize *good* only**.

But instead, they disobeyed God. In doing so, they *blindly* gave or presented their authority and freedom over to Satan and advanced his campaign of distrust in, and disobedience to, God.

Technically, Adam and Eve's initial sin *could* have been omitted IF they would have asked for forgiveness. But their overall situation was more complex than just that one bad decision. Namely, when they ate from the Tree of Knowledge, in addition to having their flesh stained with Sin, their minds were forever awakened to the knowledge or recognition of evil—adversity and uselessness.

Evil is characterized by its opposition to *good*—pleasure or peace, and a God-ordained purpose. Some of the characteristics of evil include *fear, worry, doubt, hopelessness* and many other such traits that are now common place in people's minds.

An Abundance of Sin

As the first-in-rank, Satan immediately began to influence the world in an effort to fully subdue and rule over it. He inspired the overall mindset of man*kind* in such a way that they began to ignore and, eventually, they forgot the fact they were made in God's image.

> *Now the earth was corrupt in the sight of God, and the earth was filled with violence.*
>
> *And God looked on the earth, and behold, it was corrupt; for all flesh had corrupted their way upon the earth.*

> *Genesis 6:11-12*

Through the process of procreation, the Earth was being filled with Sin-stained people; and, because of Satan's influence, the *world* or people quickly became more selfish and violent. So much so that God decided to place a cap on everyone's already limited lifespan.

> *Then the Lord said, "My Spirit [Breath or Mind] shall not strive [rule, judge (as umpire), contend or plead (the cause)] with man forever, in so much as he is flesh; nevertheless, his days shall be one hundred and twenty years."*

> *Genesis 6:3*

By drastically reducing everyone's lifespan, God shortened the duration people would suffer at the hands of their fellowman.

Case in point, due to an abundance of selfishness and violence, death was being forced on people prematurely through acts of murder. The first murder occurred very early in human history.

Following are a few background passages:

> *...Abel was a keeper of the flocks, but Cain was a [farmer].*
>
> *So, it came about in the course of time that Cain brought an offering to the Lord of the fruit of the ground.*
>
> *And Abel, on his part also brought of the firstlings of his flock and of their fat portions. And the Lord had regard for Abel and for his offering;*
>
> *But for Cain and for his offering He had no regard. So, Cain became very angry and [frowned with displeasure].*

Genesis 4:2b–5

The fact that Cain's offering was bloodless or breathless may *or* may not have been an issue. If it was an issue, it wasn't the main issue. **The main issue was the condition of Cain's heart** at the time he offered up his sacrifice to God.

In the Holy Bible's NT's book of Jude, verses 10 and 11, Cain is associated with men who verbally belittled Godly things, which they did not understand. Such men are described as *evil doers*, which mean they are hurtful, greedy and selfish; and, they are carnally-minded, which means they act on physical instinct or fleshly desires, much like an unreasoning animal.

This description of Cain is also repeated in the NT's book of 1-John 3:12. In that Scripture verse, he is described as being *of* [the same mind (-set) as] Satan. That meant the following: Cain did *not* highly esteem or value the ways of God; and, although he presented his sacrifices to God, he did so **un**willingly.

However, his brother, Abel, offered up a better—more than required—sacrifice to God *willingly* and **faith-fully** (Hebrews 11:4).

At that time, Cain and his <u>unnamed and unnumbered brothers and sisters</u> were already influenced, on some level, by Sin. Most likely, they often behaved in petty, selfish, and hurtful ways towards one another.

But, this time, a more brutal expression of **Sin was crouching**—as a dangerous animal does when stalking prey—**at the door of Cain's heart and it desired to rule over him**. Sin and Satan desired for Cain to commit an *act* of murder.

Before anything really bad happened, God personally told Cain that it *was* possible to **resist and overrule** the harmful desires of Sin by *doing what was right*, on a regular basis. This meant, **Cain could still choose** to change his character or the direction in which his overall life (-style) was going (Ref. Genesis 4:6-7).

But Cain chose to ignore God and continue down the wrong path in life. As a result, he willingly allowed that brutal expression of Sin to overtake his heart; and, eventually, he murdered his brother (Genesis 4:8b).

After that first murder, the social and moral condition of the world declined. Man*kind* intentionally and unintentionally forgot God's appeal to Cain, and the **battle for self-control was lost**.

> *Where there is no vision [spiritual insight or revelation (of God)], the people are [unrestrained or dismissive of morality].*
>
> Proverbs 29:18a

Humanity was unrestrained and out of control. People *physically* did whatever they wanted, whenever they wanted, and to whomever they wanted.

That being the case, God had to take even more drastic action to preserve man*kind*:

> *And the Lord said, "I will [erase or destroy] man whom I have created from the face of the land,*

from man to animals to creeping things and to
birds of the sky; for I am sorry that I have made
them."

Genesis 6:7

Despite the social chaos, somehow, Noah, did not completely forget God (Ref. Genesis 6:8-9). Therefore, God told Noah of His plan to flood the Earth with water, in order to destroy all the breathing creatures or souls (Genesis 6:7, 13 & 7:4).

God then instructed Noah to build an Ark, which is literally a *box* [in which sacred things are kept]. The purpose of the Ark was for Noah, his family, and each *kind* of beast and bird to be saved from God's judgment or His *decision against the world*.

Noah was 600 years old when he entered the Ark (Genesis 7:6).

For forty days and nights, water fell from above, *and* water gushed forth from fountains beneath the ground, in order to completely cover or flood all dry ground (Genesis 7:11-12). When Noah was 601 years old, dry ground was visible again (Genesis 8:13).

After Noah came out of the Ark, he built an altar and offered up burnt sacrifices in worship to God. When God smelled or sensed the aroma of worship, He said to Himself, *"I will never again [despise] the ground [because] of man, for [their hearts are filled with images of adversity, affliction, and calamity the moment they are born]* " (Genesis 8:20-21a).

God then said to Noah and his family, *"Be fruitful and multiply, and fill the earth"* (Genesis 9:1). Once again man*kind* was blessed or verbally adored by God to *fill*, decorate or adorn the Earth.

But this time they were not instructed to subdue the Earth or to rule over the other creatures. Adam had already given that privilege away. And, this time, the other creatures would only *fear* humans (Genesis 9:2).

God also gave man*kind* more food options: they could eat the meat or flesh of certain animals (Genesis 9:3). This meant there would be less of a dependency on planting and harvesting, in order to survive.

However, man*kind* was forbidden to eat an animal's meat *with* its blood; because, **the breath of life is in the blood**. In other words, spirit or *wind* is the primary source of breathing; and breathing is the primary source of life *for* the physical body.

Wind, *air,* or oxygen is **in** the **blood** (-stream), which flows throughout the entire body, EVEN **PRIOR TO PHYSICAL BIRTH**. As Leviticus 17:11 and Deuteronomy 12:23 says, ***the [life, breathing, or vitality] of the body is _in_ the blood***.

It is *not* so much the blood itself that is the *life* of the body, but it is **the spirit, air or oxygen *in* the blood that gives *life* to the body**. For that reason, the Scriptures sometimes define *death* as the spilling or *shedding of blood*; which is actually describing *the outflow of life's breath or oxygen in the blood* when a person dies from a fatal wound.

For obvious reasons, God also said, "*Whoever sheds man's blood, by man his blood shall be shed, for in the image of God He made man*" (Genesis 9:6). The shedding of **human blood** or, really, the shedding of human life-breath was not intended to satisfy a person's hunger for revenge or an animal's hunger for food.

Therefore, as a deterrent and as a sign of respect, God instituted a **punishment** (*i.e.*, an immediate onetime unpleasant event) **of Death** for any person that committed *premeditated* murder, and for any animal that killed a man-*kind*. God was reminding Noah and his family of their importance—that they were *originally* made in His image, and the potential was still there for them to be in His likeness. This despite the fact their God-consciousness and God-ordained purpose were being hidden by Sin.

SECTION II

Israel & the Law

Chapter 7

COVENANTS & TESTAMENTS

The implied definition of a Biblical covenant is *an agreement or union between two or more parties*. Those involved have made or taken an oath, and they have shed the life-blood of an animal as a **sign**ature of their commitment, to bring about a mutual goal.

In a covenant between *two individuals*, very often those two individuals represent other relatives and/or countrymen who were alive at the time the covenant was made and, in many cases, represented those who were *yet* to be born. If at any time, one of the *original* representatives succeeded or failed in his part of the covenant, then *all* those whom he represented—those who were alive and those yet to be born—received the same advantages or disadvantages.

One major benefit of a covenant was this: the resources and strength of one party become the resources and strength of the other. Of course, that benefit meant a great deal more to the lesser or weaker of the two; because, their strength and resources were immediately improved upon.

A Last Will and *Testament* is written authorization that expresses the determination or *will* of a person—called the benefactor—as to how his/her valued possessions are to be distributed among surviving heirs. As such, a Testament does not go into effect until after the benefactor has died (Hebrews 9:17).

After the flood, God began to make covenants with man*kind* to further the process of salvation and redemption for *all*. Some of the covenants He made also contained a Testament of His *Will* towards humanity.

The first covenant God made was with Noah *and* all the animals from the Ark. In that Covenant, God assured the Earth's inhabitants that He will never again destroy *all* living souls (animals) or the *entire* Earth (ground) *with water* (Genesis 9:11). God's *sign*ature on that Covenant is the rain*bow* that often appears in the sky after, and sometimes during, rain-fall (Genesis 9:12 & 13).

Next, God made a covenant with a man named Abram. The Covenant He made with Abram and all subsequent covenants were conditional: man*kind* had to exercise self-control over their inherited Sinful nature, by obeying God's Word. As previously stated, God's conditions or terms are not based on human emotions. He does not give commandments, so He can then handout treats for good behavior or punishments for bad.

Of course, God knew man*kind* could never successfully keep a vow or oath, in regards to self-control, as long as their *inherited* Sinful nature and Satan's position as first-in-rank remained intact. That's why the initial covenants and testaments God made were *only* intended *to prepare* the way for reconciliation between Himself and man*kind*.

Abram Believed God

Now the Lord said to Abram, "Go for yourself from your country, and from your relatives and from your father's house, to the land which I will show you;

"And I will make you a great nation, and I will bless you, and make your name great; and so be a blessing.

"And I will bless those who bless you, and the one who curses you I will curse. And in you all the families of the earth shall be blessed."

Genesis 12:1-3

The Holy Scripture does not specifically indicate or suggest that a relationship, of any kind, existed between God and Abram before that initial contact. But Jehovah God chose one man with whom to enter a covenant and began something new, instead of choosing from among the nations that already existed, at that time.

The Covenant God made with Abram contained a primary part, which had a more *spiritual* or non-physical meaning; and, it also had a secondary part, which was meant to be taken in a *physical* or literal sense.

First, let's examine the secondary or physical part of the Covenant.

> **On that day the Lord made a covenant with Abram, saying,**
>
> **"To your [seed] I have given this land, from the river of Egypt as far as the great river, the river Euphrates:"**

> *Genesis 15:18*

Since **the secondary part of the Covenant was physical in nature**, it literally involved Abram's biological descendants. This part of the Covenant described them *possessing* the territory or land of Canaan, as outlined by God in Genesis 15:18-20.

> **"And I will establish My covenant between Me and you, and your [seed] after you throughout their generations for an everlasting covenant, to be God to you and to your [seed] after you.**
>
> **"And I will give to you and to your [seed] after you, the land of your sojourning, all the land of Canaan, for an everlasting possession; and I will be their God."**

> *Genesis 17:7-8*

When God announced this Covenant, which centered on future generations, Abram, who was 85 years old, and his wife Sari, who was 75 years old, had no biological children. In desperation, Sari, who could not have children, told Abram to use her maid, Hagar, as a surrogate, to have a son; and, **Abram listened to her.**

But *the way* in which they went about trying to fulfill the details of the Promise was not God's way; because, Hagar and her son, Ishmael, were not the ones God chose to carry out His Promise. That and other examples of human assumptions and desperate acts of weakness are why the physical or secondary part of the Covenant was not expected to endure.

God later changed Abram's name to *Abraham*, and changed his wife's name from Sari to *Sarah*, in order to accurately reflect the true spiritual meaning of the Covenant (Genesis 17:5 & 15). The name *Abraham* (H85) means *the father of a multitude*. God then defined exactly what the "multitude" was when He called Abraham *the father of a multitude "of nations."*

Specifically, Abraham was the first to have abiding faith, which was meant to be an example for others, specifically his descendants, to follow. Through Abraham, people from every family or ethnic group on Earth can be blessed or adored by God (Ref. Genesis 12:3).

Therefore, **the spiritual or primary part of the Covenant was made with Abraham, the father of Isaac**—the Promised son, who was conceived by Sarah, with God's help. This part of the Covenant was expected to endure until the end of time, as we know it.

Primarily, God said to Abraham, "I will establish My Covenant between **Me** and **you** and **your seed** after you throughout their [revolution of time or age] for an everlasting Covenant, to be God to you and to your seed after you. And I will give to you and to your seed after you, the land... for an everlasting possession; and I will be their God" (Genesis 17:7-8). This part of the Covenant was *not* exclusively for the Israelites or Jews, because Abraham was neither an *Israelite* nor a *Jew*. (The origin of these names or terms will be revealed, shortly.)

In both the primary and secondary parts of the Covenant, the word *seed* is singular—referring to *one son*.

In the secondary part, the word *seed* referred to the many biological descendants of Abraham (through the lineage of Isaac), all of whom God would look upon, collectively, as His son (Exodus 4:22); meaning, **those who would carry on or be called by His (family) name**. Again, since this part of the Covenant was physical (*i.e.,* involving biological sons and daughters and a geographical place), it was *not* expected to last or endure, because of Sin and its influence on the world.

In the primary part, the word *seed* referred to Jesus Christ (Galatians 3:16), who, at the time this Covenant was originally made, was not yet born the unique Son of God. Since this part of the Covenant was spiritual (*i.e.,* faith-based and heavenly), it was expected to supersede the physical part and become a perpetual or ongoing Covenant. Shortly we will see *how* and *why*.

Even though the secondary part of the Covenant was not expected to last, God fully intended to *remember* Abraham's biological descendants; so, He connected them to the spiritual part of the Covenant with the physical **sign**ature of circumcision (Genesis 17:9-11). Circumcision represents the cutting away of an old fleshly covering, in order to reveal new or clean flesh.

The Father of Faith

Sometime later, after Isaac was born, God chose to document Abraham's faith, which had steadily developed over the twenty-five years or so he and Sarah waited for their Promise to be fulfilled. Abraham was instructed to offer up Isaac—his long awaited and Promised son—as a Sin offering. Abraham made the necessary preparations to obey God (Genesis 22:1-19).

It was necessary for these results to be documented; because, like the first man Adam, Abraham was also establishing a standard of living for his descendants, who were yet to be born. The only question on the exam was: *did Abraham trust God more than he feared the loss of Isaac, his beloved and Promised son?* (Ref. Genesis 22:12) Abraham chose to completely trust Jehovah God without questioning the commandment; and, as a result, God blessed (eulogized or spoke well of) Abraham and called him His friend (Ref. 2 Chronicles 7:20 & James 2:23).

But Abraham did NOT have to carry out the sacrifice; because, it was never God's will for Isaac to be a living sacrifice, which had to die for someone else's Sin. No! **God wasn't being fickle or erratic**; instead, He was establishing the blueprint for *faith*: complete loyalty to one's commitment or confidence in Jehovah God.

If Abraham's descendants would possess his *kind of faith*, then they would be allowed to *keep* every Promised possession given to them by God, just like Abraham was allowed to keep Isaac, his long awaited and Promised son. More importantly, through this ordeal, **God demonstrated that He fully intended to *provide the appropriate substitute* necessary for Abraham's descendants to carry out the sacrifice *He* required for their Sins**, just as He had provided the appropriate sacrifice and substitute *for* Abraham and Isaac that very day (Genesis 22:12-18).

By faith, Abraham recognized that a Promise from God could never be taken away or made void by obeying a commandment from God (Galatians 3:17). Abraham was fully persuaded of the following: *if* **he had completed the sacrifice and killed Isaac, then God would have had to raise Isaac from the dead; because, it was through Isaac that the Promise (of being a father of multitudes) was to be carried out** (Hebrews 11:17-19).

Chapter 8

...ONE NATION, UNDER GOD?

Isaac had twin sons, Esau and Jacob (Genesis 25:23-26). God preferred and, therefore, chose the younger son, Jacob, to continue His dealings with man*kind*, instead of choosing the elder son, Esau.

God changed Jacob's name to *Israel*. The name *Israel*[15] means *he will rule as God*; and, the character or nature of the name Israel is described as *a prince that prevails with God and men* [to obtain something desired] (Genesis 32:28).

Israel (Jacob) had twelve sons: Reuben, Simeon, Levi, Judah, Dan, Naphtali, Gad, Asher, Issachar, Zebulun, Joseph, and Benjamin. From these came the original *twelve tribes of Israel* or the *Israelites*.

Bondage in Egypt

Israel and his sons settled down in Canaan. However, after being there for a while, that region of the country suffered a long-drawn-out famine. After a chain of events, which were orchestrated by God, Israel, his sons and their families took up residency within the kingdom of Egypt. (Ref. Genesis 41-46)

While living in Egypt, the Israelites continued to increase in number; and, on many levels, they became more prosperous than the Egyptians. But after the two cultures lived peaceably together for many years, the Egyptians decided to enslave the Israelites and use them as **forced laborers**. They did so despite the fact an Israelite named Joseph had saved the entire kingdom of Egypt from the great famine, which devastated that region and brought the Israelites into Egypt many years earlier. (Ref. Genesis Chapter 41)

---

[15] Strong's Exhaustive Concordance Of the Bible, Hebrew reference # 3478

The Israelites were enslaved for two reasons: *envy* and *fear*. In addition to their envy of the Israelites' divine ability to gain material wealth, the Egyptians were afraid that the Israelites might choose to fight against them if a neighboring enemy attacked (Exodus 1:6-14).

The bondage, affliction and forced labor the Israelites suffered at the hands of their Egyptian taskmasters were difficult to bear. But that painful ordeal should *not* have come as a complete surprise to them. Long before the Israelites ever became a *people*, God told Abraham that his descendants would be forcibly humbled by another nation; but He would then *judge against* that nation. Because of God's judgment, His people would *prevail* (Genesis 15:13-14) and be *redeemed*[16], which means *to ransom, deliver or rescue* a relative or other person from an enemy.

After 430 years of bondage, God's plan to *redeem* Israel was set into motion. God chose an Israelite by the name of Moses to communicate His intentions to save or to deliver His people out of Egypt.

As one might expect, Egypt's king or Pharaoh, who did not know or worship God, naturally resisted (Exodus 5:2). But unexpectedly, at least to Moses, the Israelites themselves also ignored God's intentions to save them, because they were too consumed with, and exhausted from, their endless labor (Exodus 5:6-9 and 6:9).

Even though Moses reminded the Israelites of God's Word concerning their exodus (departure) from Egypt, they still respected, feared and honored the physical or military strength of the Egyptians more than they respected, feared and honored the spiritual power of God. However, as a result of God's determination to keep His Promise to Abraham, their exodus from Egypt did take place; but, only after God performed miraculous signs and wonders to humble both the Egyptians *and* the Israelites (Exodus Chapters 5-12).

---

[16] Strong's Exhaustive Concordance Of the Bible, Hebrew reference # 6299

Journey to the Promised Land

Once the Israelites were **made free from their forced labor in Egypt**, they began the journey *to* the land of Canaan. Canaan had always been **the place of God's Promised rest**; however, this time, the Promise of *Rest* took on a different, more obvious, meaning than ever before, and rightly so.

But physical rest was not the only intention God had. Once again, **He desired a place to meet with His people**. Still, the full meaning of His Promise will be addressed later.

The Israelites also began a mental and spiritual journey of worship and *obedience to God*, whom they—that generation—had not known before. But, that part of their journey proved to be very difficult. Although the Israelites were made physically *free*, mentally they still saw themselves as being physically inferior and *powerless*.

During their 430 years of bondage in Egypt, generations after generation of Israelites were born into slavery. On an individual level, their *wills* were broken; and, on a collective level, their cultural pride was eventually stripped away. At some point, during those 430 years, the blessing (adoration) and Promises of God eventually became a source of wishful thinking and mere folklore, instead of being a trusted source of hope.

In reality, with each passing generation, **physical labor and mental affliction became** more routine and, thus, **a way of life** for the Israelites. Except for Moses, **every Israelite** that left Egypt **was born *and* raised in captivity** as a slave-laborer. Therefore, **their outlook on life was gloomy** and grim.

As such, their past experiences and hardship as slaves were **mental road-blocks**, which prevented the Israelites from reaching a destination of **courage and trust** in God. On several occasions, they actually wanted to return to the burdensome, but familiar, routines of their forced labor and captivity (Exodus 14:10-12). They even longed-for Egypt's meager food and water rations (Exodus 17:1-7, Number 11:1-6) rather than trust God and grow up in **the faith**—persuasion and loyalty—**of their forefather Abraham**.

Despite the miracles they saw before *and* after leaving Egypt, the Israelites repeatedly provoked God to anger with constant complaining (Numbers 11:33, 14:11-37, Psalms 78:17-64). Worst of all, they dishonored (devalued) the Word and strength of God when they disobeyed His instructions, the first time, to *go and forcefully take [back] possession of the land* of Canaan. The Israelites remained fear-filled, even though God assured them of victory over the mighty men that occupied the land (Numbers 13:31-14:4, Deuteronomy 1:21-33).

They naturally found it easy to obey God immediately *after* an awesome miracle was performed, but difficult to obey Him *before* they saw His strength with their physical eyes. Collectively, the Israelites did *not* see or recognize that God's Promise of Rest (in the land of Canaan) was to those who were of the *same faith-line* of Abraham and *not* simply to those who were of the *same biological bloodline* (Romans 9:7-8).

Abraham believed and obeyed God *before* he saw the birth of his son (Genesis 17:4-5, Romans 4:16-17) and *before* he saw the ram in the bush (Genesis 22:13) with his physical eyes. Similarly, his descendants needed to believe they were the victorious people God said they were, and that they could forcefully take *back* the land.

But, of the million-plus Israelites that left Egypt, a significant number of them—everyone twenty years and older—were not allowed to enter the place of Rest God prepared for them, due to their disbelief and disrespect (Ref. Numbers 14:22-24, 32:11-13 and Psalms 95:11).

Therefore, **the entire nation of people remained in the wilderness** for forty years, **until the older, more stubborn, or set-in-their-ways, generation died off**. It was the younger or newer generation of Israelites who, eventually, believed enough that they could possess or seize the land because God said so.

These were the ones who did not have time to develop a strong slave mentality in Egypt. These were also the ones who were born *free* in the wilderness during the forty years of wandering.

Chapter 9

GOD'S COVENANT WITH THE ISRAELITES

In the Covenant God made with Abraham, Isaac, and Jacob, He Promised them that their descendants—the Israelites—would *continually* possess the land of Canaan. However, the fulfillment or realization of *that* Promise depended upon the Israelites obeying or keeping the *separate* Covenant God made with them.

Moses spoke to all the people of Israel just before they entered the Promised Land.

> *"The Lord our God made a covenant with us at Horeb.*
>
> *"The Lord did not make this covenant with our fathers, but with us, with all those of us alive here today."*
>
> *Deuteronomy 5:2-3*
>
> *"So, the Lord commanded us to observe all these statutes, to fear the Lord our God for our good always and for our survival, as it is today.*
>
> *"And it will be righteousness for us if we are careful to observe [this whole] commandment before the Lord our God, just as He commanded us."*
>
> *Deuteronomy 6:24-25*
>
> *"For you are a holy people to the Lord your God; the Lord your God has chosen you to be a people for His own possession out of all the peoples who are on the face of the earth.*

"The Lord did not set His love on you nor choose you because you were more in number than any of the peoples, for you were fewest of all people,

"But because the Lord loved you and kept the oath which He swore to your fathers, the Lord brought you out by a mighty hand, and redeemed you from the house of slavery, from the hand of Pharaoh king of Egypt."

Deuteronomy 7:6-8

"Then it shall come about, because you listen to these judgments and keep and do them, that the Lord your God will keep with you His covenant and His loving-kindness which He swore to your forefathers.

"And He will love you and bless you and multiply you..."

Deuteronomy 7:12-13a

As previously stated, **commandments are instructions on *how to live***. Even though the Book of the Law contained hundreds of commandments, those hundreds could be summed up by two commandments: **every Israelite was to *honor God* with their whole heart, and they were to *love and honor one another***.

Basically, the Law was a set of religious and social instructions given to the Israelites, so they could live in the Promised Land in harmony with God and with each other. Without structure from the Law, the Israelites would have lived and behaved like any other nation of people: selfish and morally deprived.

As stated in Deuteronomy 7:6, God chose the Israelites to be His earthly possession (Exodus 19:5, Deuteronomy 4:20, 7:6-9). **Collectively, they were His *son*** (Exodus 4:22), which means *a builder of the family name*. As such, **they needed to behave in a manner worthy of His (holy) Name.**

But God didn't just want the Israelites to simply *do* what He said in order to get what they wanted or needed. That would be a heartless conditional-based relationship.

Instead, **it was (and is) extremely important for God's people to wholeheartedly *prefer* or desire His *Will* and divine purpose for their lives more than they desired their inherent Sinful *will* and vain purposes in life**. They also needed to clearly see Him as the only true and living God, who was (and still is) worthy of praise and obedience.

The foundation of the whole Law was as follows:

> **"Hear, O Israel! The Lord is our God, the Lord is [the only] One! And you shall love the Lord your God with all your heart and with all your soul and with all your might"** (Deuteronomy 6:4-5, Mark 12:28-30 & 31b).

God is *not* insecure or desperate, so as to command people to love Him. That commandment, which is referred to as the "greatest" of all commandments, was spoken by Moses, the person through whom the Law came to the Israelites.

After being in God's presence, Moses recognized the importance of obeying God out of love and honor, rather than obeying out of fear of punishment or out of desperation and need. And, in case you were wondering, the Ten Commandments do not instruct people to love God; rather, it starts with instructions to *honor*, respect and worship God only (Ref. Exodus 20:3-17).

If love, trust, and honor for God *are* present, then obedience to His Word is easy and natural. That's why, before the Israelites even entered into their place of Promise, Moses strongly encouraged them to **bind the words or the terms of *their* Covenant to their hearts or minds**.

That's because God's Promise to Abraham, regarding his descendants (the Israelites) continuously possessing the land, depended upon them (the Israelites) keeping the Law.

While conveying the terms of God's covenant, Moses said to them, "...If your [collective] heart turns away and you will not obey, but are drawn away to worship other gods and serve them, I declare to you today that you shall surely [lose your place]. You shall not prolong your days in the land where you are crossing the Jordan to enter to possess it" (Deuteronomy 30:17-18).

Moses gave that warning to them in the presence of two neutral witnesses:

> *"I call heaven and earth to witness against you today, that I have set before you life and death, the blessing and the curse. So, choose life in order that you may live, you and your [seed],*
>
> *"By loving the Lord your God, by obeying His voice, and by holding fast to Him; for this is your life and the length of your days...."*
>
> *Deuteronomy 30:19-20*

To choose [long] life meant obeying God's commandments; because, **dis**obedience is Sin, and Sin naturally ends in death. To **bless** is to adore and *speak well of* someone, thereby causing that person to prosper or succeed. To **curse** is to detest and vilify or *speak ill of* someone, thereby hindering that person from prospering.

If the Israelites desired to be continuously blessed by God, and if they desired to maintain possession of the land and live long satisfied lives, then they needed to faithfully keep His commandments. With *one* collective voice, the people of Israel vowed to God that they fully understood what was expected of them (Exodus 24:7 & Deuteronomy 27:15-26).

And so, forty years after being saved or delivered from bondage, the Israelites finally entered into the Promised Land.

> *So, the Lord gave Israel all the land which He had sworn to give to their fathers, and they possessed it and lived in it.*
>
> *And the Lord gave them rest on every side, according to all that He had sworn to their fathers, and no one of all their enemies stood before them; the Lord gave all their enemies into their hand.*

Not one of the good promises which the Lord had
made to the house of Israel failed; all came to pass.

Joshua 21:43-45

Disobedient by Nature

Unfortunately, a short time after entering the Promised Land, the Israelites began to disobey God's commandments on a regular basis. They did so despite His original and many subsequent warnings of misfortune.

Like Eve, many of them allowed pride or self-inspired confidence to produce rebellion, which then supported their lust for forbidden things. And, like Adam, many of them deliberately devalued God's Word and Will to please other people.

Furthermore, since the Israelites were dishonoring their religious vows to God, they naturally begin to dishonor one another. Eventually, they formed two separate kingdoms: **Judah** and **Israel**. That division began with the arrogance of Solomon, who was the son of David. Both David and Solomon were from the family or tribe of Judah, and both were kings over *all* the children of Israel.

Like David, Solomon worshiped Jehovah God; and, like David, he made some errors over the course of his life and reign. But whereas David would quickly become repentant (sincerely sorrowful) and turn away from sinning, Solomon grew more prideful and continued to indulge his Sinful nature well into his old age (1 King 11:4).

One of Solomon's patterns was marrying foreign women (1 Kings 3:1-3). The problem was: *God forbade the Israelites from marrying into foreign or other cultures*. The reason God forbade them was simple, no other nation or culture knew the Self-Existing God, yet; which meant no other nation had His Law for guidance to recognize or define Sin, so as to avoid it.

<u>Back then</u>, **God forbade His people from marrying into other cultures** to give them a fighting chance, or to better position them, **to live a *holy* life**, by avoiding the influence of false gods; <u>it was</u> <u>never an issue of ethnicity or skin color</u>.

But, Solomon and many of the Israelite men gave in to their innate or natural desire to please their flesh; so, they disobeyed God and married foreign women. As a result, the very thing God warned against happened: *they began to worship lifeless gods or graven images* to please and appease their wives—women who came from other cultures that worshiped idols and performed perverted rituals (1 Kings 3:1, 11:1-8).

And, as if that expression of Sin wasn't bad enough, King Solomon also **forced great physical labor**—in the form of a mandatory *human tax*—**on his own people**. He required many of them to go back and forth to Lebanon to gather raw materials (1 Kings 5:13-16). He first did so to build the Temple or House of God, which took **seven years** (1 Kings 6:38). But then he also used forced labor to build his own extravagant house, which took **thirteen years** (1 Kings 7:1).

Which house do you think was more meaningful to him?

Therefore, because he abused God's people (like the Egyptians did many years before) and, more seriously, because he worshiped false gods, Solomon was told by Jehovah God that the kingdom would be torn from his family tree or tribe and given to his servant (1Kings 11:11).

God was harsh with Solomon for a good reason: he, more than any other Israelite, knew better. At the beginning of his reign, Solomon was given a once-in-a-life-time opportunity to ask God for *any*thing (1 Kings 3:5). Solomon **humbly** asked God for *wisdom* or an understanding heart, because he sincerely wanted to be a good king to the children of Israel (1 Kings 3:7-9), just as he had Promised David, his father (1 King 2:1-4).

It was because of Solomon's original intent and desire to be a good king that God gave him an abundance of wisdom *and* wealth (1 Kings 3:10-13), such as was not seen before or since that time. But Solomon got out of balance when he instinctively took ownership of, and

added more mental weight or value to, his gifts, which were, originally, in proportion to his commitment to care for God's people (1 King 4:20-28, 5:13-18).

Solomon abandoned his *original* state of humility and embraced pride. That's why God told him that *the kingdom of Israel would be torn from his family tree.*

After Solomon's death, his son, Rehoboam, took the throne and he reigned over *all* the people of Israel (1 Kings 11:43). Almost immediately, the people came to Rehoboam and requested that he ease the burdens Solomon unjustly placed on them (1 Kings 12:4).

But, in his arrogance, Rehoboam refused. He harshly told the people that he intended to increase their workload and punish them more severely than Solomon ever did (1 Kings 12:12-15). For that reason, a majority of the Israelites broke away from Rehoboam's throne or dominion and elected their own king (1 King 12:16-20). As foretold by God, their King was a former servant of Solomon.

Consequently, Rehoboam's kingdom consisted only of the tribes of Judah, Benjamin and, most likely, Levi (1 King 12:20-23). The other kingdom of Israel consisted, more or less, of the remaining **eleven** tribes. Yes, eleven; because, at the height of their existence, there was a total of thirteen tribes *plus* the Levites.

Here's why.

After the original twelve tribes of Israel entered the Promised Land, the tribe of Levi was no longer counted with the others. God set aside the Levites for Himself (Number 18:20-24). In their place, He installed the two sons of Joseph as tribes: Ephraim and Manasseh (Genesis Chapter 48, Joshua 14:4 & 16:4). So, at their peak, there were thirteen tribes plus the Levites.

Although the two kingdoms were made up of the same biological sons and daughters of Israel (Jacob), and although they were *in* the same Promised Land, *they remained divided.* They even fought against one another in battle.

However, the two kingdoms did have one thing in common: they both managed to commit the same sins and disobey the same Law of God. That's because everyone had the same inborn Sinful nature, which preferred to dishonor God's Word.

> *Yet the Lord warned Israel and Judah, through all His prophets and every seer, saying, "Turn from your evil ways and keep My commandments, My statutes according to all the law which I commanded your fathers, and which I sent to you through My servants the prophets."*
>
> *However, they did not listen, but stiffened their neck like their fathers, who did not believe in the Lord their God.*
>
> *And they rejected His statutes and His covenant which He made with their fathers, and His warnings with which He warned them. And they followed vanity and became vain, and went after the nations which surrounded them, concerning which the Lord had commanded them not to do like them.*

2 Kings 17:13-15

Separately, both the kingdoms of Israel *and* Judah were, eventually, overthrown by other nations (2 Kings 24 & 25), because they allowed Sin to captivate their hearts. Once again, they became forced laborers, who had to work by the sweat of their brows, for someone else.

As was the case with Adam and Eve when they missed out on their overall purpose, the Israelites never completely accomplished the true meaning of **their name**: they never truly *ruled [on Earth] as God*. And, they never *entered God's Rest*, because, collectively, they never *reflected the true meaning of His name on earth*: **holiness**.

Instead, they were scattered among other nations as captives and slave-laborers. Most likely, as they were absorbed into other cultures, over time, many of them began to *lose* their God-given identity, their knowledge of God's Law, and the memory of His Promises.

The only Israelites that were allowed, by their captors, to officially return to Canaan were those from the tribes of Judah and Benjamin (Ref. Ezra 1:5). These two, along with the Levites, later became known as **the *House of Judah*.**

These Israelites managed to keep most, if not all, of their heritage and the precepts of God's Law. **These are mainly the ones who were later called *Jews*,** which is short for **Ju**dah.

Chapter 10

THE LAW OF SIN AND DEATH

*Therefore, the Law [was a] tutor[17] [or servant whose task was to take children to school or] **to lead us to Christ, that we may be justified by faith.***

Galatians 3:24

On the surface, the Law was meant to provide religious and social structure, so that the Israelites could live long and satisfied lives in the Promised Land, enjoying peace with God and with each other. That was the most obvious purpose.

But the Law had a much deeper purpose and a much larger agenda. Not only was it meant to provide religious and social structure, it also became the legal framework for spiritual salvation from which EVERYONE—Jews and Gentiles—benefits.

Beneath the surface, the Law did the following:

- ✓ It exposed the presence and influence of Sin.
- ✓ It established a legal standard or precedent for dealing with Sin: Death.
- ✓ It revealed that the kindness or grace of God *will be* the only way to *have a new Sin-free life in this world.*

The Law Exposed Sin and Then *Increased* Its Reach

As stated before, after Adam and Eve lost their intimate relationship with God, the world or people naturally became more selfish and carnally-minded. That meant: individuals cared more about their own well-being than about the well-being of others; and,

---

[17] Strong's Exhaustive Concordance Of the Bible, Greek reference # 3807

most regrettably, they thought very little, if at all, about spiritual things related to Jehovah God.

As such, by the time the Law was given to the Israelites, the nature of Sin reigned supreme in the world. But that was to be expected; because, Sinful behavior was *never* thoroughly defined.

Therefore, the presence and full influence of Sin went unchecked. That meant, **a Sinful lifestyle** or a life without knowledge of, or respect for, God **was the *norm*** or natural; but that lifestyle was not, necessarily, deliberate.

Here's why.

Before the Law, God gave only two commandments to people, which, at one time, consisted only of Noah and his immediate family. He forbade them 1) from committing *premeditated* murder and 2) from eating or drinking the life-blood of animals (Ref. Genesis 9:4-6). Therefore, legally, people only deliberately sinned if they knew what God had said, but then chose to defy Him and commit one of those two acts.

The reality was: before the Law, a Sin-filled (Godless) life was more a matter of inheritance and ignorance and not defiance; because, people's knowledge of God was small to non-existent.

*The power [force or ability **of Sin] is the law;***

1 Corinthians 15:56b

The Law exposed the presence of Sin *to the Israelites* when it clearly began to define physical expressions of Sin or unGod-like *acts* and behavior. As it turns out, in addition to premeditated murder, **almost *everything* people naturally did, was influenced by their selfish-Sinful nature.** As a result, **after the Law was given, the Israelites**—God's people—**immediately had to begin living a new life**: one that was completely different from anything they or anyone else had previously known.

But, the Law did much more than define and then forbid bad behavior. It also gave the Israelites a lot of *other instructions,* **which had nothing to do with correcting bad or perverted behavior.**

For example, they were forbidden to worship lifeless idols; they were instructed on how to prepare for, and when to present themselves in, worship to Jehovah God; and; they were told how and when to carry out a multitude of sacrifices.

On the one hand, by adding those *other instructions*, the Law ensured that **the Israelites would be *holy*** or consecrated to God, in addition to being well-behaved. <u>**By being holy,**</u> **they would be unique or separate from other nations**; because, people from other nations could learn or adopt good social behavior, too.

On the other hand, by adding so many religious and ceremonial instructions, **the Law *increased* the scope and reach of Sin** to include **un-holiness**. To be *unholy* is to be *defiled* through exposure; the implication is: *to be left out in the open and made available for widespread or **common use**.* This translates into a form of ungodliness, because the ways or paths that God wants humanity to walk in are sacred, holy, or unique in comparison to the commonest of this Sinful world.

To recap, because of the Law, *Sinful behavior* for the Israelites was not just limited to, or defined by, bad social conduct; sinning also meant deliberately refusing the higher call to holiness. Furthermore, failure to perform any single-one of the social and religious instructions of the Law meant a person was guilty of breaking the whole Law. And, lastly, since certain sins (acts) were punishable by death, the Law added more occasions for immediate physical death, because of Sin.

Consequently, because of the Law, the same guilt and shame Adam and Eve experienced in the Garden after they had eaten, was immediately revived. But, like any other commandment from God, **the Law was *not* the source or cause of guilt and shame**. The guilt and shame were caused or, really, they were revived when the Israelites began to recognize their natural—inherent—fondness to oppose *holiness* unto God, as they began to see just how weak-willed they were against the naturally Sinful desires of their carnal—physical—flesh (Ref. Romans 7:7-14).

To use a present-day example, **if there were no speed limit laws**, people could drive as fast or as slow as they wanted, on any road and in any type of weather.

On one extreme, the *impulsive desire* to drive 100 or more miles per hour (MPH) would *not* be a source of guilt, nor would it lead to fear of a penalty and/or punishment. Although that excessive speed reduces a person's reaction time—putting them and others at risk, simply put, there is no law to oppose the driver's care-free desire to achieve such speeds.

But, in most cases, if there were no speed limit laws, then there would be social chaos. Also, vehicle-related deaths, not to mention *road rage* incidents, would soar. That's why, in most countries, there are laws in place to control or standardize our driving speed, routes, and conditions. These laws have been established for our safety and are proven to be profitable for long life.

Usually, when drivers are violating a speed minimum/maximum law, their conscience **initially** reacts with guilt, condemnation, and fear of a penalty and/or punishment. The law itself does not cause the guilt, condemnation or fear. The speed law is simply there to *oppose* people's desires or fondness to drive at (what has been determined to be) unsafe speeds (*e.g.,* too fast or too slow).

As is more common, guilt and fear of a penalty, for knowingly driving too fast, result when speeders **recognize their repeated inability or their unwillingness (hardness of heart) to resist** the unwise and unlawful desire to speed.

Typically, when speeders are caught by law enforcement officers, they must pay a one-time fine as a *punishment*. In special situations, usually for repeat offenders, speeders may be *penalized* by having their licenses—driving privileges—temporarily revoked; and, they may even spend a short time in jail.

However, some violators will pay a heavier price: they may be involved in a traffic accident. If that happens, they could suffer a permanent debilitating injury, or they may pay the ultimate price, death. Equally tragic, they may accidentally take the lives of other drivers, passengers and/or pedestrians, all because *they chose to allow a desire for speed to override any self-control to obey the law.*

God's Promises and the Law

Permanent salvation from Sin and victory over Death was *not* to be found in the Law, because of its limitations. Even if it was, somehow, possible for a few Israelites to never commit one Sinful *act* from the time of their birth until their death, in order to keep the whole Law, they would still need to have the Atoning sacrifice performed *for* them to cover over their *inherited* Sinful nature; even if that nature was somehow kept dormant or inactive.

As previously stated, the Law was necessary because of the Promise God made to Abraham, regarding the Israelites. **Their response**—obedience or disobedience—to the Law determined their ability to keep the "good" things God gave to them.

More importantly, through the Law, **God established a legal standard for dealing with Sin:** the sacrifice of Atonement. According to the Law, this one sacrifice outlined the complete, albeit temporary, redemption and restoration of man*kind*.

But, Atonement through the Law was imperfect, because that sacrifice needed to be performed each year. Even though the blueprint or outline for God's *primary* (spiritual) Promise to Abraham was hidden with*in* the Law, the fulfillment of His Promise was *not* dependent upon the Law.

> **For the promise to Abraham or to his [seed] that he would be heir of the world was not through the Law, but through the righteousness of faith….**
>
> *Romans 4:13*

God Promised Abraham that he would be *the father of a multitude of nations….* (Genesis 17:5). The word used for *nations*[18] is defined as *foreigners* or *Gentiles.*

---

[18] Strong's Exhaustive Concordance Of the Bible, Hebrew reference # 1471

Typically, this was anyone who did *not* come from the family tree of Jacob, who was later renamed "Israel." This meant ALL ethnic groups were included in God's Promise to Abraham, who himself was neither an Israelite nor a Jew. And, since **the Law** was only given to the Israelites, it **could *not* accomplish that *spiritual* Promise**.

God also announced or Promised that Christ, the distant seed of Abraham, would be *the heir of the world* (Genesis 17:4-6, Romans 4:13-16, Galatians 3:16). That meant, *God gave ALL the inhabitants of the Earth to Christ*, as an inheritance.

The spiritual meaning is: **God made Christ the final Authority or the final Word** (Matthew 28:18) **in all matters relating to Sin and justification from Sin**. And, since the Law could *not* permanently free or justify anyone from Sin, in that it was limited to matters of the flesh (Acts 13:39, Romans 8:3, Galatians 3, and Hebrews 10:1), the Law was *not* God's plan to accomplish that *spiritual* Promise.

The Gentiles *(of Old)* and the Law

The Law was given to the families of Israel because they were in Covenant with God. They were required to live by the Law; and, therefore, **only they were judged favorably or unfavorably by it**. The other nations did *not* have the Law. Therefore, God did *not* count or tally-up their sins against them in the same way.

Where there is no law, Sin is not charged to [a person's] account (Romans 5:13 & 1 Corinthians 15:56); because without a [divine] law in place to forbid certain acts, there can be no violation (Romans 4:15). But make no mistake, **the wage or payout for [inherent] Sin was and is physical death** or destruction.

That means, **Sin causes destruction and death**, even when there is no knowledge or awareness of it. (Ref. Genesis 2:16-17, Ezekiel 18:4c & 18:20a and Romans 6:23)

Two examples of this global standard would be the city of Sodom (before the Law was given to Israel) and the city of Nineveh (after the Law was given to Israel). These cities were inhabited by Gentiles, who knew neither God nor the Law.

In the case of Sodom and her sister city, Gomorrah, they were, eventually, destroyed; but, contrary to popular belief, it was *not just* the gross sensual perversions and immoral acts that led to their destruction. Those cities were destroyed because *the people deliberately ignored the outstretched hands of the truly poor and needy*: they refused to comfort and help those in need, even though there was an abundance of food and ample time to do so.

The point being: even if a nation or a person is *neither* aware of the specific matters of the Law nor of the original image of God in them, the natural mind still has the capacity to care for and/or work together with others of the same *kind*, as is evident in Nature by the behavior or social order of most other animals.

Of course, in time, a person may become filled with so much cultural or individual pride that he or she stops listening and consciously or subconsciously allow Sin to crush that innate measure of natural compassion in favor of being *entirely selfish*.

(There is a difference between being self-centered and being selfish. Almost every person is *self-centered*, in that his or her efforts and motivations in life are geared towards pleasing him or herself, first. But, in addition to being self-centered, *a selfish person* will deliberately neglect the needs of others, even when he or she has ample resources and can easily help. Instead, he or she deliberately chooses not to do so.)

> **Pride goes before destruction, and a haughty spirit [goes] before stumbling.**
>
> *Proverbs 16:18*

The pattern is the same:

> The people of Sodom grow **arrogant**, which was fueled by wealth and a false sense of being indestructible. In time, they hardened their hearts towards the poor, orphans, and widows; and eventually, their **arrogant** and uncompassionate hearts **made it easier for them to routinely commit unnatural acts** (Ezekiel 16:49-50).

However, it is extremely important to note that the core message of Ezekiel 16:48-50 was not about Sodom. Those verses of Scripture were, actually, **describing how the Israelites—God's own people— followed the same path of selfishness**, and they had even exceeded the arrogance of Sodom. Collectively, the Israelites neglected the needs of their poor, widows, and orphans, while enjoying an abundance of food and careless ease in the Promised Land.

Again, when the collective *heart* of *any* nation fills with so much pride that the people lose their compassion, then those who are truly in need can be *easily* ignored and the many faces of Sin— immorality and lawlessness—will become less repulsive and more common place.

Sodom and Gomorrah were completely destroyed because they were not in covenant with God. But, **if anyone assumes that it was the Judgment of the Sovereign God to condemned the people** of Sodom and Gomorrah, not to mention the untold number of people that died in the flood during Noah's day, **to *eternal* torture in the *after-life*,** I believe with all my heart and with all my understanding of God's Word, **they would be wrong!**

Remember: since the very beginning, in the Garden of Eden where Sin first came into the world, **THE *PENALTY* FOR SIN IS PHYSICAL DEATH, NOT *ETERNAL* DAMNATION IN A LAKE OF FIRE.**

> [God said to Adam and Eve,] *"For you are dust [(powdered or gray); clay, earth, mud, ashes or ground], and to dust you shall return."*
>
> *Genesis 3:19b*

Yes, I believe the New Testament's book of Revelation when it describes a Lake of Fire: a pit of **perpetual torment** in which Satan, his demons, and *some* people will be banished (Revelation 20:10-15). But that punishment is based on a very specific condemnation or judgment. The judgment involving the Lake of Fire is **different** from the FIRST all-inclusive judgment of **physical Death**, which **EVERYONE was and is involuntarily subjected to because of Adam.**

The Lake of Fire is called **THE SECOND DEATH** (Revelation 20:14). That means it is another kind of *Death*: one **more severe** than the FIRST [physical] Death.

The Second Death goes beyond the scope of this book, because it does *not* deal with *salvation* **by faith**. Instead, it *will* deal with **deliberate rebellion against a clear-cut, unmistakable warning from God**, which has *not yet been given*, at least not in the way it will be given.

Meaning, at some point in the future, EVERYONE LIVING will clearly hear and physically see for themselves a warning *directly* from God, via three angels (Ref. Revelation 14:6-13).

First, one angel will warn EVERYONE LIVING about God's approaching Judgment, and he will instruct them to worship only God; the implication being, to avoid condemnation.

A second angel will then warn EVERYONE LIVING that Sin (personified by Babylon *of old*) has already been condemned by God.

And finally, a third angel will warn EVERYONE LIVING not to receive the Marking, which will be mandated by the global ruler of *that day* (Revelation 13:16). **ANYONE who *willingly* receives that Mark**[19]—*etching*, *stamp* (as a *badge* of servitude), or *sculptured figure* (*statue*)—*in* their right hand or *in* their forehead WILL CONDEMN HIM OR HERSELF TO **ETERNAL PUNISHMENT—the Second Death**, which is THE LAKE OF FIRE.

Apparently, *some people* will deliberately choose to ignore that very clear warning system: some will cowardly choose to obey men's authority instead of God's; and, some will proudly prefer Sin and its *perverted* pleasures. But, in either case, *they* will knowingly choose to present themselves to, and *side* with, Sin, rather than muster up the courage and/or the humility that is necessary to stand with, and *serve*, God.

They and certain others WILL HAVE sentenced themselves to the Second Death with Satan, who is the father or originator of prideful

---

[19] Strong's Exhaustive Concordance Of the Bible, Greek reference # 5480

and deliberate (heartfelt) rebellion to the known—recognizable—Will and purpose of God.

Just to be clear: they will *not* be tempted or enticed to *do something wrong* in ignorance, as in the case of Adam and Eve and most of humanity. Rather, *they* will knowingly and willingly, **with eyes wide opened**, choose to *present themselves to Sin*, to stand against God, in order to get and/or keep the desires of their hearts.

Yes! There is also a fiery torment in Death that does not pertain to the Lake of Fire, but that torment is *still based on deliberate rebellion*. Jesus' account of **Lazarus and the rich man**, as recorded in the NT's book of Luke 16:19-31, proves, at least, one point: **Israelites** (those who intelligently and intimately knew God's Word but) who deliberately defy and/or despised the Word of the Lord, in this case, by neglecting the poor..., were "cut off from among their own people" in this life and in the after-life, as God said they would be.

> *[The Lord said to Moses:] "But the person who [defiantly does anything wrong], whether he is [a native Israelite] or a [foreigner who has chosen to live as one of you], that one is blaspheming [or despising] the Lord; and that person shall be cut off from among [the] people."* [The implication being: the person who knows, beyond any shadow of doubt, what I said, but then deliberately chooses to stand in agreement with Sin against My Word must be separated from the rest of the people.]

> *Numbers 15:30*

We can tell that the rich man (who was being tormented in flames that were NOT the Lake of Fire or the Second Death) was an Israelite or Jew for the following reasons:

- He recognized Abraham and called him "father" (Luke 16:24), as did almost every Israelite and Jew.

- Abraham indicated that his living family members *had [the writings of] Moses and the prophets [from which to hear]* (16:29).

The following was/is true: *Where there is no [official divine] law— Word, Sin is not charged to [a person's] account* (Romans 5:13 and 1 Corinthians 15:56b). But even **where there is no law—Word, the overall contents of a person's heart will be taken into account.**

It was always God's plan for EVERYONE to stand at tribunal—the Judgment Seat, in the *after-life*. EVERYONE will be held accountable for **what was abundantly present in their heart**.

And, as the Apostle Paul indicated, **where there was no formal knowledge of God's Word**, peoples' hearts will accuse or excuse them before God, based on how well they **instinctively obeyed or followed the heart or the spiritual objectives of His Word—love and mercy,** (Ref. Romans 2:12-15). And, since the Holy Bible® does not indicate exactly what happens to people at tribunal, I'll not go any further with that aspect of that end-time Judgment.

As a final point, regarding the judgments of God, there are passages of Scripture in the Old Testament that warned the Israelites about God's **anger** being *kindled* against them (Ref. Deuteronomy 6:15, 7:4, 11:17, 29:27, and 31:17). Those passages describe His anger as *slowly increasing or growing* over time, while being frequently fueled or kindled by their deliberate acts of disobedience. Then, at some point, His anger became *a raging fire* and they were consumed.

Of course, they were never literally consumed by fire; rather, their disobedience removed God's Hand of protection, and they were, for example, overwhelmed by some natural disaster or by an enemy's army, as if they were in the path of a raging fire. But nothing is mentioned in Scripture about God being passionate or *angry* when He judged against Nineveh or Sodom and Gomorrah, or against any other Gentile nation, who knew neither Him nor His Law.

In the case of Nineveh, God actually spared them from imminent destruction *after* they turned away from their wickedness. God then told Jonah, the Israelite Prophet who wanted those people to be destroyed, that he should have had compassion for **the Ninevites, because they did not know any better** (Jonah 4:11).

Going back even further in time, when God decided to destroy *everyone* on Earth (except for Noah and his family) and start over, there was no mention of Him being angry. **Grieved, yes;** but there was **no mention of anger!** (Ref. Genesis 6:6)

And in another case, when God instructed the Israelites to destroy the Gentiles living in Canaan, He did not appear to be angry with them either. Basically, He told Abram many years earlier, after a long period of time—about 450 years, the people who had taken up residency in Canaan would reach a point when their perverted ways would be deserving of their destruction (Ref. Genesis 15:16). Most likely, according to the same pattern: arrogance, which led to an uncompassionate heart, which effectively softened the harsh appearance of immoral behavior.

To repeat: yes; I do believe there is a Judgment Day in the after-life. But Jesus Himself said, *it will be more tolerable or more endurable for the Gentile cities of Sodom and Gomorrah, Tyre and Sidon on that Day of Judgment (tribunal) than for the cities in which God's own people rejected the good news of His kingdom, which was revealed in Christ* (Ref. Matthew 10:15, 11:22 & 11:24).

The Jew's Reaction to the Law

For the Law, since it has only a shadow of the good things to come and not the very [image] of things, can never by the same sacrifices year by year, which they offer continually, make [complete] those who draw near.

Hebrews 10:1

Even though the Law could *not* remove man's *inherited* Sinful nature to make a person innocent or righteous—Sin-free (Galatians 2:16-21, 3:11), many of the Israelites and Jews still developed a *performance mentality* towards the Law. They religiously believed *the only way to **be** purified or free of Sin was to avoid sinning* by trying to perfect the Law to the letter.

Every orthodox Jew knew the following: *the person who obeyed the Law lived a longer life* because of the Law (Leviticus 18:5 & Romans 10:5). So, in a sense, they also tried to prevail over or, at least, prolong, Death—the payment for Sin.

But even though they were faced with the *impossibility* of ever keeping the whole Law, stubbornness and pride would not allow the Jews to look for or to EXPECT a better and more permanent way of dealing with Sin.

Their obsession with trying to perfect the Law ultimately blinded them to the truth that **the Law was divinely *spirit*ual, because it came from God** (Romans 7:14); but, it was given to, and received by, carnally-minded or Sin-stained people, who naturally limited their perceptions and reality to this physical world. As it turned out, the Law, with its many works and sacrifices, was an *impossible burden* for *any*one with a Sinful body of flesh.

Long before the Israelites became a nation, their forefather, Jacob (just before he was renamed *Israel*), physically wrestled with a messenger from God. And, in accordance with his name and *prevailing nature*, Jacob refused to let the messenger go until he received a much-needed blessing (Genesis 32:26, Hosea 12:4).

Many years later, his descendants collectively engaged themselves in a mental (animal sentient nature or canal-minded) wresting match with the Law, which came from God. And likewise, in accordance with their name and (inherited) *prevailing nature*, they refuse to let the Law go until they obtain God's righteousness.

But **the righteousness of God can only be realized by faith** (Habakkuk 2:4), not by repeatedly performing tasks from the Law (Galatians 2:16).

That's so **NO ONE**, neither Jew nor Gentile, **can pride-fully say, *I am righteous because of my own hard work*** and determination (Ref. Ephesians 2:8-9).

SECTION III

The Last Adam

Chapter 11

THE BIG PICTURE

This chapter is intended to be a summary of previous chapters and an introduction to upcoming chapters. It begins with the description of the three kingdoms that are important to ALL man*kind*; and, then it elaborates on two terms that are significant to the rest of the book: **Holiness and Reconciliation**

The Three Kingdoms

According to the Strong's Concordance of the Bible, a *kingdom*[20] is defined as a *royalty*, *rule* or *realm*. The term *kingdom* is made up of two words: **king's dom**ain.

A **king** is a sovereign—self-governing—ruler, who is **first-in-rank** or holds the highest position of authority. His **domain** is the *territory* or borders *in* which he reigns or has the greatest influence. Since Adam's creation, there have been thousands of kingdoms established among the many different ethnic groups and cultures of the world. But only three kingdoms have ever affected EVERYONE, simultaneously.

The three kingdoms I am referring to are as followed: the kingdom of **Man**, the kingdom of **Satan**, and the Kingdom of **God**. The last two of the three kingdoms are spiritual, which means they can*not* be directly seen with physical eyes; still, these two spiritual kingdoms definitely affect this physical world.

First, there was **the Kingdom of Man**kind. Adam was instructed by God to *subdue* (tame) the Earth and to *rule* (reign) over the other creatures (Genesis 1:26 & 28).

---

[20] Strong's Exhaustive Concordance Of the Bible, Greek reference # 932 (root word # 935)

To be perfectly clear, the Earth and everything and everyone on it belongs to God (Psalms 24:1 and 1 Corinthians 10:26). Adam was never given ownership of the Earth; God only gave him—man*kind*—the right to be its ruling authority or first-in-rank.

Adam and Eve were **authorized to set and then maintain a standard of living for this *world***—the Earth's inhabitants. And, they were establishing a standard of living for themselves.

Unfortunately, they gave up their authority—their rights to subdue and to firmly establish the standard of "good" God set in place, when they chose to disobey God and become servants to Sin. As noted before, this principal is found, among other places, in the Holy Bible's NT's book of Romans 6:16b, which says: *whomever you chose to stand with, support, or yield yourself to in obedience, you are a servant to whom you obey; whether it be to Sin, which leads to Death, or to [God], which leads to Righteousness.*

By serving Sin, Adam and Eve—humanity—became **hostages of Satan**; because, Sin is the heart of Satan. As such, they unwittingly gave him their earthly authority (Ref. Luke 4:6). That transfer of authority brought about the second kingdom: **the kingdom of Satan**.

As one might expect, Satan quickly began using his ill-gotten authority to tame or subdue the Earth and everything that adorned it with his own rebellious nature. The first order of business was to establish an overall physical atmosphere of general hostility within this world—within the inhabitants, and establish a mental atmosphere of hostility towards God-likeness within man*kind*.

> ***Where there is no vision [spiritual insight or revelation (of God)], the people are [unrestrained].***
>
> *Proverbs 29:18a*

Mental distractions were, and still are, Satan's first tool of choice. He used man*kind*'s recognition of evil—adversity and uselessness—to overshadow or minimize the recognition of *good*—of God. In a way, Satan's reign was obvious, as fear—faithlessness, envy, immorality, and violence became commonplace.

Satan does not have physical (*i.e.*, puppet master type) control over man*kind* to make people do whatever he wants. Instead, **he has** *inspirational*- or influential-**access *to* mankind through the many desires of his flesh, where Sin resides; and, subsequently, such desires then inspire a multitude of vain mental imagines or imaginations**. As such, Sin is constantly at work in people, negatively inspiring their perceptions or overall frame of mind.

As a result, the spirit-part or God-consciousness, which once inspired Adam with concepts like *eternity, divine authority, value,* and *glory*, has been overwhelmed. And, to make sure that higher consciousness remained hidden or obscured as much as possible, Satan also added an ever-increasing assortment of sicknesses and diseases, dreads and fears, and other distractions to promote misery and anguish prior to death.

That abundance of mental and physical anguish brought about a desperate need for the third kingdom: **The Kingdom of God.** Within the Kingdom of God, man*kind* has an unobstructed view of his true value and of his *original* God-given purpose: to be the image *and* likeness of God on Earth.

A more detailed description of God's kingdom will be given, shortly. But, **the primary purpose of God's kingdom**, which is currently being established on Earth, is *holiness*.

Holiness

> *Therefore, having these promises, beloved, let us cleanse ourselves from all defilement of flesh and spirit*[G4151]*[mental disposition], perfecting holiness in the fear of God.*

2 Corinthians 7:1

True holiness is the choice of anyone who desires the presence of God. **It is not religious pretense** or mere self-control.

To be *holy* in this Sinful world is to be *clean, sacred,* or *un*common. Something or someone that is **common** can be touched or handled by *any*one, at *any* time, for any reason; but a **holy thing** or person can *only* be touched, handled, or approached by a select few and, even then, *only* at specified times, and *only* for specific reasons.

God is holy. That's why He requires those who deliberately call upon His name, in heartfelt worship, to also be holy or set apart from the *common state* of this world. That means He first requires His people to be separated from Sin, so they can worship Him in the true *spirit* of holiness—*mind and inspiration*.

Even God's name, **Jehovah (Y**ᵉ**hôvâh in Hebrew)**, which means Self-Existent or Eternal, is holy. For instance, when God instructed the Israelites not to use or take His name in vain, He was letting them know that His name was not to be spoken lightly or flippantly. When the Israelites did find it necessary speak or call upon the name of God, especially in times of worship or in desperation or need, *they should expect something awe-filled or wondrous to happen.*

In order to reinforce the principle of holiness within the Israelites' culture of worship, God even ordained certain places as holy. If commoners—people who were not ordained priests—entered a place or room that was designated as holy unto God, something awful would happen to them: they would die. They didn't die because God had something to hide or because He was psychotic about people touching His stuff; they would die because they were unclean—not properly prepared—and they were not selected.

The point being: although God could, occasionally, be near His people, as Exodus 26:33 and Leviticus 16:1-3 reveal, He could not freely dwell among them and they (*i.e.*, the common to this world people) could not freely enter into His sacred places and presence without immediate death occurring, because of inherited and personal Sin. But God had a plan to deal with Sin: **reconciliation.**

Reconciliation

For if while we were enemies, we were reconciled
to God through the death of His Son ....

Romans 5:10a

In the above verse of Scripture, *reconcile*[21] means *to change mutually* by adding-in or inserting the difference [in value]. The terms "reconcile" and "reconciliation" are widely used in the financial world; as in *to reconcile two sets of financial records, statements, or accounts*. For example, reconciling a bank statement to a personal checkbook ledger involves changing each set of records *in order to make the value of the two records agree*.

In the past, by the time a person or a company receives a bank statement in the mail, it would not reflect the most recent debts against the account, such as checks that were written, ATM withdrawals and debit card purchases made after the statement's closing date. Neither would the statement reflect the most recent credits or miscellaneous deposits that were added to the account.

Likewise, the personal or corporate checkbook ledger would not reflect recent debts, like the various bank fees that are automatically taken from the account; nor recent credits, like accrued interest payments that are automatically added to the account each month.

It is necessary, then, to mutually change both sets of records by posting these newly revealed differences to make the two accounts agree or balance equally. (Of course, this process is, now, much easier or seamless with online banking.)

When it came to *holiness*, the Law revealed just how far off the differences were between God and man*kind*. For the better part of human history, man*kind*'s portfolio or balance-sheet listed *no worth-while value*. EVERYONE was morally bankrupt and had no equity or righteousness with God.

Worse than that, man*kind* had a lingering liability or debt of death to payoff.

In the next several chapters we will see *how* and *why* the grace (kindness) of God is so amazing, as we see how God reconciled the differences between us and Him.

---

[21] Strong's Exhaustive Concordance Of the Bible, Greek reference # 2644

Chapter 12

ALL HAVE SINNED

Despite the fact there are many different races or ethnic groups and cultures around the world, and despite the fact people come in many different sizes and speak many different languages, there is still only one *kind* of human-being. In God's eyes, there is neither Jew nor Gentile, male nor female, rich nor poor (Ref. Galatians 3:28 & Colossians 3:11).

As mentioned in the previous chapter, only three kingdoms were and are relevant to EVERYONE. The first, which was the kingdom of Man, was prevailed upon by the second. The second, which was the kingdom of Satan, is, even now, being prevailed upon by the third, which is the Kingdom of God.

Each of these three kingdoms can be associated with a particular atmosphere or *spiritual state of affairs*. These spiritual states are *not* the same as a person's *lifestyle*, which tends to be based more on their cultural, social, and religious circumstances. These three spiritual states are the same for EVERYONE, regardless of race or financial status.

The first two spiritual states are described below. The third will be named at the end of this chapter and then described in more details throughout subsequent chapters.

The first state was **Divine Spiritual Consciousness by design**.

As stated before, while they were in the Garden—the designated meeting place, Adam and Eve were spiritually alive: they could easily recognize and relate to spiritual things, because they had **perpetual communion with God**, Who is Spirit and Life. However, after they disobeyed God, Sin entered the world and things changed.

The **second state** is **Divine Spiritual *UN*-consciousness through inheritance**. Sin disrupted their perpetual communion with God, and it caused them to be evicted from the Garden or meeting place.

Adam and Eve began to have sons and daughters in their own *likeness*—acting like them, after their own *image*—disconnected from divine spiritual things, and they passed on the stain of Sin to EVERYONE else. Humanity naturally lost their original God-designed connection to spiritual things (*i.e.,* being spiritually alive), as they began to focus more on natural things, including working and sweating in order to eat and live.

Sour Grapes: Guilt by Association

Then the word of the Lord came to me saying,

"What do you mean by using this proverb concerning the land of Israel saying,

'The fathers eat the sour grapes, but the children's teeth are set on edge?'"

Ezekiel 18:1-2

Although this proverb or symbolic illustration applies to the Israelites, it also gives us insight into our collective human history.

In the case of the Israelites *of old*, it was common for one or more generations to repeatedly sin, but then when they were, eventually, penalized for *their* sins, the penalty would linger or continue throughout future generations, to include **those who did not commit the same sins** of their fathers and grandfathers.

As you might image, those who did not commit the actual sins that led to the specific penalty (*e.g.,* physical captivity, famine, impoverishment, suffering, etc.) were resentful towards those who did; and, they were resentful towards God for allowing the penalty to continue for so long. But this situation is *not* as unfair as one might think, because *all have sinned* [or will sin] and miss the target of true holiness (Ref. Romans 3:23a & 5:12b).

I will explain this point in a round-about way.

Pride keeps some people from identifying with or relating to the faults of others. For example, how many times have you heard someone say, or you have said yourself, "I can't believe [he or she] did *that*"? Or, "I would *never* do something [stupid, lame, dishonest, bad, etc.] like *that*."

The term "that" refers to any number of things, such as: *eating from the Tree of Knowledge*, like Adam and Eve did after God *personally* warned them not to; or *provoking God to anger*, like the Israelites repeatedly did after seeing God work miracles for them; or *denying ever knowing Jesus*, like Peter did after seeing all the miracles Jesus did. Basically, any number of sins, which we may have read or heard about other people committing, qualifies as "that."

But, when we pride-fully say, "I would never do something like that," we are looking at or, really, we are judging another person based on *our* current level of information and from *our* own environment. In most cases, the right course of action or the more noble decision will be clear to us: we are objectively looking at, so as to see, the big picture or know the full consequences of the other person's slip-ups.

Hindsight is 20/20. In many cases, the people who made the errors in the Bible or in our community could not *see* the big picture or fully *recognize* the consequences of their sin, even if God or society's laws told them exactly what would happen. Besides all that, in most cases, the other person's environment and/or circumstances were/are different from ours: either better or worse.

To paraphrase a familiar saying: *we shouldn't be so quick to condemn people without first walking a mile in their shoes.* The problem is, **if we really could** walk in someone else's shoes, **we wouldn't know or recognize it**. To truly walk in someone else's shoes is to know as little or as much as they knew and to have as little or as much as they had, in order to accurately see things through the eyes of their understanding before they made the error.

What is **unfair** is when we judge against—condemn—others by proudly *proclaiming* that we could walk in their shoes and not make the same error. But again, such bold proclamations are usually made because we already know the outcome, in that we have a linear-timeline type of insight into the event and its consequences.

In truth, we personally may not make the *identical* error someone else in the Bible or in our community made; but we ALL have faults—we all sin.

The only difference is the *reasons* (*e.g.*, ignorance, fear, pride, peer pressure, etc.) for sinning or missing the target.

Therefore, it ***was not*** **unfair** for later generations of Israelites to inherit or share in the lingering penalties of their forefathers' sins. The point is this: **if given the time, and if presented with the same opportunities, the children themselves would, eventually, commit the same or similar sins,** which deserved the same penalties and punishments brought on because of their fathers.

Inheritance is the nature or standard of ***original*** **Sin**. Without a doubt, the most noteworthy example of this standard is when Adam and Eve ate sour grapes (sinned) and not only were their teeth (divine spiritual senses) dulled, but so too were the teeth (divine spiritual awareness) of EVERYONE who was born after them.

And, although this standard may not seem fair to some people, it is applied equally. Believe it or not, that's actually a good thing; because, as we are about to see, God also intended for man*kind* to **benefit** from another *all*-inclusive standard that was hidden within the Law: Atonement.

That term also introduces humanity's **third state** of affairs: **Divine Spiritual Consciousness, again, through faith**. And, as stated at the beginning of this chapter, the next several chapters will define and lay a foundation for that spiritual state.

Chapter 13

THE SACRIFICE OF ATONEMENT

... God demonstrates His own love toward us, in that while we were [still] sinners, Christ died for us.

Romans 5:8

Before Christ was born, the Israelites *of old* had religiously performed countless **animal sacrifices**, in accordance with the Mosaic Law, for centuries. Most likely, the average Israelite saw and participated in hundreds of sacrifices during his or her lifetime. Perhaps so many that those sacrifices were seen more as a burdensome routine, instead of being seen as the requirements necessary to worship and have some resemblance of a connection to Jehovah God.

Nevertheless, each sacrifice meant that God's *original* sentence of physical death for Sin and sins was being carried out among His people. And, more importantly, **hidden within each of those sacrifices were the love and mercy of God**.

Here's how:

Every time the Israelites were required to *pay* the price—the shedding of *life*blood—for their sins, **God mercifully allowed and faithfully *provided* a substitute or another living soul** (*e.g.*, an animal or bird) **to die in their place,** just as He had done for Abraham and Isaac (Genesis 22:10-14).

Out of all the sacrifice and offering ceremonies contained in the Law, *one* was very unique: **The Sacrifice of *Atonement*.** That one sacrifice **affected the whole nation of Israel, at the same time**.

In the Atonement ceremony, the death of *one* small animal became a substitute *for* the death of *all* the Israelite people.

Therefore, through that particular ceremony, a pattern was established: **God demonstrated His love and mercy for EVERYONE, at the same time**.

To *atone*[22] means to cover [over]. To *make atonement*[23] means to make payment for. As such, the Sacrifice of Atonement was meant to indicate the following: **the people's misdeeds were being covered [over] with life-blood and, in so doing, their debt of Death was being paid in full**.

Although the Atonement ceremony had to be repeated annually, it was meant to be both the introduction and the pattern for a more permanent and a greater sacrifice, which God planned, through Christ. That annual, albeit temporary, version accomplished the following **spiritual** works, in the eyes of God:

1. Payment was made for the people's debt of Death
2. The people's sins were removed from them
3. The inherent grip of Sin was loosened.

Despite how the people felt or saw themselves, these things were accomplished in the sight of God, where it mattered most.

God's Amazing Grace

But the Lord was pleased to crush Him, putting Him to grief; if He would render Himself as a guilt offering, He will see His offspring, He will prolong His days, and the good pleasure of the Lord will prosper in His hand.

Isaiah 53:10

Fixing our eyes on Jesus... who, for the joy set before Him, endured the cross....

Hebrews 12:2a

---

[22] Strong's Exhaustive Concordance Of the Bible, Hebrew reference # 3722

[23] Strong's Exhaustive Concordance Of the Bible, Hebrew reference # 3725

Jehovah GOD IS LOVE (1 John 4:8b).

Jehovah God is *not* a hu**man** (Numbers 23:19a). He is *not* *occasionally* overtaken with strong feelings of love, based on the right mood or circumstances; nor does He fall in and out of love, as we are inclined to do, based merely on appearances and/or desires. God *is* love and everything He does expresses love.

> *Love is patient, love [does useful things], [love] is not [insanely jealous]; love does not brag and is not arrogant,*
>
> *[Love] does not act unbecomingly; it does not [plot against others to get its own way], [love] is not [easily provoked], [love] does not take [inventory of the wrongs it] suffered,*
>
> *[Love] does not [cheer] unrighteousness, but [applauds] the truth;*
>
> *[Love silently covers over all wrongs], [it never stops believing (for good) regardless of what happens], [it never stops expecting (good) regardless of what it sees], [regardless of the situation, love will always endure].*
>
> *[There will always be a need for love];*
>
> 1 Corinthians 13:4-8a

As we can see from those Scripture verses, **love is strong and enduring**, not weak, mushy, and short-lived. One characteristic of love is *grace*.

Grace is the undeserved gift of kindness. Grace is the willful act of giving undeserving people the very thing they need the most, at your own expense.

It pleased Jehovah God to cover over our Sins at the expense of His own uniquely begotten Son, Jesus [the] Christ—the Anointed One. And, it pleased Jesus [the] Christ to obey God the Father and payoff *our* debt, at the expense of His own life, when He hung and died on the Cross.

That's why salvation from Sin and a new victorious life in this world are only possible because of God's *free gift* to ALL. The term **free gift**[24] implies a gracious act: **freely giving something good or something of value to someone, for no reason other than** *kindness*.

God was *not* obligated to save us because of something we'd done for Him. He graciously sent His Word to save us ALL, because of Love.

The Word Became Flesh

In the beginning was the Word, and the Word was with God, and the Word was God.

He was in the beginning with God.

All things came into being by Him, and apart from Him nothing came into being that has come into being.

John 1:1-3

Words are spiritual. Words are *exhaled or breathed-out sounds* that express the speaker's *will* (determination) and intentions. The Word[25] of God is the *discourse, topic, utterance* or *Divine expression* of God. Jesus Christ is the Divine Expression of God on EVERY topic relating to this physical Earth and the souls that inhabit it. Jesus Christ *is* God, because He came from God.

To illustrate this point, imagine that every word you ever spoke on a certain topic suddenly came together and formed a human person. This human formation **is** you, because it only exists as **a physical expression of your determination or** *will* to do something.

That's who and what Jesus Is: **a physical formation of every Word God spoke** on the topic of **our salvation from Sin**.

[Jesus said,] "I can do nothing on My own initiative. As I hear, I judge; and My judgment is just, because

---

[24] Strong's Exhaustive Concordance Of the Bible, Greek reference # 5483
[25] Strong's Exhaustive Concordance Of the Bible, Greek reference # 3056

I do not seek My own will, but the will of Him who sent Me."

John 5:30

Jesus said to him, "[I've been with you a very long time, Phillip, and yet you still don't know Me at all], He who has seen [stared at or clearly discerned] Me has seen [stared at or clearly discerned] the Father; how do you say, 'Show us the Father'?

"Do you not believe that I am in the Father, and the Father is in Me? The words that I say to you I do not speak on My own initiative, but the Father abiding in Me does His works."

John 14:9-10

Throughout the books of the Old Testament, the prophets of God were inspired by the Holy Spirit of God to speak out and make known God's Will or determination to save man*kind* from Sin and to give us victory over it. And, at the appointed time, those prophetic words *literally* became flesh—in the form of a Son, a Servant, and a Sacrifice.

...But now once at the [end] of the ages [Jesus] has been manifested to put away Sin by the sacrifice of Himself.

Hebrews 9:26b

During His life on Earth, Jesus spiritually and physically filled the roles necessary to accomplish His God-given purpose. But before continuing, let's examine *how* one person can fill multiple roles.

Typically, the average person will have many roles and responsibilities during his or her lifetime.

For example, at birth, a male child is a **son** to his parents and a **brother** to his siblings. As he ages, he will be a **neighbor**, a **friend**, a **coworker** and, perhaps, even an **elected official**, who represents or stands on the behalf of many other people in his community or nation. If he marries, he becomes a **husband** to his wife. And, if he later has children, he becomes a **father**.

At any given moment, this person will have different responsibilities, based on the role or position in which he finds himself. And he will relate to those around him on different emotional and behavioral levels. Still, he is *one* person who relates and/or expresses himself differently to many people.

The Son of God

And the Word became flesh, and dwelt among us, and we beheld His glory, glory as of the only begotten from the Father, full of grace and truth.

John 1:14

A son bears his father's name for life; unlike a daughter, who (usually) takes the name of her husband in marriage. But more than that, a good son will imitate or reflect the very best qualities of his father, who is his source and identity (Ref. John 5:19-20).

The Jews considered themselves to be sons or name bears of God and, in a limited way, they were. They were all proud of the fact they came from Abraham, who came from Adam (Luke 3:23-38), who was called the son of God (Luke 3:38b). In addition to that, they had the Law, which instructed them to be holy unto God.

But Jesus was *unique* from His fellow Jews; and, He was even unique from the first man Adam.

In these last days [God] has spoken to us in His Son, whom He appointed heir of all things, through whom also He made the world.

Hebrews 1:2

And He is the image of the invisible God, the first-born of all creation.

For by Him all things were [formed or created], both in the heavens and on earth, visible and invisible, whether thrones or dominions or rulers or authorities—all things [were established through] Him and for Him.

And He is [in front of or came before] all things, and [He is the authority through which all created things remain in place].

Colossians 1:15-17

In these last days, the very Word of God, Who called *all* physical things into existence, has Himself become a physical creature, in order to accomplish God's *Will* (Philippians 2:6-8).

Like the first man Adam, Jesus was also in the image and likeness of God, because He had the Authority to do and say God-like things on Earth. But, unlike the first Adam, who received authority *from* God, Jesus IS the Authority *of* God in every matter pertaining to the Earth and its inhabitants.

And [the Son] is the radiance of [God's] glory and the exact representation of [God's] nature, and upholds all things by the word of His power.

Hebrews 1:2-3a

As the Word of God in human form, Jesus was sent to spiritually and physically accomplish every *conversation*, *utterance* or *divine expression* God ever spoke regarding **His Kingdom** and man*kind*'s **salvation** from Satan and Sin. As such, He Himself was God's final **judgment** or *decision for* the world.

The Son of Man

"But in order that you may know that the Son of Man has authority on earth to forgive [Sins]...."

Matthew 9:6a

Jesus was also **the *first* Son of Adam**, as it related to **man***kind*'s *original* Sin-free condition. A more detailed explanation is in order; so, I'll give a quick example, first.

When it comes to human reproduction, medical science has known for some time that the body of a normal, healthy woman will produce millions of tiny eggs that are periodically released during a process referred to as *ovulation*. New human **life begins** when the seed—medically referred to as *semen or sperm*—of a man penetrates or fertilizes one of these eggs.

After nine months of gestation or development in the womb, a human baby is born. But everyone born eventually dies; because, the ovarian eggs from which we all develop must be fertilized by the seed or semen of a male of man*kind*.

That's how the *nature*, the *stain*, or the *poison* of Sin is passed on from the first Adam to EVERYONE.

However, it was different for Jesus.

He was *not* conceived by the *will* or semen of a man.

God chose a *virgin* named Mary to be the human vessel in which His Word came into this physical world, in the form of a Son and a Savior. One of the many eggs released by Mary's ovaries received a direct injection of life from the Holy Spirit or the Divine Life of God.

As a result, Jesus' Life (as a living soul or breathing creature) began through a **non**-sexual, yet divine, *visitation* from God (Ref. Luke 1:26-35). The **purpose** for this unique method of conception was to ensure that *this living soul* would *not* be born with a body that naturally inherited the stain of Sin from the first Adam.

As such, Jesus was *a Sin-free soul* that did *not* have a personal debt of death to payoff. That is what made Him the first Son of the *original* Man, Adam, before Adam became a servant of Sin.

Jesus was also born a Jew (which, at that time, referred to someone who was born into the tribe of **Ju**dah), through the lineage of His biological mother Mary, and through the lineage of Joseph, the man who cared for Him *like* a biological father would. That meant, as a child, **Jesus was raised and educated according to the Law** (Luke 2:22, 27 & Galatians 4:4). And, as a man, **He obeyed the full *meaning* of the Law: He wholeheartedly loved and honored God the Father and His neighbors** (Ref. Matthew 22:36-40).

However, as indicated, Jesus was *not* someone with a Sinful nature who needed to perform the many sacrifices described *in* the Law. Jesus was born *innocent* before God, just like the first Adam was created innocent. But, unlike the first Adam, Jesus remained obedient and *faithful* to God even after He was tempted by Satan (Luke 4:1-12).

Jesus' **perpetual connection to, and communion with, God** remained intact, because He was Sin-free. I say "remained intact" because the process of His physical life began in the womb by the Holy Spirit—Breath of God, which remained in Him. That meant He had an active awareness of unseen spiritual things; and, He was not limited to, or focused only on, the many cares of this physical world.

But make no mistake, **Jesus was human**. The Word of God willfully emptied Himself of His God-hood and became flesh and blood (Ref. Philippians 2:6-8).

As such, **Jesus *could* have yielded** to the physical sensations produced by His flesh, in response to the many *un*lawful worldly things, which were pleasing to the eyes and delightful to the flesh. Or, He *could* have yielded to the many delightful and worldly things that were lawful but were also capable of delaying or taking Him away from His God-ordained purpose.

Like the first Adam, **Jesus *could* have willingly obeyed** a voice that opposed God's Will for His life. And, in so doing, He *could* have *exchanged* His **dominant *spirit*ual awareness** for His dormant fleshly ability to offend God's *Will* for His life. But, when you compare the unpleasant effects of the first Adam's sin to **what would have happened *had* Jesus sinned**, the difference is heart-stopping.

In the case of the first Adam, he was empowered or authorized *by* God to become the first-in-rank and to adorn or decorate the Earth with others of his *kind*, in the image and likeness of God. And, when he fell short of that God-ordained purpose, ***a plan* to save man*kind* was immediately set into motion** (Ref. 1 Peter 1:18-20).

In Jesus' case, He was ordained to *inherit* (possess) the Earth and its inhabitants (Psalms 2:8 & 18:43). And, like the first Adam, Jesus was also expected to adorn or decorate the Earth with other of His *kind*, in the image and likeness of God. But, because He was the Word of God in human form, **Jesus Himself *was the plan* for man*kind*'s salvation**.

Consequently, **<u>IF</u> Jesus would have sinned** and offended God, then I don't think there would have been any *legal* recourse, remedy, or appeal process God Himself could have used to **redeem man*kind*** back from the bondage of Satan and Sin; at least not **with as much kindness or grace towards us as the *original* plan** had. That's because **the *only* pattern for covering over Sin was already laid-out or established in the Law,** even though the Law itself was *not* the means of our permanent salvation from Sin (Ref. Romans 8:3).

Therefore, **<u>IF</u>** Jesus *had* sinned, then **God's Word** or His expressed determination to save us **would have become inferior or subordinate to Satan and Sin**. As such, the man Jesus would have become just another person who needed to have the atoning sacrifice performed *for* Him (on a routine basis), in order to please God. And like the first Adam, Jesus would *not* have accomplished His God-ordained purpose.

But praise God forever more! **Jesus did *NOT* sin**.

Even though the weight of the world, which is to say ALL of humanity, was placed squarely on His shoulders, Jesus did *not* buckle or give-in. He remained obedient and faithful to God's *Will*. And, as a result, **He was qualified to become the sacrificial Lamb of God**.

Leviticus Chapter 16 describes the annual ceremony of *Sacrifice for Atonement*.

This sacrifice required the use of three animals, which had neither a spot nor a blemish in or on their bodies. In the case of these sacrificial animals, a flaw**less** body was symbolic of being Sin**less**— free from the effects or defects of Sin.

The three animals consisted of **two lambs and one ram** (Leviticus 16:5). Although *three* separate animals were used in this ceremony, it was still viewed as *one ceremony of sacrifice* in the sight of God.

(Note: In some of the sacrifices described in the Old Testament, a *young male goat* or *kid*[26] was used. In the New Testament, the corresponding word for this sacrificial animal is translated as *lamb*[27] and, therefore, I have used, and will continue to use, the word *lamb*.)

In preparation for the sacrifice, two *lambs* were chosen from among the people's common livestock.

> ***For [Jesus] grew up before [God] like a [tender shoot], and like a root out of [dry] ground; He has no stately form or majesty that we should look upon Him, nor appearance that we should be attracted to Him.***

Isaiah 53:2

During His thirty-three years on Earth, Jesus physically looked like the average Jew of His day. He did not have a heavenly glow.

To jump ahead a bit for a moment, He was so average looking that, when the Temple guards came to arrest Him, someone who knew Him had to identify Him from among His disciples (Ref. Matthew 26:48).

The Lamb of God

> ***"Behold, the Lamb of God who takes away the [Sin] of the world!"***

John 1:29b

Through a selection process, one of the two lambs, which were taken from the common stock, was then set aside *for* God. And, as unlikely as this may sound, *that* lamb embodied or represented Sin.

As a result, *that* lamb, which was **God's lamb, was put to death because of Sin** (Ref. Leviticus 16:8-9).

---

[26] Strong's Exhaustive Concordance Of the Bible, Hebrew reference # 7716 & 8163

[27] Strong's Exhaustive Concordance Of the Bible, Greek reference # 286

> *[God] made [Jesus], who knew no Sin to be Sin on our behalf that we might become the righteousness of God in [Christ Jesus].*

> *2 Corinthians 5:21*

As Leviticus 16:15-16 describes, the high priest then **sprinkled the life-breath that flowed in the blood of that lamb** throughout the Sanctuary of God, on the following things:

- On the *Mercy Seat*. This seat was actually the lid to the Ark of the Covenant, which was kept at the back or West end of the Temple in a partitioned off area referred to as the Holy of Holies—the Most Holy of all Holy places. On occasion, God's presence would rest or settle on that seat when He wanted to meet with His people, temporarily.

- Within the *Tent of Meeting or Temple*. This was a large tent structure (before the brick and mortar Temple was built by Solomon) that surrounded the Holy of Holies. This was an area consecrated by God for the priests, who ministered or serviced the sacred things of God.

- On the *Altar of God*. The Altar was positioned in the courtyard, outside the entrance of the Tent or Temple. The priests would come out from the Temple and offer up the people's **personal** sacrifices and burnt offerings to God for the sins they knowingly committed.

That physical Sanctuary was fashioned after a spiritual Sanctuary in Heaven (Exodus 25:9, 40). Therefore, by comparison, when it came time to present the life-breath of the atoning sacrifice to God, the blood of countless lambs that died year after year could only be presented from a distance and sprinkled on replicas of things in Heaven; whereas, **the precious blood or the divine mixture of the life-breath that flowed in [the] Christ was presented directly to Jehovah God, in Heaven**.

...Christ...entered through the greater and more perfect Tabernacle [or Tent], not made with hands, that is to say, not of this

[physical] creation; and not through the blood of goats and calves, but through His own blood, He entered the holy place [before God in Heaven] once for all, having obtained [perpetual ransoming] (Hebrews 9:11-12).

The People's Lamb

The other lamb was *for* the people. In the second part of the atoning ceremony, the high priest confessed all of the people's Sinful *acts* and rebellious *behavior* onto the head of their lamb. Their lamb or scapegoat was then *sent* to an isolated place or wilderness far away (Leviticus 16:21-22).

Spiritually or symbolically, *that* lamb carried upon itself *all* of the people's moral impurities to that far off place (Isaiah 53:4-5). Likewise, Christ carried all of our sins *in* His body up onto the cross and then to a far-off place: the grave. And, because of that, *if we confess our sins, God is faith and just to forgive us of our sins and cleanse us from all unrighteousness* (1 John 1:9).

The Ram

The Ram was the last of the three animals used in the atoning ceremony. This animal, along with the lifeless body or remains of *God's Lamb*, was required as a burnt offering. Destruction of the body is the only way to destroy Sin, which inherently resides in man*kind*'s flesh.

Since these animals were substitutes *for* the people, spiritually or symbolically, the following occurred, IN THE SIGHT OF GOD:

   ✓ **Collectively, the people were forgiven of Sin when God's lamb die**

   ✓ **The people were free of the sins they committed when their lamb carried those sins to a far-off place**

   ✓ **The only evidence that proved *inherited* Sin ever existed among them was destroyed by fire.**

As a result, the peoples' Sin was legally covered [over], at least, temporarily, in the sight of God.

And according to the Law, one may almost say, all things are cleansed with blood, and without shedding of blood there is no [forgiveness of, or freedom from, Sin].

Hebrews 9:22

In Hebrews Chapters 7-10, Paul describes the overall spiritual meaning of the *sacrifice for Atonement*. According to the precedents or standards set forth in the Law, Jesus Christ was appointed by God to be **our continual High Priest** (Hebrews 7:17-21) and **His Lamb**.

As such, **He offered up Himself** in death. He did so after choosing to become [as] Sin **for ALL man*kind***, just as in the Law one small animal was made to become [as] Sin **for all the people** (Ref. Hebrews 10:5-12 and Titus 3:3-5).

Chapter 14

PHYSICAL EXAMPLES OF OUR SPIRITUAL SALVATION

Now these things happened to them as an example, and they were written for our instruction, upon whom the ends of the ages have come.

1 Corinthians 10:11

As previously defined in Chapter 1, a *shadow* is an image or an outline of something more real and greater than itself. In the right *light*, anyone or anything will cast a shadow.

From the *light* of God's written Word, the shadow or outline of **mankind's spiritual state of affairs** was cast upon the Earth in the form of the **Israelites' physical state of affairs**. More specifically, God used their physical captivity and long-term bondage in Egypt to demonstrate man*kind*'s spiritual or non-physical captivity and inherent bondage to Sin; and likewise, He then used their physical salvation and exodus (*i.e.*, departure) from Egypt to demonstrate man*kind*'s spiritual salvation from the bonds of inherited Sin.

That physical example of salvation is more on target than it may seem, at first glance. Meaning, the Israelites were not the only slaves serving in Egypt; subsequently, when Pharaoh reluctantly leased all of the slaves, every person that left Egypt with Moses was not an Israelite.

A *mixed multitude* of people (*i.e.*, various ethnic groups) left Egypt that day (Ref. Exodus 12:37-38). Overall, the entire collection of people that left Egypt was a snapshot of humanity, as a whole.

But the Israelite people were unique; and, they were the main focus of the Exodus for the following two important reasons:

1. Every Israelite was held captive in Egypt; whereas, many of the other ethnic groups that existed, at the time, were merely represented among the other slaves.

2. The Israelites were Abraham's descendants; and, God was certainly going to honor the Promise He made to His friend, Abraham.

Although the Israelites were probably one of the youngest nations on earth when they left Egypt, their brief history, somewhat, mirrored that of humanity's history, as a whole. For instance, the nation of Israel, ultimately, came from one man and his wife: Abraham and Sarah. The human race also came from one man and his wife: Adam and Eve. As a result, *one* couple set the tone or created the atmosphere for all of their *kind* or *kin* that followed.

In the early stages of their existence, the Israelites were overtaken by a more experienced and cunning nation, Egypt, because of envy and fear of their potential (Exodus 1:9-10). Likewise, man*kind* or Adam and Eve were overtaken in the early stages of their growth by a more experienced and cunning spiritual creature, Satan, also because of envy and fear of their potential.

While being held captive within the kingdom of Egypt, the Israelites were forced to perform burdensome tasks that glorified and achieved the desires of their captors. **Every Israelite was intimately acquainted with physical and mental exhaustion**: they were hopeless and had little **Rest** (refreshment), because of the endless tasks they routinely performed (Exodus 1:13-14). Therefore, **hopeless**ness and **restless**ness *were* their way of life; which is why the Israelites naturally developed *a perfect slave mentality*.

In a roundabout way, here's why:

In the OT, Proverbs 22:6 instructs us to train-up or start off a [young boy, girl, or servant] in the way [or on the road] you want them to travel, because when they [become an adult] they will, most likely, not [turn off that road].

The implication of that verse is: we should teach our children to travel on the path of Godliness or good, so they will recognize and, therefore, instinctively choose to walk that same path when they are older, regardless of the situation they're in and/or what they have achieved. But that same principle also applies to other areas of life.

For example, when I was very young, I once heard someone describe how circus elephants were tamed—restrained. I don't remember where or how I heard the information, or who told it; nor have I personally researched and verified this information to be factual. But I believe it to be true or, at least, some form of the truth.

An elephant must be *tamed* while it is still a calf or baby!

If **a baby elephant** has a heavy shackle placed around its leg, and that shackle is attached to a heavy chain, and that chain is fixed firmly to a securely anchored pole or ground stake, the elephant can be held in place indefinitely. Naturally, it will repeatedly try to free itself or escape; but, try as it may, *the baby elephant* cannot escape, because **the chain is stronger**. At some point, *the young elephant* will just give up and stop trying to free itself.

Even when the elephant is older, heavier, and stronger than most chains, it will *not* try to escape, because **it remembers past failures**. So, if *an adult elephant* has been tamed in that way, supposedly, a heavy chain is no longer needed: as long as there is a heavy shackle around its leg, the elephant can be held in one place by a common rope, due to **an inferiority complex associated with the shackle**.

Similar to the elephant in the illustration, the first few generations of enslaved Israelites, probably, thought a lot about their freedom; but, most likely, they never tried to escape, because they were outnumbered by the armed Egyptian military. Over time, the Israelites continued to increase in numbers *and* in strength, as a people (Exodus 1:15-20).

But, by the time they significantly outnumbered the Egyptians, they had abandoned *all* hopes and thoughts of freedom, like the elephant. At some point, they'd mentally settled for, or accepted, that way of life and simply focused on their daily tasks.

That's why when Moses came and announced that the time for their **freedom** was near, they didn't make any effort to believe him or to have any hope of freedom. They remained too exhausted from their continuous but familiar workload (Exodus 5:6-9 and 6:9).

Based on those circumstances, it is accurate to say: the Israelites were held captive in a physical *kingdom of darkness*, which purposely hid or obscured their true strength and identity as God's chosen people. Even their captor, Pharaoh, recognized their potential greatness; which is why he enslaved them in the first place (Exodus 1:9-10).

Spiritually, the bigger picture was the same. But, instead of just one entire nation of people being physically held captive by another, ALL man*kind* was being spiritually held captive within Satan's kingdom of darkness. To some degree, *everyone* **instinctively** (without question) labored to accomplish Sin's desires and intentions to oppose Godliness. And, to varying degrees, *everyone* was personally acquainted with **restless**-ness and the miseries (*e.g.*, sicknesses, diseases, and the many pains) of death.

As for the Israelites *of old*, before God could **give them** *physical* **Rest** from their endless labor, and before He could **make it possible for them to freely worship Him**, He first had to save or deliver them *all* from their *physical* captivity. After God announced (through His servant Moses) that He was ready to **make them free**, He did not allow the predictable opposition of the Egyptians, nor did he allow the fearful unbelief of the Israelites stopped Him from redeeming or taking back what was rightfully His.

Israel's deliverance was based solely on the Covenant Promise God made both to Abraham *and* to them—the collective seed of Abraham, before they ever existed as a nation (Deuteronomy 7:8-9). The question was never *if* He would deliver them, but *when*. Their deliverance took place after **God's last judgment of death was carried out against the firstborn sons of their enemy**.

As for the whole of humanity, before God could fulfill His Promise of *spiritual* Rest from our inherited servitude to Sin and Death, and before He could bring us all to a place where it was *possible* to freely worship Him, He first had to save or deliver us ALL from captivity, too. After God announced (through His servant John the Baptist and then through His Son Jesus) that He was ready to **make us free**, neither the predictable resistance of Satan nor the prideful unwillingness *and* ignorance of humanity stopped Him from redeeming what was rightfully His.

While God was working out man*kind*'s salvation, religious-minded people pride-fully resisted the plan or, really, they resisted the man, Jesus, whom God selected to achieve the plan. As for the Gentiles, they didn't have God's Law; which meant they didn't know or care about the need for salvation (Ref. 1 Corinthians 1:23).

Man*kind*'s collective salvation from the grip of inherited Sin was based solely on the Covenant Promise God made to Abraham and to his *seed*, Jesus (Genesis 17:7 & Galatians 3:16). Jesus was ordained by God to become the very foundation on which stood the true meaning of God's Promise: **Abraham would be the father [of faith] to a mixed multitude of nations** or ethnic groups.

Similar to the enslaved Israelites' situation long ago, man*kind*'s deliverance also took place after God carried out a judgment of death against the *firstborn* son. But this time the punishment was carried out against His own uniquely firstborn Son.

As described in the previous chapter, Jesus [the] Christ, the only-begotten Son of God, was *made to **be**come* [as] an enemy when He voluntarily chose to embody Sin for us ALL, as God's Lamb (2 Corinthians 5:21 & Galatians 3:13). As such, **He was able to pay off our debt of Death**.

Christ accomplished **our collective salvation or deliverance from the grip of inherited Sin.** That one accomplishment **placed us ALL in a better position** from which to move forward in God, into a Sin-less place.

Still, **each person must work/walk-out** (*i.e.,* maintain) **their own individual salvation**. Meaning, upon hearing this good news, *each person must choose* for him or herself to *be* <u>*completely free*</u> from Sin.

So then, my beloved, just as you have always obeyed, not as in my presence only, but now much more in my absence, work out [accomplish, finish, perform] your salvation [rescue or safety] with fear and trembling.

Philippians 2:12

An Image of Grace for the Israelites

The following is an analogy that I hope will further illustrate the grace of God in action and demonstrate how a *way* was provided for man*kind* to live free from Sin.

Overall, the analogy applies to ALL man*kind*; but, this **first version**, more so, describes **the circumstances of the Israelites**. In a later chapter, I will add to the analogy and describe the circumstances of the Gentiles.

Imagine a hot desert where there is little to no water or shade for comfort. In the distance is a shimmering silhouette of what appears to be a tall person walking through the desert.

However, a closer look reveals something very abnormal. There are two travelers. One of the travelers is a cruel taskmaster, who is being carried on the back of the second traveler. The second traveler is a slave of the taskmaster.

The slave is bent over because, obviously, he is burdened by the weight of the taskmaster and by heavy shackles that bound him. The slave also has a horse's bit in his mouth. The bit is attached to a set of strong chain-link reins, which the taskmaster uses to obstruct the slave's speech and to influence his direction.

According to reliable sources, the slave is in this situation because of a huge debt, which he inherited from an ancestor long ago. As such, the slave is attempting to earn his personal freedom by applying the credits he receives from the religious works he does.

Unfortunately, the slave is in a "no win" situation. He routinely increases the amount of the original debt with the errors he himself makes daily, but only because of the taskmaster's presence and influence.

The slave is always tired, and his body is usually bruised and sore; mostly because he himself adds extra religious works to an already burdensome workload. By his extra work, the slave is erroneously trying to please God, whom he believes is angry with him because of his personal faults and imperfections.

The slave's goal is to fill every waking hour of his day with religious works. His plan is simple: the busier he is, the less opportunity there is for the taskmaster to influence him. That way he could, at least, stop the additional debt to his account; and, he could then take <u>all</u> the credit he earned from God and apply it to the original debt. The slave is convinced that this course of action is <u>the only way</u> to obtain his freedom.

But, by the end of each day, the results were always the same: no matter how hard he worked, he only earned enough credits to pay off the additional debt he himself added. And, to add insult to injury, that's the exact time of day the taskmaster begins to taunt the slave by repeatedly telling him, "You are a worthless slave and you will continue to be a worthless slave until we reach our final destination." So, as if paying off an ever-increasing debt wasn't enough, there was also a deadline, which could present itself at any moment: Death.

One day, the slave heard another traveler approaching from afar off. At first, he doesn't bother lifting his head up to look and see. He knew there was another slave also aimlessly wandering through this desert, and that slave was burdened with an even bigger taskmaster.

Soon, this other traveler began to call the slave by his given name, telling him to, "Be of good cheer." The slave was somewhat confused as to how this person knew his name; especially since he and the other slave did not personally know each other. Actually, they purposely avoided one another.

As the other traveler continued calling out to him, the slave actually became annoyed. So, with great effort, he slowly lifted his weary head up to look at the other traveler. As the distance between them lessened, the slave began to notice that this person was somehow different—shorter—than the other slave he had seen before.

As he continued to stare through the constant flow of sweat that fell from his brow, it looked as if this person did not have a taskmaster riding on his back as he and that other slave did. The slave's first thought was, "that's pretty amazing." But, almost immediately his thoughts changed from admiration to jealousy, and then from jealousy to hatred.

With more determination than ever before, he pride-fully said to himself, "I am almost to the point of perfecting my religious works and prevailing over this taskmaster. Soon, I too will earn my own freedom as this person has obviously earned his." After speaking those self-inspired words, he lowered his head and vowed never to look at the approaching traveler again.

When the traveler finally stood before the slave and his taskmaster, he immediately expressed concern for the slave's difficult situation. After speaking to the slave for a long while, the traveler did something totally unexpected.

As a sign of love and respect, he humbled himself by bowing his head down to the exact eye level of the slave. He did this even though he knew about the jealousy and contempt the slave had for him.

He then announced the following:

> *"Although I am a King, I have agreed to be your substitute. I have already gone ahead to your final destination, and I have paid your debt in full. Therefore, this taskmaster can neither hold you accountable for what your forefather did long ago, nor can he continue to keep you in bondage for the slip-ups you make, because of his influence. Legally, he can no longer hinder your speech and influence your path in life, unless you give him permission to continue doing so."*

Question: If you were that slave, what would you do after hearing the good news of your freedom?

The average, so-called, sane-minded person might say something like, "I would immediately throw off that horrible taskmaster and start enjoying my freedom." While that may be a commonsense response, this is one of those times when a majority of the people are ONLY stating the obvious, because it is obvious.

Unfortunately, most people never, really, act as heroic, as bold, or as rational as they think they would in tough physical situations. And, if it is often difficult for us to be rational in most physical situations, then imagine the level of difficulty there is in spiritual— **often indiscernible** and without physical proof—situations.

Even after the gospel is thoroughly explained to people and they, for the most part, logically understand it, *rarely* will the results be mature faith—enduring loyalty—and corresponding actions. The reason is simple: **the truth of humanity's spiritual bondage to Sin and Christ's spiritual work of salvation are not as obvious to our naturally-carnal mind** as I hope the previous illustration was.

No More Sour Grapes or Guilt by Association

"The soul who sins will die. The son will not bear the punishment for the father's iniquity, nor will the father bear the punishment for the son's iniquity; the righteousness of the righteous will be upon himself, and the wickedness of the wicked will be upon himself."

Ezekiel 18:20

"In those days," [declares the Lord], "They will not say again, 'the fathers have eaten sour grapes, and the children's teeth are [dulled].'

"But everyone will die for his own iniquity; each man who eats the sour grapes, his teeth will be [dulled]."

Jeremiah 31:29-30

CHRIST MADE A WAY to legally cancel **inherited** Sin's grip on everyone; and, He made a way to cancel its penalties: physical death and the absence of perpetual inspiration and communion with God.

For the love of God [takes hold of and compels] us, having concluded this, that one died for all, therefore, all died;

2 Corinthians 5:14

That is the <u>FIRST</u> and the most important part of the human salvation experience: **CHRIST DIED FOR ALL**; therefore, **ALL died in Him and are SAFER than before**.

> <u>That does NOT mean EVERYONE has a new Sin-free life</u>. It means, for the first time since man*kind*'s eviction from the Garden, **it is**, once again, **possible** for a person to walk and talk with God in the newness of life, **if** he or she wholeheartedly *choses* to do so. It also means that a system of **personal accountability** went into effect.

The New Testament's version of *no more sour grapes* (*i.e.*, the two Scripture references that opens this section) is as follows:

> **Since the message of the cross is now being preached everywhere**, God is requiring INDIVIDUALS everywhere to turn from inherently following Sin; because, as people are hearing the message of the cross, ignorance (about inherited Sin) is no longer a valid reason for God to turn a blind eye, so as to avoid seeing our slip-ups (Acts 17:30 paraphrased).

After Jesus' Death on the cross, **everyone is accountable for their own actions**, based on what they did or did not intimately know about God—His Word.

What It Means to be Saved

According to the Strong's Dictionary, **to be saved**[G4982] **is to be delivered, protected, preserved, or made whole (*e.g.*, healed)**. The overall implication is: ***a person is <u>made safer</u> [than before]*** when he or she is *delivered, protected, or preserved from harm or danger*.

So, in addition to the popular Christian term, *new-life experience*, the Holy Bible's New Testament also uses the word ***saved***[G4982] to describe being *physically healed* and being *rescued or delivered* from harm or danger, as in the following scenarios:

> ▧ *[Jesus] went about curing all those* [He encountered] *that were sick or were oppressed by the devil* (Matthew 4:23, 9:35 and Acts 10:38). One such example was a woman who had internal bleeding; but she was then ***healed***,

which is the same word *saved*,[G4982] from that adverse condition after she touched [the edge of] Jesus' clothing (Ref. Matthew 9:20-22).

- When Jesus was dying on the cross, some of the crowd taunted Him, by saying, *He* **saved**[G4982] *so many others* [by delivering them from the pains of sickness, disease, and oppression by the devil], *why can't He* **deliver** *or save*[G4982] *Himself* [from the pains of death] (Luke 23:35).

- The Apostle Paul and others were caught in a fierce storm at sea; and, their lives were in danger. After the ship had been tossed around by a fierce wind and monstrous waves for many days, they lost hope of ever being **rescued** or *saved*[G4982] [from the danger of the storm and/or from certain death] (Acts 27:20).

Contrary to some modern teachings, the sum total of the Christian salvation experience is *not* the results of a one-time event, whereby an individual is *all-inclusively* saved because of a prayer. **Salvation is a conditional ongoing process**: we *were ALL made safer*, because of what God did through Christ; **and then, IF we change our minds** and have a faithful response to what God did, **we are** perpetually *being saved* from the same fate of this Sinful world.

- o **The beginning** of the process is: through Christ, *God saved us ALL* from the legitimate grip of *inherited Sin—* guilt by association or *kin*ship.

- • **The middle** of the process is: INDIVIDUALLY, if, by faith, we *put on* the life *of* Christ, then *we are constantly being saved or* **kept safe** from blindly fulfilling the lingering desires of Sin, which are still in our flesh, for now.

- ∞ **The End** of the process is: IF we remain *in* Christ until the end of this age, then *we will be completely safe* from God's wrath; and, **we will receive new Sin-free bodies**, like Christ, to complement our new life.

Under normal circumstances, **perpetual safety is based on a series of choices**. And, such choices are made more successfully based on our ability to know or recognize the truth—the outcome. That's why the basis of **a true and honorable sacrifice** is to *willingly forego one's safety and/or comfort, even one's life, with eyes wide open*: having a complete knowledge of the harm, danger, and/or discomfort that is to come.

Just because a person was saved (*e.g.*, healed or delivered) from a specific threat does not mean he or she will remain safe from *all* threats, nor does it even guarantee that he or she will remain safe from *the same threat* that was experienced before.

For example, a person who was healed or saved from cancer (through a genuine miracle, through modern medicine, or through some other remedy or combination thereof) can still die from a heart attack, later on in life, if he/she chooses not to change bad personal habits. In some cases, the same strain of cancer can recur if, for example, no significant dietary changes are made. In most cases, a person has choices in regards to the quality and *possibilities* of their future.

The people that were healed by Jesus from various sicknesses, diseases, and demonic oppression were freer or safer from those adverse conditions; and, in some cases, their sins or misdeeds were forgiven. **But at no time were they ever considered to be immune to sickness or incapable of committing the same sins as before.**

Whether the quality of a person's life was improved or a person was given a new lease on life, because he/she was healed or saved, it was, and still is, up to the individual to take advantage of a second, third, etc., chance. In some cases, that means either a subtle or drastic course correction in life to avoid the same or similar adverse circumstances that led to the previous need or predicament.

> *But God demonstrates His own love towards us, in that while we were yet sinners, Christ died for us.*
>
> *Much more, then, having now been justified by His blood, we shall be saved from the wrath of God through Him.*

> *For if while we were enemies, we were reconciled to God through the death of His Son, much more, having been reconciled we shall be saved by His life.*
>
> *Romans 5:8-10*

The implication of what the Apostle Paul wrote in Romans Chapter 5, and what this section is intended to convey, is this:

Christ died to save us ALL from the grip and penalties of inherited Sin; those of us who have heard and have believed that message are **benefiting more** (*i.e.,* we are receiving the full or intended benefits) from His Death, by **continuing to express** that salvation, which we have come to know. We must *continue being saved* or being set free from Sin, by continuing to live a new CONSECRATED and VICTORIOUS life over Sin, which means **living a different—Christ-like—life** in this world. By doing so, we are also *being saved* from God's wrath, which is soon to come against Sin.

Again, whether we are using physical or spiritual terms, **the totality of the Christian salvation experience cannot be summed up by a one-time event**—a single prayer or an emotional confession. **Christian salvation is *the process of perpetually living a new life*,** *after recognizing that we were saved from the old life of Sin, first.*

Imagine the following:

You're at home during a long fierce storm. The storm is so violent that your house is destroyed; so, you pray or cry out to God and, eventually, the storm stops. **Although your life was saved, you still must take action**; because, that was not the last storm you'll ever face.

Therefore, after the storm, you decide to build a **new** house in the cleft of a large rock-face to protect yourself *and* your house from all future storms.

Spiritually, that process describes a person who has heard and has come to understand what God did, through Christ: He loosened Satan's grip on man*kind* (*i.e.,* He changed our position) enough to give us all a little more breathing room. Those who believe, now, see *Christ as the rock* of protection from the furious satanic-like storms in this Sinful world.

And, while we are *in* Christ, we **continue to fortify** (dig in) **our position to remain there—safe, until the end**. But again, that is only possible because of what God did, first: He saved us ALL.

Universal Salvation: The First Part

And we have beheld and bear witness that the Father has sent the Son to be the Savior of the world.

1 John 4:14

God had EVERYONE in mind when He sent Christ to die on the Cross. The first part of the salvation process is: **CHRIST PAID EVERYONE'S DEBT OF DEATH**, in full.

Now, EVERYONE is legally safer from the grip and penalties of inherited Sin; and, as such, the way, the potential, or the possibility now exists for EVERYONE to have a new and better life, in Christ: *...It is for [Godliness] we labor and strive, because we have fixed our hope on the living God, who is* the Savior of all men, especially of believers (1 Timothy 4:10).

As that Scripture indicates, EVERYONE benefits from what God did, through Christ; but **those who believe will get the FULL benefit**.

UNIVERSAL SALVATION IS NOT THE SAME AS TODAY'S VERSION OF *UNIVERSAL RECONCILIATION*, which says, for the most part, that *everyone is in right-standing with God, because of Christ's death*. **Controversy on the topic of Universal Salvation exists because of how the term "saved" is typically explained and viewed by mainstream Christianity**.

Today, in many church pulpits, the term "saved" or "receiving Christian salvation" is usually applied to a person after he/she says *a one-time personal prayer or confession of faith, which, supposedly, brings about spiritually-mature life-changing results*. And, immediately after a person prays that prayer, he or she is considered, by mainstream Christianity, to be spiritually reborn and have a new and better Christ-like life in this world. As a result, they have victory over Sin, and they are seated in heavenly places.

Yes, the blood of Christ *is* **capable of immediately bringing about such changes** and more. **BUT WE ARE NOT**. (Note: the proper context for Romans 10:9-10 will be covered, later, in Chapter 18.)

In the beginning stages of our Christian conversion, we have neither mature faith nor a renewed mind, so as to immediately and confidently start valuing spiritual principles above natural ones. As such, *we* fall short when it comes to immediately walking in such spiritual victory.

So, even though it is possible, it is not very likely that one simple emotionally charged prayer, added to a single act of belief, will be enough for a spiritual infant in Christ to immediately build and properly maintain the spiritual separation that must exist between a consecrated believer and this Sinful world. Yes! Something does immediately happen after a person says that kind of a prayer or makes a confession of faith: our Sinful nature will begin to overwhelm and attempt to devalue anything that opposes it.

Unfortunately, because mainstream Christianity tends to favor a flawed or incomplete template for salvation by traditionally taking certain verses of Scripture out of context, most people are never properly equipped to overcome and pushback the ungodly thoughts and desires that continue to be generated from their un-renewed minds. As a result, **people have difficulty bringing about real Christ-like changes or spiritual maturity in their lives**.

For that and for scriptural reasons, we must stop promoting a traditional template that over-simplifies the Christian salvation experience, for the sake of getting as many people as possible to accept what we're presenting, as quickly as possible, for the sake of *counting* converts. The gospel was not meant to create competition among ambitious believers: our mandate or directive is not to *merely* fill up our churches with people.

The purpose of the gospel, which means *good news*, is to TEACH AND, THEREFORE, TO MAKE victorious faith-filled believers, who are capable of overcoming this Sinful world.

> *And He died for all, that they who live should no longer live for themselves, but for Him who died and rose again on their behalf.*
>
> 2 Corinthians 5:15

To restate the key point of this section:

🗝 The **FIRST** and the most important part of the salvation process is: **CHRIST DIED FOR ALL; therefore, ALL died in Him** (2 Corinthians 5:14).

> But CHRIST'S **DEATH** DID **NOT** AUTOMATICALLY PRODUCE NEW LIFE FOR ANYONE. NEW LIFE FOR CHRIST AND FOR US REQUIRED **RESURRECTION**,[G386] which mean to stand up again from death; and, that **ONLY HAPPENS THROUGH THE ENABLING POWER OF GOD**.

> *Therefore, we have been buried with Him through baptism into death, in order that as Christ was raised from the dead through the glory of the Father, so we too might walk in newness of life.*
>
> Romans 6:4

Work Out Your Own Salvation: The Middle Part

> *So then, my beloved... [work fully, accomplish, finish or fashion] your own salvation with fear and trembling;*
>
> Philippians 2:12

> *But if the Spirit of Him who raised Jesus from the dead dwells in you, He who raised Christ Jesus from the dead will also give [new] life to your [earthly] bodies through His Spirit who indwells you.*
>
> Romans 8:11

The middle part of the salvation process is where we take advantage of, and individually benefit from, what God has already done, through Christ. This middle part is **SANCTIFICATION AND NEW LIFE, BY FAITH**. This part starts to become more evident as we hear and, in time, as we fully believe the good news that God wants to dwell or live in us, by His Holy Spirit.

When we have enough faith in what we've heard, spiritually, through the enabling power of God, **we CAN be made progressively freer from Sin** or the ungodly demands of our flesh, which naturally connects and ties us to this Sinful world.

And, with many other words [the Apostle Peter] solemnly testified and kept on [inviting or appealing to] them, saying, "Be saved from this perverse generation!" (NAS version) The King James and other versions of the Holy Bible translate Peter's appeal as: "**Save yourselves** from this [stained, defective, or blemished] generation." (Acts 2:40)

We work- or live-out the free gift of salvation by agreeing with God: we begin to recognize Sin and its passions as being bondage and the very thing that keeps us from clearly seeing God. Therefore, at some point, we begin to change our thinking or renew our minds enough to *progressively* put an end to the mental and physical reign of Sin, while still living in this Sinful world. Again, this is necessary, because **being consecration to God**, or being separated from the bonds of Sin, **is the proof of our new life**, in Christ.

Also, within this middle part of salvation, God will then call *some*—not all—believers into His service, in order to preach this good news to others. As such, it is especially important for those who have been called by God to maintain the integrity and not just the appearance of their freedom from Sin, so that they can be living proof of what God has done for us all.

> ࿋ [The Apostle Paul told Timothy, a young minister of the gospel, to...] *Pay close attention to yourself and to your teaching; persevere in these things; for as you do this **you will ensure salvation** both for yourself and for those who*

hear you (1 Timothy 4:16). *...If somehow, I [Paul], might [make my countrymen jealous] and save some of them [in the process]* (Romans 11:14). *To the weak, I became weak, that I might win the weak; I have become all things to all men, that I may by all means save some* (1 Corinthians 9:22).

Glorification: The Finalé

As for the completion of the salvation process, it's when those who have remained *in* Christ or have lived a Christ-like life in this Sinful world will literally receive **NEW SIN-FREE OR GLORIFIED BODIES**. (Ref. 1 Corinthians 15:35-55)

Those new bodies are only intended to **finalize the salvation process** that was, or is now being, accomplished in our minds or hearts, first, by faith. Those new bodies are for the new Heaven and the new Earth that are to come, later (Ref. Revelation 21:1-2).

∞ Therefore, my beloved brethren, be steadfast, immovable, always abounding in the work of the Lord, knowing that your [laboring to work out your salvation] is not in vain in the Lord (1 Corinthians 15:58).

∞ Blessed is a man who perseveres under trial; for once he has been approved, he will receive the crown of life, which the Lord has Promised to those who love Him (James 1:12).

Just to Be Clear...

The Beginning of the Salvation process made EVERYONE safer, because **Christ died for Sin, in accordance with the Law, and EVERYONE**—past, present, and future—**died with Him**. But, since the Law was limited to dealing with Sin in only ONE way, Death, (*i.e.*, either the death of the offender or the death of a substitute animal) **EVERYONE does NOT have a new life** in this world.

The Middle of the salvation process establishes A NEW, JUSTIFIED, and CONSECRATED LIFE, ACCORDING TO OUR

FAITH IN CHRIST (Romans 1:17 & Galatians 3:11) and ACCORDING TO THE ENABLING POWER OF GOD.

So, as for the question of Universal Salvation, **IS EVERYONE IN THE WORLD SAVED or MADE <u>SAFER</u> FROM SIN?**

The answer is, **Yes!**

Again, **THIS IS NOT <u>TODAY'S VERSION</u> OF UNIVERSAL RECONCILIATION, NOR IS IT A GOSPEL OF INCLUSION**; because, I'm NOT implying that everyone is in right-standing with God. I am **NOT** implying that everyone is automatically Heaven bound and, therefore, no one has to repent.

To further illustrate the point of true universal salvation:

> **EVERYONE is saved in *the same sense* that EVERY slave was, first, delivered from <u>forced</u> bondage in Egypt** and then led into the wilderness; and, even though the wilderness was never meant to be **their** final destination, at least, *there* they were ALL *safer* and *freer* than before. But they still needed to move forward, by faith, into the Promised Land, where God's full provision for a new and better life of consecration awaited them.

In *that* same way, today, through the atoning work of Christ, **ALL of man*kind* has been ransomed or saved from a hopeless and <u>forced</u> inherent state of servitude to Sin**; and, EVERYONE has been **made safer** and has been placed in [a type of wilderness, which is] a better position from which to move forward in Godliness.

Again, THAT DOES **NOT** MEAN EVERYONE IS SIN-FREE or RIGHTEOUS or HAVE NEW LIFE; because, just like the slaves from Egypt, **NOT** EVERYONE WILL CHOOSE TO MOVE FORWARD, BY FAITH.

> *Now I [Jude] desire to remind you, though you know all things once for all, that the Lord, after saving a people out of the land of Egypt, subsequently destroyed those who did not [entrust themselves to His Word].* [The implication being: they did not die as slaves in Egypt; but they still died

prematurely, because of Sin and a lack of faith in what God did and wanted to do for them.]

Jude 5

Today, as in the past with the slaves *of old*, people still die without experiencing new life or the peace and presence of God. The reasons range from **ignorance**—never hearing the gospel or good news of their salvation, to **unbelief**—never quite believing what they have heard or seen, to **disbelief**—refusing to believe and do what they know to be true.

Therefore, even though Christ died for us ALL, so that we don't have to be held captive by Sin, some people will still die in servitude to Sin. That just means, for whatever reason, they never took advantage of what God did for us ALL, through Christ.

The Free Gift Is *for* Everyone!

God... is the Savior of [every-one], especially of believers.

1Timothy 4:10b

Finally, here is the primary example that is intended to reveal or describe our *initial* salvation from Sin. Hopefully, this example will show just how all-inclusive the first part of salvation was.

This example was mentioned before: The Sacrifice of Atonement. It describes how the Israelite people (who, in a spiritual sense, represented the whole of humanity) did not have a role in **the ground work** that led to their *initial* salvation from Sin.

Keep in mind the following point: although our salvation was *not dependent upon* the Law, it was patterned after the Sacrifice of Atonement, which is contained *in* the Law.

When reviewing the Atonement sacrifice's original guidelines, which are found in the OT's book of Leviticus, Chapter 16, the following becomes clear:

  ☙ **The ceremony was carried out *by* the high priest *for* all the people**. As far as I can tell, during the first part of the ceremony, when God's lamb was being put to death, INDIVIDUALS NEITHER DID NOR SAID (as to confess) ANYTHING IN ORDER TO BENEFIT FROM THE *ALL*-INCLUSIVE SACRIFICE. They just needed to know and believe that they benefited from what was happening.

- **The people's Sinful acts**—perversities, iniquities or evil deeds—**were confessed** onto the scapegoat *by* **the high priest** *for all* **the people** (Leviticus 16:21). The scapegoat then took the people's sins with it, into a far-off place, away from them. (Note: This is why we acknowledge or confess the Lord Jesus Christ as our Savior, instead of confessing our sins (Ref. Romans 10:9-10).

During that entire ceremony of sacrifice, *all* the people—commoners and (regular) priests—were *the same* **in the sight of God**: all were sinners. But the blood of God's lamb covered them *all* when it was sprinkled on the Mercy Seat by the one chosen to be their high priest (Leviticus 16:15-16).

Yes, it is true that the Israelites were already in covenant with God, which is why they had the Law in the first place. But the bigger picture was: **God graciously established both the pattern and the standard for man*kind*'s atonement long before the Law** was ever given to them.

> *And the Lord God made garments of skin for Adam and his wife, and clothed them.*
>
> Genesis 3:21

At the beginning, in the Garden, God Himself carried out **the first sacrifice** that temporarily covered or atoned for EVERYONE. Of course, at that time, Adam and Eve was "EVERYONE" or the whole of man*kind*. Therefore, later, at the appropriate time, it was fitting for God to then carryout **the final sacrifice** necessary to cover EVERYONE or to make Atonement for ALL of man*kind*.

To repeat: Jesus [the] Christ was both the High Priest (Hebrews 6:20, 7:17-25) and the sacrificial Lamb of God (John 1:29, Leviticus

16:8-9). As such, He *personally* offered up Himself in Death for EVERYONE and His blood covered the whole world, in the sight of God.

Again, I submit the following for consideration: If, in His love, God permitted the life-blood/breath of a small four-legged animal to cover-over *every Sinful soul* in the nation of Israel, **how much more precious and qualified was the life-blood/breath of His own *uniquely* begotten human Son to cover over ALL Sinful souls**, past, present, and future?

> *For while we were still helpless, at the right time Christ died for the ungodly.* [The implication being: EVERYONE was considered Sinful or ungodly.]
>
> *For one will hardly die for a righteous man; though perhaps for the good man someone would dare even to die.*
>
> *But God demonstrates His own love toward us, in that while we were [still sinful], Christ died for us.*
>
> Romans 5:6-8

We no longer share accountability for the first Adam's *original* **sin**; which means, we are no longer inherently liable for its penalties. ***The way***, **the potential**, or **the possibility** for complete restoration has been made available to ALL: **Jesus** [the] **Christ**.

Now that's really good news.

That is the message or *gospel* we have been commissioned by God to preach in order for ALL people to actually enjoy a life of freedom from Sin and restoration, now!

Personal Salvation

> *So then, my beloved… [work fully, accomplish, finish or fashion] your own salvation with fear and trembling;*
>
> Philippians 2:12

Figuratively speaking, after God's firstborn Son died as the ransom for Sin, ALL of humanity was spiritually led away from Satan's kingdom of darkness into a type of wilderness or common ground, just like the slaves *of old* were physically led away into a geographical wilderness. Physically then and spiritually now, **the wilderness is a place of solitude, wandering, and restlessness**.

It is only meant to be a transition point and proving ground, *not* **a long-term resting place and safe-haven.**

On one side of the wilderness—looking backward—is the border where the kingdom of darkness ends. On the other side of the wilderness—looking forward—is the border of God's Kingdom, wherein is the lifestyle and authority God has prepared for us.

But, *if* some people don't recognize or realize the gift of *their* salvation, because of either ignorance or unbelief, then they will remain in the wilderness long term; and, most likely, they will die there. People in the wilderness may be *safer* than before, but they're still **neither completely safe nor completely at rest** until they're inside of God's Kingdom. More accurately, they're neither completely safe nor completely at rest **until God's Kingdom is *inside* of them**—their hearts or renewed minds.

As such, those in the wilderness are still naturally inclined to believe **Satan, who continues to erroneously insist that we are *all* powerless** against him, because he's still the first-in-rank. But, although he is called the *god or prince of this Sinful world* (2 Corinthians 4.4 and John 14:30, respectively), **believers** in Christ should recognize that they **can be free from the bonds and limitations of this Sinful world**.

Satan's lies, which says we are powerless against him, appear to be credible, because these lies are supported by life's many matter-of-fact miseries. Misery and hopelessness have always been routine distractions that keep people from *seeing* what God has done, first, and has made possible for us *all*.

Such miseries include, but are not limited to, the various sicknesses, diseases, and disasters that are common to this world;

which means, these affect everyone in one way or another. And, then there's Death. Everyone is familiar with Death, which is a tremendous source of hopelessness and fear.

At this point, let's ask the following question: Based on what has *initially* been done through Christ, **IS EVERYONE AUTOMATICALLY PLEASING TO GOD?**

Answer: NO!

Again, ALTHOUGH EVERYONE HAS BEEN *MADE FREER* or SAFER **FROM THE BONDS OF SIN**, EVERYONE IS **NOT** DELIBERATELY FAITHFUL AND LIVING A SIN-FREE LIFE; and therefore, EVERYONE IS **NOT** IN A "RIGHT" RELATIONSHIP WITH HIM—WALKING IN HIS *LIKENESS*.

Just like the slaves *of old* were required to believe or entrust their well-being to God and *collectively* move forward out of the wilderness into the physical place He prepared for them, we too, although on an *individual* basis, must believe, in order to spiritually move forward, into the place He has prepared for us—His Kingdom. Only there can we have a new spiritual life in this Sinful world.

Below is **an excerpt from Chapter One** that relates to man*kind* being *originally* created in the image and **likeness** of God. It is fitting for this section and bears repeating.

The *image* part, which referred to [mankind's] higher consciousness and connection to eternity, was something God did. **The *likeness* part**, which referred to Adam's God-like authority on Earth, was something **Adam had to... workout to completion.**

The word *likeness* implies something identical [in composition or makeup], or something that has the same mannerism and/or purpose as the original. Since Adam was an image of God, it was possible for him to **physically behave and sound *like* God** on Earth.

...This is the same principle Jesus touched on when He said:

> *"[Anyone] who has seen [stared at, clearly discerned or took notice of] Me has seen [stared at or clearly discerned] the Father;"*

John 14:9b

God does not look *like* Jesus' physical form. As a man, Jesus willingly chose to know and to have the Mind of God. As a result, He naturally behaved and sounded *like* God, because His only purpose was to do God's Will.

Therefore, when people took notice of Jesus, in reality, they were *seeing* and *hearing* a physical form or version of God—His image and likeness. *That* is the opportunity and glorious **potential** the first Adam had in the beginning; and, that is the opportunity and glorious **potential** we have, now, in Christ, by faith.

Chapter 15

FAITH

...Faith^{G4102} is the assurance of things hoped for; the conviction of things not seen.

Hebrews 11:1

Since the 19th Century, generations of **believers have, undoubtedly, had negative religious experiences, based on a common misunderstanding of Hebrews 11:1 and the definition of faith**. For years, I, too, held a widely accepted Christian definition of faith and, subsequently, I learned to misapply it. As a result of our misuse of faith, we have become spiritually stagnant, because we have unintentionally sidestepped God.

For decades, churches have erroneously referred to Hebrews 11:1 as the *definition* of *faith*: typically, we are taught that faith is an act of our will, whereby we choose to believe in the unseen spiritual God and His spiritual Promises. More specifically, **we are taught to have <u>blind conviction</u> for what we hear about, and read from, the Holy Bible** and, then, we must immediately train ourselves to mentally rest assured **that the things we need and want will be provided to us**. I say *blind conviction* because most of us have yet to see, first hand, any *undeniable proof* that Jehovah God exists.

Before continuing, I must define and then explain the term **undeniable proof**, in order to distinguish my use of it from the widely accepted and watered-down definition of some believers:

> Scripturally, undeniable proof is to *physically* hear an audible voice, or see a visible expression of God, or to PERSONALLY witness a supernatural event, or have a dream that is credited to God in which there is no hint or possibility of it being a *coincidental- or common-occurrence*. Meaning, *anyone* who experienced what happened would agree that it **reliably proves God IS** Who and What He says He IS.

Since most of us have *not* experienced undeniable proof of God, it is likely we have, instead, merely given our consent to His existence and His Authority. Meaning, most of us *have mentally accepted* the existence of God through family-religious traditions and/or varying emotional responses to what we've heard, read, and learned from the Holy Bible. Then, instinctively, we've learned to cling to *chance occurrences* and we readily accept *common events* as being miraculous proof. This is mostly done subconsciously or it is unintentional; but, it can also be intentional, because it allows us to avoid asking the hard question: *where are the [signs or wonders]^G4592 we were promised would follow the believers*? (Mark 16:17-18)

Simply put: <u>most of us are struggling to believe or even to imagine *that* God exists</u>, mostly, because we lack undeniable proof. (Of course, that is but *one reason* we, also, struggle to obey His Word and live in accordance with His Promises.)

If *faith*^G4102 and *belief*^G4100 are not properly defined and followed, then we will neither confidently run nor finish the spiritual race that is set before us. (Of course, religious people are always *competing* with one another, *as if they are in a secular race to finish first.*)

- **FAITH^G4102 is NOT merely the will or the mental ability to believe *for* the physical things we want or need**, and...

- Even though it is a religious social norm to verbally *say* that God is Who and What He says He IS..., **mere mental consent or mental assent^G3982 *for* Him is NOT the same as being fully persuaded through undeniable proof.**

Defining Faith and Belief

There are three Strong's Dictionary New Testament Greek words that will be used to define the meanings of *belief* and *faith*.

The first is the Greek word *pisteuō*, Strong's reference number G4100, and it means: to have faith (in, upon, or with respect to, a person or thing); by implication **to entrust (especially one's spiritual well-being to Christ):** - **believe (-r)**, commit (to trust), **put in trust with**. The primary translation for this word is **believe (-r)**.

G4100 comes from the word pistis, **G4102**, which is defined as: **persuasion**, [**confidence**]; moral **conviction (of religious truth, or the truthfulness of God** or a religious teacher), especially reliance upon Christ for salvation; by extension the system of religious (Gospel) truth itself - assurance, belief, believe, faith, **fidelity**. In the Holy Bible, <u>the primary translation for this word is **faith**</u>.

G4102 come from the Greek word peithō, Strong's reference number **G3982**, which means: **to convince (by argument, true or false)**; by analogy, **to pacify or [appease]**; also, it means **to assent** (to evidence or authority), to rely (by inward certainty), to agree, assure, believe, have confidence, obey, persuade, trust, or yield. This word has <u>multiple translations in the Holy Bible</u>, including the following: to **convince** or persuade (as in the context of providing evidence, or through argument, debate, or swaying a crowd's opinion), to **trust in** (something, such as riches), to **obey** (either the truth or a lie), to have **confidence** in (*e.g.*, a person or a movement).

<u>Those three words describe various types of agreement with someone and/or a Cause.</u> The agreement may vary from an individual being caught up *in the moment* (*e.g.*, an immediate crowd or mob mentality, or the occasional emotional and inspirational jolt), to an individual having a *perpetual* agreement that bring about a complete renovation of his/her mindset.

<u>In general</u>, the process for perpetual agreement is as follows:

- We are Convinced,[G3982] by discussion or by experience, that <u>someone</u> seen or unseen is *who* and *what* they say, or that a crusade or a Cause is worthy and/or is Just.

- **Faith** or Persuasion[G4102] refers to our mind**set: how confident are we** that the person can do what is proclaimed and/or promised? This, then, <u>determines the level of our *obedience* to the authority the person</u> is perceived to have, and it reflects the level of *loyalty* or *respect* we choose to give to the stated Cause...

- **Beliefs**[G4100] are **our first** thoughts or mental **response** to what we hear or read (e.g., fear, worry, courage, joy, etc.); beliefs indicates how much or how little we **trust what we hear or read** (*e.g.*, regarding unseen things that are reported, promised, or declared by or about someone); **beliefs are often fluid,** because **they are based on our *current* state of mind**, which *can* be changed to form and support new or different beliefs.

Generally, when it comes to supporting unseen things, a **mindset that is based on mental consent-only** must often attempt to override an individual's nature doubts. That's because an individual who has merely given his/her **mental consent** about someone or something unseen is still *unsure*; because, he/she was convinced by something other than undeniable proof (*e.g.*, by family tradition or strong emotions). That's why an individual *can* give controlled agreeable **responses**[G4100] in public, but then, express doubt in private, especially about God.

By comparison, an individual whose **mind has been *set* and satisfied with undeniable proof** will almost always verbalize *natural* or mind-renewed responses[G4100] of agreement **IF** he/she honors and chooses to stand with the unseen person and/or the Cause. Therefore, when the individual thinks and, then, speaks or acts in accordance with the person or Cause, it is *natural*—not pretense.

Scripturally, as it relates to having **faith *in* God**, here is how the process *should* flow:

- **We are Convinced**[G3982] **that God Is** Who and What He says He IS, **because we are, first, humbled by an undeniable sign or a wonder** that followed a true believer, who was preaching the good news of our salvation. If we sincerely crave or desire Jehovah-God and His Ways, **we will make a quality decision to honor Him**; subsequently...

- **We have Faith**[G4102] *in* **God:** ① we are **persuaded** to submit to His Authority, ② we **trust** what He said *has* happened, and ③ we have **confidence** *in* what He said will happen; as such, **our mind is being reset or renewed**.

For example, following are several significant events that has happened and one requirement that must happen:

- o Satan and Sin infected the world through the first Adam

- o The world has already been judged, because of Sin;

- o God has already provided a means of salvation from Sin: [the] Christ, Who also happens to be the very sign of His judgment against Sin

- o As such, we are required to *see* and understand eternal and spiritual concepts, in order to live a victorious Christ-like life over Sin, because there is an impending tribunal against Sin and anyone who *deliberately* stands with [the] Satan—the adversary of godliness.

Because we have confidence *in* God, **our immediate response**[G4100] **to this life or to any situation** (*e.g.*, our first thoughts) **perpetually agrees with** ① Who He IS and His Authority, ② His Promises for today (*e.g.*, our new spiritual life and His Holy Spirit *in* us, etc.), ③ His Promises for tomorrow (*e.g.*, Christ's imminent return for us and unfathomable things He has prepared for those that love Him), and ④ His Warnings of judgment.

Scripturally, **faith is NOT for the purpose of assuring us that God exists** (*i.e.*, He is real). Rather, **faith was/is needed for an individual to willingly and deliberately ACT** (*i.e.*, to obey, to do, and/or to say something), based **on God's Authority and His revealed Word** (*e.g.*, His Plans, His Promises, AND His Judgments); because, **the faith-filled are persuaded that Jehovah-God is faithful to His Word**: He did what He said and He will do exactly what He said.

Hebrews 11:1

Hebrews 11:1 is identical to 11:7. Of course, all of the faith examples in Hebrews Chapter 11 are related to 11:1, in one way or another, but 11:7 actually clarifies for us a key term: *things not seen*.

> *By faith, Noah, being warned by God about <u>things</u> <u>not yet seen</u> {specifically, God's judgment—the flood waters}, [in reverence or in fear]^{G2125} [he] prepared an ark for the salvation of his household, by which he condemned the world, and became an heir of the righteousness which is according to faith.*

> *Hebrews 11:7*

For the sake of clarity, the following points must be highlighted:

- Before the Ark, the world was already condemned because of man*kind*'s preference for expressing Sin (*e.g.*, premediated and spontaneous murders, violence, etc.) (Ref. Genesis 6:5-7, 11-12)

- First, God personally **warned** Noah about <u>things not seen</u> (*i.e.*, the flood waters—His impending judgment)

- In reverence or fear, Noah ACTED, based on his confidence in God's Authority and His Words: he obeyed and built the Ark—the means *of* salvation; therefore...

- Noah's or man*kind*'s **salvation happened because of obedience** to God's instructions, **and that pleased God**

- So, because of his obedience to God, Noah became **an inheritor or possessor of the *kind* of righteousness** (*i.e.*, equity of character) **that is of God**: he was **justified or** acquitted **through or by his obedience** and, therefore, he was saved from that particular judgment against Sin.

So then, there are two aspects or parts to Hebrews 11:1 that faith supports and proves: ① **Promises** we expect to be fulfilled and, ② the **Warning** of impending judgment—<u>unseen things</u> yet to come.

> *...**Faith**^{G4102} {or persuasion and confidence <u>in</u> God} is the [... (support) or assurance]^{G5287} of things {(i.e., His Promises we've)} [hoped for or we expect]^{G1697} {has already been done and/or will be done; faith is also} the [proof, conviction, evidence]^{G1650} of things {He has Warned will happen (i.e., impending Judgment, which we have)} not {yet} seen.*

Hebrews 11:1

Hebrews 11:1 is not defining faith; instead, **11:1 is describing faith**[G4102] **as an applied Standard** (*i.e.*, a rule or a principle that is used as a basis or an authorized starting point) for Justification, Righteousness, and Salvation.

The Standard is: we are confident[G4102] **that God did what He said and we fully EXPECT**[G4100] **every one of His Promises to be fulfilled**; therefore, because of that, **we willingly obey His Authority and we reverently ACT** on His Warnings of things not yet seen, from which we are saved.

To illustrate the application of a corporate Standard, consider the familiar term, *gold*. Gold is a widely accepted *precious or valuable yellow-ish metallic element* that is not subject to corrosion or decay. **That is its basic *definition*.**

But, **the application of gold as a standard describes a monetary system** in which the face value of a currency (*e.g.*, paper and coins that are being circulated) is backed or supported by a fixed quantity of physical gold. That financially sound standard was widely used by many nations before it was abandoned for the more convenient and manipulative credit-based system where credits and debits are, almost literally, generated out of thin air, and we have learned to give universal *consent* to that virtual financial system.

Alone, paper currency is just that: paper with numbers, words, and, in most cases, pictures or icons printed on it. In the past, **gold supported** (*i.e.*, it **gave the necessary weight or added-in the actual worth** to) the numeric-value printed on the currency. **Without mature faith,**[G4102] **many of our religion-based words** (*e.g.*, our prayers, declarations, confessions, etc.) **and our actions**—good deeds—**are weightless or have little to no spiritual worth**. But, **true persuasion** or confidence[G4102] *in* God **will add-in the necessary value** or spiritual weight to our words and actions. And, like God's Word, our words will succeed or accomplish their intended purpose.

Faith is necessary to please Jehovah-God, because His Will (*e.g.*, humanity's protection, salvation, etc.) is accomplished through **the**

standard of faith—our assurance of His Word. In order for faith[G4102] to be effective, the one who worships or draws near to God must ALREADY be convinced[G3982] that He IS...; because, faith is confidence[G4102] *in* His Authority and His ability to do what He says He will do. The results are perpetual beliefs,[G4100] based on Jehovah-God being a **Rewarder** of [...or He provides protection and salvation *for*] them that diligently seek or crave him. (Ref. Hebrews 11:6)

Is Faith Blind?

Faith is NOT blind, especially not in the way we *might* think or are led to believe. **God never expected anyone to serve Him blindly— never having <u>undeniable proof</u> of His Authority and/or Power**, as it would *seem* the Church has, for centuries, insisted people do. Without undeniable signs and wonders following the believers, **especially church leadership**, there is little to no difference between the Holy Bible and any other religion-based writings, or even a fictional story (*e.g.*, Santa Clause).

In the Old Testament (OT), whenever God asked or required people to do something, He would, first, show that person or people a sign (*e.g.*, an appearance) and/or speak to them directly or through a person of His choosing. Even after the Law was given, those Israelites who were born after the *original* signs and wonders—the supernatural manifestations that got the Israelites from Egypt to Canaan—were to have undeniable proof through the unmistakable signs and wonders that *were supposed to follow* their faithful or obedient parents. Collectively, the Israelites *were supposed to live a distinctively blessed life* that was to be envied by non-Israelites. (Ref. Deuteronomy 28:1-14.)

In the New Testament (NT), Jehovah-God did miraculous things— signs and wonders—through Jesus [the] Christ. He wanted the people to *see* for themselves that He was *with* or among them, first, before He gave them *right-now* Promises and *eternal-spiritual* Promises in which to have HOPE; and before He warned them of unseen things or impending judgments to avoid.

But, as is evident in Scripture, **signs and wonders can and will be dismissed**, resulting in little to no faith—obedience to His Authority, **if a person and/or a people do not willingly humble themselves and honor Jehovah-God as Lord and Savior**. Subsequently, if a person or a people will not honor God, then they will neither desire Him nor His holy Ways, regardless of what they hear and/or see from Him.

In both the Old and New Testaments, despite the various signs and wonders from Heaven, despite the miracles (*e.g.*, the healings), and despite the deliverance events from demon oppression (*e.g.*, people being set free from seizures, hearing and speech issues, and other mental related adverse spiritual conditions), **people still had an issue with faith** (*i.e.*, confidence *in* God's Authority and *in* what He said), **because they did not honor Him** (Ref. Romans 1:21-25).

But unlike today, in Bible times, the issue of faith rarely centered on the question of whether Jehovah-God existed. The issue of faith back then was, primarily, about **the mindset** of the people. Ultimately, many were **unwilling to love, prefer, and fear the invisible God** *more* **than the visible things of this world**: they remained carnally-minded. And today, while that can also describe the people's overall state of mind, there was more accountability back then, because of the signs and wonders they physically saw.

So, in many ways, it is unfair for a sermon to suggest that the average unbeliever, today, is being a "Doubting Thomas" (*i.e.*, the disciple who would not believe Jesus was resurrected from the dead until he saw physical proof). Typically, in such sermons, the implication or warning is: *we must have blind faith and believe what the Bible says, even if there is no physical proof.*

But **that noteworthy situation with Thomas was not about having blind faith** *in* something he did not personally see happen. It was about *disobedience to God's Authority or disbelieving the truth.*

> Then [Jesus] said to Thomas, "Reach here with your finger, and see My hands; and reach here your hand and put it into My side; and do not be unbelieving,[G571] [disbelieving, or without Christian

faith (specifically a heathen); untrustworthy (person): - that believeth not, faithless] **but** *[be]* **believing**[G4103] *[trustworthy; trustful:* faithful, true]."*

{After recognizing Him <u>by</u> His wounds,} **Thomas answered and said to Him, "My Lord and my God!"**

Jesus said to him, "Because you have seen[G3708] [or because you have *stared at*, or <u>you have discerned or perceived clearly (either *physically or mentally*)</u> or because you have personally *experienced*] **Me, have you believed?**[G4100] **Blessed are they who did not** {or do not personally} **see**[G1492] {this glorious event}, **and yet believed"**[G4100] {based on what they have already known and seen}.

John 20:27-29

There is little to no comparison between most of us and Thomas. Thomas was one of the original twelve Disciples, so he was with Jesus for several years. **By that time, he had physically SEEN countless miracles** and he had personally heard Jesus explain many of the **mysteries** of the Old Testament that the general population of that day could or would not hear, even though they were looking right at the things He did. So, even though he did not personally see the glorious resurrection of Jesus, **by that time, Thomas should have been fully convinced**[G3982] **that Jehovah-God is Who He said He IS,** which meant, *he should have been* fully PERSUADED[G4102] or faith-filled enough to believe[G4100] and obey, what was being reported to him about Jesus' resurrection from the dead.

From faith to faith:

FROM the faith—the persuasion and confidence—that is <u>based on what was **already** seen and heard from God</u>, **TO** the kind of **faith that is, itself, the sole proof of what is now being heard/reported**.

That's why faith is never blind:
1) It is, first, established through undeniable miraculous events and through the truth the individual *already* holds to or knows,

2) Then, as the mind is progressively renewed, day by day, **the renewed mind itself can sustain greater expectations**[G4100] and more readily **accept greater manifestations** of His Presence and Plan.

Naturally, Thomas believed the amazing things Jesus did in the past, because he personally saw or witnessed those miracles. But, apparently, even after all he saw and heard, his faith—his confidence to obey and support the truth that *ALL THINGS REALLY ARE POSSIBLE WITH GOD*—remained conveniently small. So, <u>when Jesus reprimanded Thomas</u>, **it was not because he was merely skeptical when he heard about something new, glorious, and/or amazing** (*i.e.*, resurrection from the dead).

Unfortunately, like many of the proud-minded religious leaders of his day, **Thomas made a conscious decision to disbelieve that Jesus could do something so seemingly impossible, like defeat Death**, even though God Promised through David (Ref. Psalms 16:10), in a round-about-way, that *He would raise up His Holy One on the third day to prevent His body from seeing decay*, which occurs on the fourth day, after death. And, even though Thomas personally witnessed Jesus' God-given Authority over sicknesses, diseases, and demonic forces (*i.e.*, when Jesus was healing and freeing the people) on countless occasions.

More importantly, even though Thomas had already witnessed that same Authority over Death when Jesus raised up Jairus' daughter (Luke 8:54-55) and Lazarus (John 11:41-44) from the dead, **he still deliberately disbelieved Jesus when He plainly told him and the other disciples** that *He would be struck or killed, but then He would be raised up [by God] on the third day*. (Ref. Matthew 15:21, 20:19, 26:31-32, and Luke 18:33-34)

Faith Comes...

Scripturally, both of the following statement are true:

- **Seeing is believing** - (1 Kings 10:6-7, Matthew 27:42, John 10:38, 20:29a, James 2:19b)

☞ **Believing is, eventually, seeing** - (Matthew 21:22, Mark 11:22-24, John 11:25-26 & 40, John 20:29b, James 2:19a)

Man*kind* is first carnal (*i.e.*, we are predominantly physically-minded). So, **if** we give mental consent[G3982] to the existence and Authority of the *unseen* God **based only on** audibly hearing and reading His Word—without any undeniable proof, then that decision will, most likely, be easily and frequently overwhelmed by other decisions[G3982] to respect and, subsequently, to fear something or someone physical with more *perceived* power and authority.

> *However, the spiritual is <u>not</u> first, but the natural [sensitive or animated];*
>
> 1 Corinthians 15:46a
>
> *The first man [or Adam] is from the earth [soil or ground], earthy [dusty or soil like];*
>
> 1 Corinthians 15:47a

Because of our naturally-carnal mindset, there are few truths that can be successfully revealed without ever being demonstrated, first. The truth about Jehovah-God is NOT one of them, nor was it meant to be; especially given the requirement for radical change.

A **mature application of faith**—a willingness to obey the Authority and Word of God—*initially* **requires visual and/or audible manifestations from Heaven**, because a person must willingly humble him/herself before he/she will choose to perpetually honor someone claiming to be greater. (I say *initially* because, as in the case of Thomas, at some point, **faith MUST lead to greater faith**—it MUST **be**come self-evident.)

And, without heartfelt honor—after recognizing that Jehovah-God IS Who and What He says He IS, mature confidence[G4102] in what He has said will be difficult to establish.

> <u>So then</u>[G686] *Faith comes from hearing, and hearing by the word of God.*
>
> Romans 10:17

Yes, faith[G4102] does come from [repeatedly] *hearing,*[G189] the Word of God. The Strong's dictionary defines G189 as followed: *(the act, the sense or the thing heard), preached, reported, [or] rumored.* **But, again, it's NOT quite as simple as merely reading the Holy Bible and/or audibly listening to sermons about God's Word that leads to [mature] faith.**

To get the complete picture of *how* faith truly comes, you cannot start with Romans 10:17; you have to consider 10:16, first:

> **But they** *[specifically, the Israelites of old]* **have not all obeyed**[G5219] **the gospel. For** *[in Isaiah 53:1]* **Isaiah** *[indicated that everyone did not believe the good news; therefore, he made that point clear by asking the question, "Lord, whosoever or whichever one believe*[G4100] *or has put trust" in our report]*?

> *Romans 10:16 (KJV)*

The word *obeyed*[G5219] is defined by Strong's as: **to hear** *under* **(as a subordinate),** *to listen attentively; by implication to heed or* **conform to a command or authority;** *be obedient to [what is said].* The word *obey* is made up of two other words: G5259, which means, **under or inferior to**; and G191, which means, **to hear or understand**.

That is why the first two words in Romans 10:17, literally, *draws a conclusion* from 10:16: **"So then"**[G686], **faith** (*i.e.*, being persuaded enough to make a quality decision to humbly and willingly submit to a Higher Authority) **come from hearing….** But, unless we have humbled ourselves, first, after being convinced that God IS Who and What He said He IS, we will not hear His Word (*i.e.,* his Promises and Warnings) **in the right mindset—as a subordinate.**

Isaiah 53 indicates, *obey* **ALSO means to look for and expect**[G4100] God to keep His Promise of *complete* salvation that, ultimately, leads to His *kind* of Justification and Righteousness: being Sin-free.

> **For in** *[the gospel or the good news of Jesus Christ]* **the righteousness of God is revealed {FROM a faith** *that is based on what was seen and heard from God,*

TO the kind of faith that is, itself, the very evidence or proof of God's Promises and Warnings that are yet to be seen}; as it is written, "But the righteous man shall live by faith."

Romans 1:17

The Status Quo

Today, it seems the average churched-person is merely being **encouraged**[G3982] **through inspirational and enticing words or alluring promises of men**. Also, it seems people are **merely being convinced**[G3982] **of God by traditional means**: most commonly, through the testimony of someone whom they consider to be a reliable source (*e.g.*, a close relative, a trusted family friend, a pastor, etc.). But that reliable source is *usually* someone who is merely conveying what he/she has heard from another reliable source, and/or has read for him/herself from the Holy Bible, and/or has learned from a reputable institution.

That means, in most cases, **neither we nor our reliable sources can base our faith on a personal encounter with God's glorious presence or on personally experiencing a genuine miracle**.

But that's not how it is supposed to be.

[Jesus said,] *These [indications or signs will follow near, attend to, conform to, or fully know] those who have believed: in My name they will cast out demons, they will speak with new tongues;*

They will [take away, remove, or atone for maliciousness, especially Satan], and if they drink any deadly poison, it will not hurt them; they will lay hands on the sick, and they will recover."

Mark 16:17-18

[In a letter to the church at Corinth, the Apostle Paul wrote,] *And my [speech] and my preaching were not in [enticing] words of man's wisdom, but <u>in demonstration of the Spirit and of power,</u>*

> *So that your faith [should __not__ stand {or ripen or bear fruit}] on the wisdom of men, but {stand} on the [dunamis: force, miraculous power, ability or meaning] of God.*

1 Corinthians 2:4-5

Since the days of the original Apostles, there has been only a few documented men and women of God who have had signs and wonders *closely* following them. But, because of hubris and/or idolatry, **it was necessary** for the frequency of such glorious signs and wonders to lessen and eventually stop; or, in some cases, the person suddenly died. During or immediately after those *glory-days*, a major ministry was established and was managed by or, at least, bore the name of that man or woman, who was viewed by the masses as an authoritative voice of God to the Church.

In that person's latter days, he/she would speak about, and consistency encouraged others with, the miracles that happened **in the past**. And, as was often the case, other major and minor ministries were birthed from that one to carry a similar version of God's Word to their generations; but, they did not, necessarily, carry on the same glorious power of God. So, without the frequency of miracles, that major ministry and many of its offspring **conveniently made adjustments** to gain, retain, and refresh the masses.

Even though the Church at large *sounds* more intelligent than it did in past generations, the reality is: **from the pulpit to the pews, the people have mostly substituted true faith**[G4102] **with virtual faith**.[G3982] Simply put: we are doing **faith impersonations to support the selected parts of God's Promises** that we have conveniently chosen to hold or value more. The purpose is to, at least, *appear* to have great faith by routinely doing and saying faith-like things.

In most religious circles, ***faith* itself is a form of competition that is measured by the amount of knowledge someone has**. This concept is a natural progression of our innate desire for convenience and approval: learning a lot of facts is easier and gains recognition more quickly **than the process of renewing one's mind**.

Today, most believers support a common **mis**-conception: if people talk like they have mature faith, then they will, eventually, DESERVE the benefits of mature faith. So, when we have financial and/or health problems, **we are taught** to avoid saying that *we are poor* and avoid describing *how badly we actually feel*. Instead, **we are taught** to only say what we *want* to happen.

Therefore, we will routinely answer the question, "how are you...?" with a faith-sounding response, such as, "I'm blessed," or "I am in good health;" and, we will often add to those faith sounding declarations the phrase, "... and I am highly favored of the Lord."

Yes, mature faith[G4102] does *sound* **like that**. But *words* that are spoken through fact-gathering and/or learned speech training do **not** have **the same impact and effectiveness in the spiritual realm as do** *words* **spoken through courageous doubt-free expectancy**: a genuine inner-confidence that what we are saying will happen.

By impersonating faith, yes, a person will *sound* spiritual or faith-filled. But the reality is, there will be little to no evidence or fruits; because, the required authenticity of, and confidence in, what is spoken or declared will be missing. **Learning** *faith-talk* **can be a good starting point** for any believer to become **more mindful** of Who God Is and who He says we are, in Christ; **but,** *mastering* **the art of faith-talk should never be the goal**.

So, why are we merely learning faith-talk and not true faith?

Because even though the Church is mostly impotent—devoid of the Presence and Power of God, instead of people repenting and seeking God, subconsciously, they've learned to see and accept an environment that is nearly devoid of His Presences as being normal.

Man*kind*'s Original Fault: Ignoring the Will of God

Sometimes our reasons for disobedience are so subtle and natural that the resulting sin is almost unrecognizable, at first. For example, the first Adam sinned when he *instinctively* desired to please the other one of his *kind*, Eve, whom he could physically see, more than he desired to please God, Whom he could not see.

That impulsive decision gave way to Sin; and, Sin caused man*kind* to be **evicted from the Garden of Eden**.

As previously indicated, the Garden was the original place God intended for man*kind* to have perpetual rest, while knowing or recognizing only good—free of adversity. More importantly, **the Garden was the place God chose to meet with man*kind***. But, after Adam and Eve submitted themselves to Sin—each for different reasons, they were removed from that meeting place.

Then, God ordained other places or temples where He could meet with His people, as dictated in the Mosaic Law. And finally, through Christ, His people became *living temples* for Him to dwell in.

However, **collectively**, God's people have yet to truly follow His original plan for their lives, **unity: being one with each other, in Him**. Although there may have been several occasions when some people came close (Ref. Act 2 and 4:32-35), to this day, **God's people are still ignoring His Will, by remaining divided:** like Eve, many are obviously deceived; and, like Adam, many are impulsive.

But, if a group of people, who think and speak the same way (*i.e.*, they are of one mind), can accomplish *anything* they set out to do, *even if* God was not with them (Genesis 11:1-6), then it is easier to see why *nothing would be impossible* to the Church when **we are of one mind, in Christ**, (*e.g.*, we could literally move mountains).

So then, if disobedience gives place to Sin, and Sin separates us from Jehovah-God, then **our new spiritual Sin-free-obedient lives will invite and ignite His Presence in us ALL** (Ref. Act 2:43-47, 5:12).

> *[Jesus said,] "A new commandment I give to you, that you love one another, even as I have loved you, that you also love one another.*
>
> *"By this all men will know that you are My disciples, if you have love for one another."*
>
> John 13:34-35

JESUS CHRIST IS THE WORD OF GOD: He is our prime example of spiritually-mature-obedience to God the Father.

He is the true image of God; and, while on earth, He behaved and sounded just *like* God. Jesus loved His fellowman, because God *is* Love.

The God-*kind* of love is the source of the UNITY that *will* bind true believers together in this world. And, as Jesus said, **LOVE is the ultimate sign of TRUE discipleship**.

The world cannot duplicate God's *unconditional love*. A carnally-minded person has fears and is perpetually suspicions; as such, he/she naturally places conditions on love—affection, so as to avoid being hurt by others. **That's why that NEW spiritually-based commandment leads us to war, in subtle and in not so subtle ways**.

The battleground is the *un*-renewed mind and the enemies are the carnal thoughts (passions and fears) that still occupy it. And, just as God instructed the Israelites *not* to allow ANY of the former inhabitants of Canaan to physically remain among them, **we must** *not* **allow ANY part of <u>our former Sinful selves</u> to mentally remain and live *within* us**.

In order for God's Word to be firmly established in us, we need to **continue the work of salvation**, which God started through Christ Jesus: <u>we must **forcibly drive out the enemies of our new spiritual**</u> **<u>lives</u>**. Our enemies include *selfishness, pride, bitterness, envy, hate, lust, lying, **un**-forgiveness, complaining, idolatry*...; and, that's just a few of **the characteristics that prevent us from truly loving one another** like Christ loved us when He died for us on the Cross.

If **we cannot love** other consecrated servants **the way God instructed us**, then there is no way we will truly experience the Plans and Promises of God in this world. As a result, we will *remain* in a state of <u>RESTLESSNESS, DISUNITY, and IMPOTENCY</u>—without Godly power, especially in our collective worship.

Today, there are many forms of **religious preferences**; which is to say, there is little unity in the Faith among those who call themselves *Christians*. It is not uncommon for each person or group to only worship with, and relate to, other people with whom they agree in the most convenient of ways.

And that is the perpetual problem: what may have started out as subtle differences in religious views, has easily morphed into complacency and contempt for others with opposing viewpoints.

Before going to the Cross, Jesus washed His disciples' feet, so that He could give them an example of *how* to **love and serve one another**, regardless of rank or position (Ref. John 17:4-5).

Afterward, **Jesus prayed** one of His last and most notable prayers, which included the following Words:

> "I do not ask on behalf of [just these disciples that are currently with Me, now], but also for those who will believe in Me through their words; **that they may *all* be one**; even as You, Father, are in Me and I in You, **that they also may be in Us, so that the world may believe that You sent Me.**

> "The glory [or the honor or reputation] which You have given Me I have given to them, that they may be one, just as We are One; I [Your Word] in them and You [Love] in Me, **that they may be perfected in unity, so that the world may know that You sent Me, and loved them** [John 3:16], even as You have loved Me. Father, I desire that they also, whom You have given Me, be with Me where I am, so that they may see My glory which You have given Me, for You loved Me before the foundation of the world.

> "O righteous Father, although the world has not known You, yet I have known You; and these have known that You sent Me; and **I have made Your name known to them, and will make it known, so that the love with which You loved Me may be in them, and I in them.**" (Ref. John 17:20-26)

God Is Love, and **HIS PEOPLE ARE SUPPOSED TO BE *LIKE* HIM**, in this world: just *like* Christ was *like* Him.

Based on Jesus' description of the Church's role in this world, **did YOU see the undeniable PROOF of God's unconditional Love *in* His people while YOU were first being convinced of the gospel** or, per the status quo, were you made to be convinced of your sins—guilt and shame, first**?**

Even today, **does the world REALLY know**, understand, and trust that God sent Jesus into the world because **He *is* love**?

Sure, the world *has been informed* that God loves EVERYONE, because that information (*i.e.*, John 3:16) has become a familiar, generic, and religious **catch phrase**, through repetition, by churched people. But, the passage **John 3:16 was NOT meant to be an overly used convenient religious statement *directed at* sinful people**, so as to get them to confess their sins.

> *For God so loved the world that He gave His only begotten Son…,* is an accountability statement: it was **meant to be PROVEN by His people**. The type of love God has for the world, or for the people that adorn the earth, should also be *shown by* His people for one another; because, CHRIST, as the Word or Commandment of God, IS SUPPOSED TO BE IN HIS PEOPLE and they *in* Him (Ref. John 17:26).

This is not referring to superficial fellowship that happens only while attending a church service. It is a God-like love that only the mature in Christ are capable of fulfilling (1 Corinthians 13:1-8).

There is *Still* the Need to Repent

"Repent,[G3340] *for the kingdom of Heaven [or the rule of spiritual things is nearby]."*

Matthew 3:2, 4:17, Mark 1:15

Repenting is more than expressing grief. Based on its Scriptural use, *repenting* implies, *thinking differently and/or reconsidering your current condition* {or your current course or direction}, based on either new information or an ultimatum you've received. True repenting *often* begins with a moment of clarity, usually, regarding the truth we ALREADY know. *At some point, we must have an unwavering agreement with God's Word,* based on what we have seen from Him.

To continue from the previous section, the reason we are not seeing signs and wonders is: **The Church is STILL sidestepping the heart of God in favor of our religious and cultural differences.**

Jesus prayed to the Father for the Church to be UNIFIED in their LOVE one for another, and He instructed the Church—believers—to be unified or to be as *one*. So, WE KNOW THAT *BEING AS ONE* IS HIS AND THE FATHER'S WILL FOR US ALL.

But, <u>even back in NT Bible days</u>, when there were more signs and wonders, <u>Jesus' desire for oneness was still difficult to comply with</u>. Even elder believers in the past had trouble overcoming learned cultural preferences and subtle forms of prejudice behavior for and against others, especially regarding outward appearances:

- The Apostle Paul corrected the Apostle Peter and others for allowing themselves to be culturally intimidated: they sought to please their Jewish brethren, at the risk of offending new Gentile believers (James 2:1-7)

- The Apostle James, the biological brother of Jesus (Mary's son), warned Christians believers to avoid showing preferential treatment to the rich, while instinctively looking down on the poor (James 2:1-7).

To this day, such preferential treatment still exists. And today, as in the early church, when it comes to *sitting under someone* to hearing the Word, there are/were also personal preferences *for* the one preaching the gospel, probably, for the same reason as it was back then: people prefer to have their ears tickled by a certain speaking styles or there is a cultural connect to a particular person.

> *[The Apostle's Paul's letter to Corinth]* **And I, brethren, could not speak to you as to <u>spiritual</u> men, but as [carnal]**[G4559]**, as to infants in Christ.**
>
> **I gave you milk to drink, not solid food; for you were not yet able to receive it. Indeed, even now you are not yet able,**
>
> **For you are still [carnal]**[G4559]**. For since there is jealousy and strife among you, are you not [carnal], and are you not walking like mere men?**
>
> **For when one says, "I am of Paul," and another, "I am of Apollos," are you not [carnal]**[G4559] **men?**

What then is Apollos? And what is Paul? Servants through whom you believed, even as the Lord gave opportunity to each one.

I planted, Apollos watered, but God was causing the growth.

So then neither the one who plants nor the one who waters is anything, but God who causes the growth.

1 Corinthians 3:1-7

Interesting enough, that erroneous favoritism occurred when most of the Church was being persecuted. One might think there would have been a *natural* **sense of solidarity and appreciation among those who were**, possibly, **being persecuted** and oppressed; especially, if they were being persecuted for the same reason.

But, to this day, **the Body of Christ remains fragmented** for one reason or another. We seem to think we can afford to separate from those with whom we have the slightest of disagreements or differences (*e.g.*, subtle Biblical interpretation, political affiliations, economic status, ethnicity, etc.). Yes! In some ways we are *grouped together* locally but, usually, only in ways that are convenient to us.

That means, overall, **the Church at large has never really grasped Jesus' commandment for unification and unconditional love**, at least not long-term. As such, there are fewer manifestations of His genuine Presence and Power in our midst.

[The Apostle Paul wrote:] *Therefore I urge you, brethren, by the mercies of God, to present your bodies a living and holy sacrifice, acceptable to God, which is your spiritual service of worship.*

And do not be conformed to this world, but be transformed by the renewing of your mind, so that you may prove what the will of God is, that which is good and acceptable and perfect.

Romans 12:1-2

So, because of the Church's **impotency and low sense of eternity**, at some point, the *faith*-movement was redirected from *having faith IN God*, so that His Will be done on earth, to desperately trying to apply *faith FOR things* (*e.g.*, **our** healing, **our** finances, **our** relationships, **our** houses, **our** happiness, etc.), *in* Jesus' Name, solely for the betterment of our lives in this world. But, again, **our individual needs and wants** are NOT the primary application of faith.

It is the responsibility of the Body of Christ to BE Christ-like in the earth—to the world, so that the world will know that God loves them/us. People need to *see* the proof of His love. YES!! Pray for revival *in* the Church; because, **we ALL need to *see* signs and wonders**, including the proof of His love for us, so that our faith can stand on more than just the persuasive and enticing words of men.

> *Let love be without hypocrisy. Abhor what is evil; cling to what is good.*
>
> *Be devoted to one another in brotherly love; give preference to one another in honor;*
>
> *Not lagging behind in diligence, fervent in spirit, serving the Lord;*
>
> *Rejoicing in hope, persevering in tribulation, devoted to prayer,*
>
> *Contributing to the needs of the saints, practicing hospitality.*
>
> *Bless those who persecute you; bless and do not curse.*
>
> *Rejoice with those who rejoice, and weep with those who weep.*
>
> *Be of the same mind toward one another; do not be haughty in mind, but associate with the lowly. Do not be wise in your own estimation.*
>
> *Never pay back evil for evil to anyone. Respect what is right in the sight of all men.*

If possible, so far as it depends on you, be at peace with all men.

Never take your own revenge, beloved, but leave room for the wrath of God, for it is written, "Vengeance is Mine, I will repay," says the Lord.

"But if your enemy is hungry, feed him, and if he is thirsty, give him a drink; for in so doing you will heap burning coals on his head."

Do not be overcome by evil, but overcome evil with good.

Romans 12:9-21

And, while we are faithfully practicing ALL of that, in love, we trust or we have faith *in* Jehovah-God and *in* His Authority to meet our needs. Meaning, **it is not necessary for us to focus on or desperately attempt to muster up faith *for* OUR needs**.

And [Jesus] said to His disciples, "For this reason I say to you, do not worry about your life, as to what you will eat; nor for your body, as to what you will put on.

"For life is more than food, and the body more than clothing.

"Consider the ravens, for they neither sow nor reap; they have no storeroom nor barn, and yet God feeds them; how much more valuable you are than the birds!

"And which of you by worrying can add a single hour to his life's span?

"If then you cannot do even a very little thing, why do you worry about other matters?

"Consider the lilies, how they grow: they neither toil nor spin; but I tell you, not even Solomon in all his glory clothed himself like one of these.

"But if God so clothes the grass in the field, which is alive today and tomorrow is thrown into the furnace, how much more will He clothe you? <u>You men of little faith</u>!

"And do not seek what you will eat and what you will drink, and do not keep worrying.

"For all these things the nations of the world eagerly seek; but <u>your Father knows that you need these things</u>.

"<u>But seek His kingdom</u> {His reign and rule within you}, <u>and these things will be added to you</u>.

Do not be afraid, little flock, for your Father has chosen gladly to give you the kingdom {the rule and reign of spiritual principles and concepts}."

Luke 12:22-32

The truly called and sent-out ones of God must set the example. The local pastor must humble him/herself and unite his/her church members to be as one, as Christ and the Father are One; then, signs and wonders will follow those believers. Local pastors must unite with other local churches to be as one, as Christ and the Father are One; then, signs and wonders will follow those believers. The Church as a whole must unite to be as one, as Christ and the Father are One; then, signs and wonders will follow ALL true believers.

The Victory that Overcomes the World …

The apostles said to the Lord, "Increase[G4369] our faith!"

Luke 17:5

Before I began to see the true definition of faith—that it was not blind conviction *for* the existence of God and spiritual concepts, I routinely asked God to *increase my faith [for Him]*. Based on personal conversations with other believers and on personal observations, I'm certain that other believers have asked Him for the same. So, when I read that Jesus' apostles asked Him to increase their faith, I was very interested in His response.

Until recently, it did not seem like Jesus' response directly addressed their request for *increased faith*.[G4102] Meaning, at first, I thought we—them and I—wanted the same thing: for Jesus to *do* something miraculous, so as to provide proof of spiritual things. But surely, unlike me, the apostles were not asking to *see* something, in order to believe in spiritual things.

By that point in time, they had seen many miracles by Jesus (*e.g.*, devils being casted out and various types of healings for many people), and many of them had personally done the same in His name (Ref. Luke 10:1-17). Actually, I believe they wanted Jesus to *give* them *the gift of faith* (Ref. 1 Corinthians 12:9a). But that gift did not fit the occasion for which they were asking: a readiness to cheerfully obey, what seemed like, a difficult commandment.

> Again, to have faith[G4102] *in* God is to be fully **persuaded**, fully **confident**, or fully **assured** of His Authority and His Word—He is faithful and well able to do what He said He will—after being convinced that He is Who He says He IS. As such, **faith is a mindset of humbled-obedience to Jehovah-God** in support of HIs Promises, and faith provides evidence for the Warnings—impending judgment—of things not yet seen, which cause us to obey His instructions for our salvation and for the salvation of others.

The *gift of faith* is given by the Spirit of God to the believers He has appointed for spiritual heavy-lifting or extremely difficult and, realistically, unbearable works that would, understandably, threaten or weaken the resolve of someone not gifted. The apostles wanted Jesus to immediately ***increase***[G4369] [or to *lay beside (extend the range or reach of)* or add to] ***their faith***—their readiness to submit to His Word—supernaturally or, perhaps, **unnaturally**. But, in *that* particular situation, they were capable of increasing their own faith, based on what they had already seen and heard from Him directly.

That's why Jesus addressed their request with two scenarios describing God's Authority, Kingdom, or Reign, which must be *in* us.

One: The Authority—Kingdom—of *God at <u>work</u> in us*:

> *And the Lord said, "If you had faith like a mustard seed, you would say to this Sycamore [or fig] tree, 'Be uprooted and be planted in the sea'; [then or indeed] <u>it would obey^{G5219} you</u>."*

Luke 17:6

Meaning, if a subordinate is instructed by a superior to do something beyond his/her means, the subordinate has the superior's authority and resources at his/her disposal to get the task done. In our case, once we know the Heart and Will of God for us and others, we have His Authority and His Name to make specific things happen. Basically, Jesus was saying, **we can EXPECT the same Authority God used to create this physical universe to be at work within us**, because He's the One through whom it was given to us.

As such, we should have a living expectation^{G4100} that **things** in both the physical and spiritual realms **will obey us**, too, <u>if we are working in accordance with the known Plan and/or we are doing the known Will of Jehovah-God</u>.

Two: The Authority—Kingdom—of *God at <u>rest</u> in us*:

> *"Which of you, having a slave plowing or tending sheep, will say to him when he has come in from the field, 'Come immediately and sit down to eat'?*
>
> *"But will he not say to him, 'Prepare something for me to eat, and properly clothe yourself and serve me while I eat and drink; and afterward you may eat and drink'?*
>
> *"He does not thank the slave because he did the things which were commanded, does he?*
>
> *"So, you too, when you do all the things which are commanded you, say, 'We are [merely] slaves; we*

have done only that which we ought to have done.'"

Luke 17:7-10

Both of those examples are about obedience to the Will and/or Plans of God: obedience from created things, including us. Not only *do* we have God's Authority *at work in us*, **we *must* also have His Authority *at rest in us*;** because, **we must remain faithful to His Will until the end,** regardless of how inconvenient it may seem.

But first, there are several points that must be clarified in that second example, understandably, due to our modern-day mindset against slavery:

- Slavery has been *acknowledged* in the Holy Bible—Old and New Testaments, because it was/is a part of the human experience. But just because something is mentioned in the Bible does not mean it is approved of by God. Like taxes, slavery was a part of most societies' economic systems, whereby debts were paid off: rather than throwing a person in (debtor's) prison, they or a relative would, instead, work off the debt. In most cases, it was also better than killing the debtor in anger. Of course, like most human experiences, people were **exploited in an untold number of abusive and forceful ways** (*e.g.,* conquered nations of people, orphans, women, the homeless, etc.) through slavery **for the convenience of others**, because of man*kind*'s Sinfulness; but...

- In that second example, Jesus was not giving permission for people to abuse and overwork their servants to death

- Jesus did not call those who served God *unworthy or useless*, as if they/we did not deserve anything good in this life. The term He used only indicated that this was *just a servant* in the grand scheme of things, his role was to serve the master, as instructed.

The point of the second illustration **was not about** the *treatment* of the slave; rather, **it was about** the heart of a servant.

In this case, His *apostles*—the disciples He chooses to *sends out to do what He did*—must **willingly respect or obey God's Authority** more than their personal desires for convenience. That's because <u>**the TRUE REST and the TRUE REWARD of a TRUE SERVANT of God will come when ALL of the required work is completed**</u>. That *is* the reality of the matter.

So, why did Jesus' disciples ask Him to increase their faith—their readiness to obey? Because, **Jesus had just given them a new spiritual—higher or greater—commandment that** *seemed* **to contradict their familiar comfort zone**, as practiced under the Mosaic Law (*e.g.*, *an eye for an eye*). At the time, the Law was still the acceptable rule for the Israelites and Jews, but it was being done away with or superseded by higher spiritually-based laws.

Here's what was said just before they asked Him for more faith:

> *[Jesus] said to His disciples, "It is inevitable that [snares or an occasion to fall, through stumbling]^{G4635} will come, but [grief] to him through whom [trap-sticks]^{G4635} come"!*
>
> *It would be better for [that person] if a millstone were hung around his neck and he were thrown into the sea, than {to cause an immature person to stumble and fall in his pursuit of God's grace and love}.*
>
> *"Be on your guard! If your brother sins {against you}, [warn] him; and if he repents {or reconsiders his actions}, forgive him {or overlook the offense}.*
>
> *"And if he sins against you seven times a day, and returns to you seven times, saying, 'I repent,' forgive him."*
>
> Luke 17:1-4

The main subject is still *faith*—a mindset of humbled obedience to Jehovah-God's Authority. **The application of faith, here, is in the form of** *forgiveness*.

And, just to be clear, the trap-stick or the snare of offense is *not* the person who sins against you. **The trap that the enemy sets is for YOU not to forgive the person** (*e.g.*, a brother or sister in the faith) **who sins against you, thereby, making YOU the wrongdoer**—the one holding a charge of offense to *their* account.

In order to willingly forgive anyone who repeatedly sins against you, and to willingly decline setting a convenient self-determined limit on how many times you will or should forgive them, you need Christ-like faith to look into eternity to see the bigger picture—the reward at the end. As such, you choose **not** to lay or charge offenses to peoples' account, regardless of whether or not they are aware of what they did, and whether or not they've reconsidered their actions against you.

> *When they came to the place called The Skull, there they crucified [Jesus] and the criminals, one on the right and the other on the left.*
>
> *But Jesus was saying, "Father, forgive*[G863] *them [lay aside, leave, let (-alone, -be, -go), omit {or decline to add this charge to their account, so they will not have to receive its payout}]; for they do not know what they are doing" {the implication being: if they knew Who I was and what I was doing for them, they would reconsider their thoughts and actions}.*
>
> Luke 23:33-34a

As our example, Jesus willingly interceded on man*kind*'s behalf. He requested Jehovah-God to forgive the people, because they were not able to clearly see that they were wrong. **Jesus knew the Will of the Father**; and, **by faith, He looked beyond His personal pains** and, instead, **He saw God's plan and Promise of salvation for the world as being fulfilled, through His obedience**.

So, at the height of His suffering, while He was dying on the Cross, Jesus accurately transmitted to us the Will and Heart of God: **LOVE forgives**; LOVE patiently endures and bears all things; LOVE expects the best, even when things and people look and act their worse. (1 Corinthians 13:4-8)

Forgiveness is one of the primary expressions of LOVE; and, God is LOVE. Therefore, forgiveness is one of the primary expressions of God towards ALL man*kind*. So, if we are determined to have faith *in* God, then we must whole-heartedly show others His Ways:

> *[Dear ones], let us love [or have social and moral compassion for] one another, for love [compassion] is from God; and everyone who loves [or has social and moral compassion] is born of God and knows [perceives or understands] God.*
>
> *The one who does not love [or the one who has no compassion, {for whatever reason}] does not know God, for God is love [compassion].*
>
> *1 John 4:7-8*

Even now, Christ is still expressing to us the Love of God:

> *If we confess our sins, He is faithful and righteous to forgive[G863] us our sins and to cleanse us from all unrighteousness[G93] [(legal) injustice (properly the quality, by implication the act); moral wrongfulness (of character, life or act): - iniquity, unjust].*
>
> *1 John 1:9*

But, **if we do NOT forgive other people** from their intentional or unintentional wrongs against us, then we have deceived ourselves or **we have allowed ourselves to be deceived into thinking we know God** and/or that we have been forgiven by Him.

> *For if you forgive[G863] others [lay aside, leave, let (alone, be, go, have), omit {remove or forgo adding charges}] for their transgressions,[G3900] [sideslips (lapse or deviation), that is, (unintentional) error or (willful) transgression: - fall, fault, offence, sin] your heavenly Father will also forgive you.*

But if you do not forgive[G863] others, then your Father will not forgive your transgressions.

Matthew 6:14-15

<u>In addition to signs and wonders</u>, **the way WE increase OUR faith is with Christ-like characteristics**—building one upon the other, as instructed by the Apostle Peter. (It would not surprise me if Peter was the one who initial asked Jesus to *increase our faith*.)

> *Now for this very reason also, applying all diligence,[G4710] ["speed", eagerness: haste] [add[G2023] to [furnish besides, that is, fully supply, (figuratively) aid or contribute: - add, minister (nourishment, unto)]] your faith... moral excellence, and [to] your moral excellence, knowledge,*
>
> *And [to] your knowledge, self-control [(especially continence, {which is self-restraint or abstinence, especially regarding sexual activity}], and [to] your self-control, perseverance, and [to] your perseverance, godliness,*
>
> *And [to] your godliness, brotherly kindness, and [to] your brotherly kindness, love.*
>
> *For if these qualities are yours and are increasing, they render you neither useless nor unfruitful in the true knowledge of our Lord Jesus Christ.*
>
> *For he who lacks these qualities is blind or short-sighted, having forgotten his purification from his former sins.*
>
> *Therefore, brethren, be all the more diligent to make certain about His calling and choosing you; for as long as you practice these things, you will never stumble;*
>
> *For in this way the entrance into the eternal kingdom of our Lord and Savior Jesus Christ will be abundantly supplied to you.*

2 Peter 1:5-11

Again, when a person knows the truth about God and His Promises, he/she also knows his/her TRUE REST and REWARD comes after all of the work is done. But **I would NEVER imply or assert that God intends for His faithful servants to be poor in this life**.

However, a person with mature-expectant-faith[G4102] will not **limit his/her perception of good to the material things of this world**: his/her **mindset** will NOT think or naturally assume the BEST rewards are in *this* life. That's because the truly faithful **do NOT limit their reality *to* this world**, as those with small faith naturally do.

Yes, I am referring to today's popular prosperity sermons. Yes! I believe God's people CAN be wealthy in this life. But, despite the core message of *some* prosperity sermons, **God does NOT promise us that we all will be wealthy**. The popular, but often misused prosperity passage, 3 John 1-8, is clarified in Chapter 19.

Yes! There should be financial compensation for faithful ministers or servants to God's people. After all, we are still *in* the world and **we still take part in its financial system**.

But, a servant, who has been truly called by God, should be mature enough in his/her faith[G4102] to operate within this world's financial system **without being entangled by it or enticed by material possessions** like so many believers who are still *of* this world. It seems as though some servants **cannot see beyond this life: it is as if they do not, necessarily, expect any inheritance or reward, later**, so they desire to gain all they can, now.

> *'To him who overcomes, I will grant to eat of the tree of life which is in the Paradise of God.'*
>
> *Revelation 2:7*
>
> *... 'To him who overcomes, to him I will give some of the hidden manna, and I will give him a white stone, and a new name written on the stone ....'*
>
> *Revelation 2:17b*

'He who overcomes will thus be clothed in white garments; and I will not erase his name from the book of life, and I will confess his name before My Father and before His angels.'

Revelation 3:5

'He who overcomes, I will make him a pillar in the temple of My God, and he will not go out from it anymore; and I will write on him the name of My God, and the name of the city of My God, the new Jerusalem….'

Revelation 3:12

'He who overcomes, I will grant to him to sit down with Me on My throne, as I also overcame and sat down with My Father on His throne.'

Revelation 3:21

'He who overcomes will inherit these things….'

Revelation 21:7

Teachable Moments in Faith

Through *faith*, we can confidently or boldly speak to **Natural events or the Elements**, and we can EXPECT these to obey and change accordingly.

Through *faith*, we can confidently or boldly speak to **natural or physical circumstances**, and we can EXPECT these to obey and change accordingly.

Through *faith*, we can confidently or boldly **command demonic forces to release** the oppressed, and we can EXPECT them to obey.

According to the first four books of the New Testament (NT), a large number of people were healed by Jesus. For the most part, there was no indication that the majority of them had faith enough (*i.e.*, confidence in His Authority and/or an expectancy) to be healed.

The Scripture indicates, those miracles occurred:

- So, the people would pay closer attention to the announcement that the Kingdom of Heaven was among them (Ref. Matthew 10:7, John 4:48, Mark 16:20).

- So, the people would, perhaps, recognize that God gave Jesus the Authority to forgive sins (Ref. Matthew 9:6).

But there are also several passages in the NT that are considered to be *teachable moments* on faith. In these, Jesus is recorded to have said to several people, something along the lines of: *Your faith^{G4102} has made you whole,* or *be it done to you according to your faith^{G4102}* (Refs. Matthew 9:20-22, 9:27-29, Mark 10:46-52, Luke 17:12-19). The people about whom Jesus made such statements were persuaded enough in His God-given Authority to *fulfill God's Promises;* and, subsequently, **they said and/or did what was necessary to express their expectations of good**. At the very least, they chose to *believe^{G4100}* Jesus was able—He had the Authority and/or Power of God—to heal or deliver them or a loved one.

Following are four teachable moments, one of which is the primary example from Jesus Himself, revealing the following truth: mature **faith, first, sees and sustains the desired change; and then, natural corresponding action follows, based on our expectations**.

First, consider Jesus' encounter with two desperate people, each exhibiting a different level of faith, based on what they had seen and heard about Jesus. (Note: These two encounters are recorded in the Books of Matthew (9:18-25), Mark (5:22-42), and Luke (8:41-56); and, each Book records unique details about these encounters.)

A Ruler or Leader of the Synagogue—a local Jewish assembly, named Jairus (Jay-i-rus), came to Jesus, fell at His feet, and begged that He come to his house and deliver his 12-year-old daughter from death. Of course, Jesus agreed.

While in route to Jairus' house, a large crowd followed them. Somewhere in the crowd was a woman, who had been [frequently] bleeding (presumably from her vaginal area) for 12 years; but, the medical community of that day could not cure her.

According to the Mosaic Law, this woman should not have had any physical contact with other people, due to *that* type of blood loss: she was considered to be *unclean*, and anyone who came into contact with her was also made to be unclean (Ref. Leviticus 15:25-33). Legally, she could have been put to death for breaking the Law, had she been discovered.

But, after being nearly isolated for 12 years, and having spent all of her money without being cured, she was desperate enough to risk immediate death, as opposed to the lingering certainty of death, due to [frequent] blood loss. Most likely, after being convinced[G3982] that God was healing other people through Jesus, **she was persuaded**[G4102] **in her heart/mind to give life to the truth**[G4100] **of His Word**—that He was willing to heal her. And, she did not let go of that truth.

> *"But for you who fear My name, [says the Lord], the Sun of righteousness will rise with healing in its wings;"*[H3671]

> *Malachi 4:2a*

Jesus is the *Sun of Righteousness*: He is the *Light of the world* (John 8:12), and He is the *Dayspring*—the rising of light from the East—*from on High* (Luke 1:78). And because of the Authority and the Power He received from God, He had healing, even in His *wings*,[H3671] which describes the fringe, edge, or outermost part of a garment or cloth.

The woman, first, made **a declaration of faith**: she expressed her inner conviction and expectation of what the Authority of God could do for her. **She said,** *If I merely touch His garment I will be healed* (Matthew 9:21). So, **she acted**[G4100] **or did what was necessary to give life to her faith and expectation.**

> *And Jesus said, "Who is the one who touched Me?" And while they were all denying it, Peter said, "Master, the people are crowding and pressing in on You."*

But Jesus said, "Someone did touch Me, for I [(absolutely) know] that <u>power had gone out of [or away from] Me</u>."

When the woman saw that she had not escaped notice, she came trembling and fell down before Him, and declared in the presence of all the people the reason why she had touched Him, and how she had been immediately healed.

And He said to her, "Daughter, your faith has made you well; go in peace."

Luke 8:45-48

The teachable moment is HOW the woman was healed:

- Jesus did not touch her; **she touched Him** or, rather, she touched the fringe or hem of His clothing (8:44).

- Jesus did not send forth virtue[G1411] or **the miraculous power of God**, as was the usual manner when people were healed through Him; **she accessed *it* and then pulled or withdrew *it* directly from Him with her *living* faith**[G4102] and an expectation[G4100] of *good*.

And, when she was discovered, she came and fell before Jesus trembling. She was not afraid because she was healed; she was afraid because she had just confessed to breaking the Law—being out in public in an unclean state, especially in the presence of a Synagogue leader, Jairus.

But Jesus did not condemn her; because, she had actually done or demonstrated exactly *what* He had come to do: **to show God's people how to fulfill and then surpass the Mosaic Law, by using the same *kind* of faith**[G4102] **Abraham used long before the Law was given**. That's why Jesus used a unique term when He addressed her; He called her, "Daughter." She wasn't just a biological descendant of Abraham, which was a hollow claim many of the argumentative and religiously-minded Jewish leaders would often boast to Jesus (Matthew 3:9, John 8:33, 39).

In that moment, **she was a spiritual descendant, according to the faith of Abraham.** And, that living faith made her whole (Ref. Romans 4:16-22).

Ideally, Jairus was *seeing and hearing* all of this and his faith was being increased. As a ruler of the local Synagogue, he probably knew of this woman's situation—her 12 year-ordeal; but, in that moment he, more than anyone, understood her desperation.

But, during Jesus' interaction with the woman, someone came from Jairus' house to confront him. They tried to convince him not to harass Jesus any further, regarding the matter, because death had already won.

Here is the first part of this teachable moment:

> **Jesus instructed Jairus not to be frightened by** what he heard: **the antagonizing and hopeless report he was just confronted with** doesn't have to be the end of this matter, so don't automatically settle on or buy into it. *Only believe[G4100] [or continue ONLY to give credibility to the original reason and the hope you had in seeking Me out and getting Me to come to your house: to deliver your daughter]* (Ref. Luke 8:50).

Quite often, Jesus' first words to people were, *don't be alarmed [by what you just heard or by what you are seeing in the natural]*. Typically, when people are hopeful, it is because they **can** logically *see* or even desperately *imagine* the possibility of a solution to their problem. But **they can easily become alarmed by new or reaffirming adverse information; and, they can quickly lose hope**, because, really, they have little to no faith for, seemingly, impossible things.

If they choose to believe the report, at that point, they've placed more credibility either in the person who is reporting the information or in the information itself. And, because of that, a new belief—response—will spring up in **their un-renewed mind**.

If that happens, then they will express emotions and/or **speak corresponding words** of fear or dread, because of that which they are, now, convinced. And finally, this all too common process, usually, concludes with lingering dread-filled expectations or predictions about what happens next.

Small faith cannot easily maintain a belief that a person can actually live, again, once dead; but it could *naturally* support the belief that a person is actually dead. And naturally, from that belief[G4100] would come the expectation of living life without them. But **Jesus wanted Jairus to <u>see beyond</u> what he knew** in the natural, even though the situation was being reinforced by someone else.

When Jesus entered the house, He attempted to comfort the mourners that were already inside. HOW He attempted to comfort them and the parents is the second part of this teachable moment:

- ∞ **Jesus tried to change their natural perspective**, from one that caused continuous mourning and despair, **to His God-ordained spiritual perspective**, which *would* result in rejoicing and glorifying God for His goodness.

- ∞ He asked the mourners, "*Why are you crying?*" And, as He had also done with Lazarus (John 11:11), **Jesus announced His spiritual perspective**, by saying, "<u>*The child is not dead, **she is merely sleeping**</u>,*"

According to His Higher perspective, Jesus really could instruct Jairus not to be afraid or alarmed by what he was seeing in the natural—the breathless or lifeless body of his daughter. Yes, on the one hand, <u>in the natural</u>, the child was dead. (In a moment, there will be a Scriptural reference indicating that her spirit or life-breath had left her body.)

But, on the other hand, **Jesus was looking at the situation**, as He did all situations, **from a mature-faith-expectant point of view. <u>He saw and then confidently sustained His perspective, first, in His mind,</u>** <u>even though it was contrary to what physically happened</u>.

Unfortunately, those with little or no faith could not *see* from His perspective. They were looking at things from a carnal point of view; they even ridiculed or *laughed at Jesus* for suggesting the situation could be something other than what they were physically seeing.

Had Jesus been *just* some guy off the streets making that claim, their resistance would be understandable. But surely some of them had heard reports about Jesus healing other people in that city and in the region. After all, that's why Jairus sought Him out.

But they, as many people all too often do, only placed credibility[G4100] in what they could physically see or, at least, what they could understand, within reason. To them, Death was too strong and its rank in this world was too high for it to be given a command to *let go of someone*.

Therefore, Jesus had the mourners leave, in order to remove their unbelief and natural stubbornness—their **unwilling**ness to change their minds. **Jesus** then took the young girl by the hand and **spoke to her according to His faith-based perspective**: He commanded her to *wake up* [from sleeping]. Her spirit,[G4151] then, came back [in]to her (Luke 8:55a), and she stood up (Mark 5:35-42).

Today, when people with naturally small faith pray about certain situations, they may not ridicule or mock Jesus with laughter *when* they fall short of *seeing* the situation from a faith-based perspective. But, in many ways, they are doing something very similar.

They are dismissing any spiritual or Higher perspective **by insisting, through their unbelief, that this natural universe is either EQUAL TO or is MORE real than the spiritual one that created it**. (A common thought pattern for an **un**-renewed mind.)

The Book of Mark, Chapter 9, records the next teachable moment and it is, probably, **relatable to most believers**, today. It involves a conversation between Jesus and the father of a young boy, who was possessed by a demon. Just before that encounter took place, Jesus had taken three of His disciples with Him atop a high mountain where He was transfigured or gloriously changed; and, there Elijah and Moses (of the OT), who had physically died long ago, talked with Him [about things to come] (Ref. vs 2-8).

When they came down from the mountain, Jesus saw that a crowd of people had gathered around the remaining disciples, and that some of the religious leaders were interrogating them.

When Jesus asked why His disciples were being questioned, the boy's father explained that he brought his son to be delivered from a demonic spirit. However, since Jesus was away, His disciples attempted to deliver his son, but they could not do it (Ref. vs 14-18).

> *[Jesus responded to him* and probably to His own disciples] *and said, "O [disbelieving] generation, how long shall I be with you? How long shall I put up with you? Bring [the boy] to Me!"*

> *Mark 9:19*

Jesus then asked how long the boy had been like that. The father indicated he had been that way since infancy; and, he proceeded to described what the evil spirit would often do to his son. I'm sure those in the crowd, who were listening, could hear the desperation in this man's voice when he made the following emotional plea that, perhaps, by that time, was filled with uncertainty:

> *But if You can do anything*[G1536 G1410] *[or if you are able or if it is possible],* *take pity on us* *[or feel compassion]* *and help* *[aid or relieve] us!"*

> *...Jesus said to him, "[If I can?], All things are [possible or capable]*[G1415] *to him who believes."*

> *Immediately the boy's father cried out and said, "I do believe {that you believe}; help my unbelief."*

> *Mark 9:22b-24*

Then and now, most people will readily announce they believe that God can do *anything* (*i.e., nothing is impossible for Him*). People were/are convinced[G3982] of this, mostly, because of religious-rhetoric. However, when it comes to their own lives, then, **they're not so sure *if* He will do *anything for them*.** Typically, it is in those moments when people realize that *dis*belief has always been there; it was just being suppressed by religious conviction.[G3982]

Here's the key difference between what Jesus did and did NOT say, and what the man's small faith was *saying*:

🗝 Jesus DID say: *all things are possible to him who believes.*[G4100] But what He meant was: *faith in God's Authority will sustain and give life to* **the truth** *we believe; and, that means* **anything you or I believe**— *have an expectation for*—**is possible**.

🗝 Jesus did **NOT** say: *in order for something to happen, you only have to believe or give mental assent*[G3982] *that all things are possible.* The distinction was made clear in the man's response: *I do believe [***all things are possible** or* **anything <u>can</u> happen**, <u>*because God can do all things*</u>; *but, if my faith is the key for my son's deliverance, then I know I don't have that kind of faith. Help us!!]*

Here's a paraphrased version of what Jesus said:

Of course, it is possible—I am capable. **The disbelief of My disciples** *and, subsequently,* **their inability** *to have an expectation for God's Authority, His Power, and His Willingness to deliver people* **is not a reflection of Me***.

But, My question to you is: based on what you have seen and, at least, heard, do <u>you</u> believe[G4100] *that God's Authority and Power is at work in Me?*

The principle example of loyalty to one's expectations, regarding Jesus' God-given Authority and Power, can be clearly seen in an encounter He had with a Roman Military Captain. And, it is the last teachable moment in faith using other people in the Bible.

(Note: Below, I used the version of this encounter as recorded in Matthew 8:5-10; but, Luke 7:1-10 is a slightly different, more detailed, version of the same encounter. The difference between the two versions is neither a contradiction nor a flaw; it ONLY reveals a lost principle of that day: **talking with a servant or an ambassador, who was sent to speak to you** *in* **the name of a superior—on someone else's behalf—was, literally, considered to be talking directly with the superior, who sent the servant.)**

...When Jesus entered Capernaum, a [Military Captain] came to Him, [pleading with] Him,

...Saying, "Lord, my servant is lying paralyzed at home, fearfully tormented."

Jesus said to him, "I will come and heal him."

But the [Captain] said, "Lord, I am not worthy for You to come under my roof, but just say the word, and my servant will be healed.

"For I also am a man under authority, {and I am a man in authority} with soldiers under me; and I say to this one, 'Go!' and he goes, and to another, 'Come!' and he comes, and to my slave, 'Do this!' and he does it."

Now when Jesus heard this, He marveled [or admired him] and said to those who were following, "Truly I say to you, I have not found such great faith^{G4102} with anyone in Israel."

Matthew 8:5-10

Unlike the people of Israel, Judah, and even Samaria, this Gentile or non-Jew, most likely, never had the gospel *intentionally* preached or taught directly to him by Jesus or by His disciples. And yet, Jesus marveled and said He *had not found such great faith^{G4102} [in quantity or amount] in Israel (i.e.,* among those whom He taught directly).

It is not recorded anywhere that Jesus ever marveled at anyone else for having matched or surpassed that level of faith. There were many people whom Jesus physically touched, and there were many to whom He spoke directly into their situation (*i.e.,* He spoke directly to the demonic forces that bound them) and they were delivered. But, up to that point, apparently, <u>no one had every recognized the</u> <u>magnitude of Jesus' Authority over sicknesses in such a way, so as</u> <u>to say to Him**, no physical contact is necessary, YOU NEED ONLY**</u> ***SPEAK or GIVE THE COMMAND and I confidently expect that it*** *(e.g., healing, change, etc.)* ***will happen***. (Peter came close, had he continued to walk on the water or, really, walk on Jesus' Word for him to "come". Ref. Matthew 14:22-33)

But, just to be clear, **this is not indicating that the Roman Military Captain had** *perfect* and *eternal* **loyalty** to his belief in God and His Ways. But, <u>compared to those in Israel</u>, **he had** *greater insight* **and more confidence in Jesus' Authority over sickness**.

The juvenile saying, *it takes one to know one*, was applicable in this situation, in a good way. The Military Captain, who **knows what it means to be a subordinate**—to listen *under* authority, and to have authority over others, **related to Jesus' Authority** over sicknesses, most likely, by observing Him.

It is extremely likely that the Roman Government and its Military had Jesus (or anyone who spoke to and incited large crowds) under surveillance. As such, this Captain probably observed Jesus for many days and/or he read reports, including eyewitness accounts, about how He went throughout the region teaching and healing people.

But this soldier was, somewhat, unique: ❶ he had enough mental clarity to identify with Jesus' Authority in a way the religiously stressed Israelites of that day did not; and, ❷ he loved God's people (Luke 7:5) enough to care about their well-being, unlike the other Gentile soldiers. (Most likely his servant was a Jew.)

The reason the Roman Military Captain could more easily recognize this spiritual principle—authority over sickness—is because **he did not have a Sin-consciousness** (*i.e.*, the same deep awareness of, and condemnation for, bad behavior) like the Israelites. **That's NOT to say the Captain never committed sins.** In fact, it is safe to assume he did not live a godly life, which is why **he considered himself to be unworthy for Jesus to come to his house**.

But, unlike the Israelites, **he did not have the Mosaic Law to condemn him**. This is the same principle the Apostle Paul described in Romans Chapter 7, specifically verses 7-24.

Today, a person with a renewed mind or *maturing* Christ-like faith would be in a far better position to see God's Authority more clearly than that Roman Military Captain:

- Such a person can both **supernaturally and obediently see** him/herself as having died with Christ; and, therefore, his/her expectation of being **spiritually dead to Sin** would be more complete.

- So, despite being keenly aware of his/her own imperfections, this person will have less of a Sin-consciousness and more of a clean-consciousness, so as to **clearly see Jesus' Authority over ALL things**, including sicknesses, diseases, demonic oppression, and death.

- Therefore, from a position of victory, **this person fully expects to also have access to the same Authority and power**, in Jesus' Name.

And Jesus answered saying to them, "Have faith[G4102] *in God.*

"Truly I say to you, whoever says to this mountain, 'Be taken up[G142] *and cast into the sea,' and does not doubt*[G1252] *in his heart, but believes*[G4100] *that what he says [shall happen or come to be, he shall have whatsoever things he says, calls, or commands].*

"[Because of that,] I say to you, all things for which you desire or ask, when you pray, believe[G4100] *that you have [taken hold of, accepted, or obtained those things, and to you, or by you—by your faith, it will be]."*

Mark 11:22-24

The primary part of what Jesus said is as follows: *Have confidence in God's Authority and His faithfulness to keep His Word and/or Promises*. And, because of that we can:

- **Confidently speak or call out commands with the Authority of God at work in us** and expect[G4100] physical and spiritual obstacles—even mountain sized ones—to move out of the way (vs. 23).

- **Confidently pray or worship based on loyalty to our belief in God and His goodness**, in order to receive personal needs, desires, and wants (vs. 22 & 24).

Without undeniable proof—signs and wonders, Mark 11:23 is nearly impossible for the believer today, <u>due to the condition Jesus gave</u>. The word *doubt* is not just *a feeling of uncertainty.* G1252 means, **to separate thoroughly** *from, that is, (literally and instinctively)* **to withdraw from,** *or (by implication) to* **oppose;** *to* **discriminate,** *or to* **hesitate, contend, stagger, waver.**

That, of course, describe <u>the more common pattern of naturally *small* faith</u>: we sincerely speak out *or* pray and declare something we want or need to happen, only then to have our **un**-renewed mind withdraw from, or stagger in unbelief at, the very things we declared will happen, because of natural opposition to it and/or feelings of inadequacy or unworthiness. Generally speaking, it is hard for a person with an **un**-renewed mind to *see* or fully expect *good* things to happen in the midst of opposition or adversity, especially when it comes to time-sensitive matters.

Worst still, **because many believers seldom recognize "the disconnect" between their prayers** (which they believe obligates God to do everything *for* them) **and their thought-life** (which they often discount as being of little to no consequences), they are often disappointed when nothing favorable happens for them. So, **they erroneously assume** and are even taught to say one of the following cover-phrases: *it was NOT God's will for me to have what I asked for*; or, *it must NOT be within His timing for me to be delivered from what I was praying against.*

Unfortunately, after that same cycle is repeated multiple times, at some point, believers become frustrated with their relationship with God and they settle for a life of religious pleasantries. They may still go to church, as a matter of obligation, possibly, to secure their place in Heaven; but, all the while, they continue to live in spiritual and, in most cases, physical defeat, using learned faith-talk as a filler to blend in with others believers.

Equally as bad, too many **believers naturally choose to adopt self-inspired methods to get want they want,** similar to Sari (Sarah), Abram's (Abraham's) wife (Ref. Genesis 15-17). God Promised

Abram that he would have a son; something they both desired above all else. But, after years of nothing happening, Sari's expectation decreased and unbelief increased, causing her to *become* impatient. So, she decided to *get things going* by choosing an alternate resource by which their desire and God's Promise would be accomplished; and, like the first Adam, Abram obeyed the voice of his wife.

Due to their haste, they caused long-term issues and perpetual conflict for the ones—the Israelites and Jews—that were actually born in accordance with God's Promise. That conflict still exists today, in the Middle East: Israelis and modern Arabs.

Again, it is essential that our small faith be transformed into a reinforced-mature faith,[G4102] which gives man*kind* the ability to agree with God. We must begin to *see* beyond the limitations of this physical world, so as to expect the same Authority and power that created this physical universe to be at work *in* us.

That means, **by faith**—persuasion and confidence—*in* **God and a progressively renewed mind, we can be *like* Christ in this world**:

    ☙ We must **change from our predominantly physical perspective to a predominantly spiritual perspective;** because, **THE TRUTH OF WHAT WE SAY AND WHAT WE PRAY WILL <u>FIRST EXIST</u> IN OUR RENEWED MIND** before it is ever seen or realized in the natural.

    ☙ **As such, <u>WE BECOME BOTH THE SOURCE AND THE SUSTAINER OF *THAT* TRUTH</u> BY PROVIDING THE NECESSARY PROOF OF, AND SUPPORT FOR, IT, FIRST.** And, since we have access to the Authority of God, through Christ, we will have whatsoever things we say, if we do not doubt or become overwhelmed in our mind.

Yes, *whatsoever things* you say *and* expect in your heart are brought into existence, according to *the power and principle of agreement* (*i.e.*, both self-agreement and agreement with God's Word); and, **there are no limitations to that principle**.

But <u>this has little to do with simply having our material wish-lists fulfilled</u>. Yes, it does mean "whatsoever things;" but, a person who has developed a mature-humbled-obedient-expectant-Christ-like-faith also WILL HAVE **a renewed mind**, so as to think more like Christ. Meaning, **old carnal-only thinking and desires are no longer primary**.

As such, this person is no longer selfish—thinking of and caring only for one's own needs, while neglecting the needs of others. But this person wholeheartedly agrees with the purpose God has for his/her life: we are more than conquerors over Sin and its many expressions of misery and Death.

To be *more than a conqueror* is to both **win (defeat)** *and* **reign (lord-) over your enemies**. That's the new victorious Christ-like life every born-from-above believer is supposed to live in this world, first. Then, all of the other things we have need of will *naturally* be added to that victorious life, by God Himself.

Chapter 16

YOU MUST BE BORN AGAIN?

In the Holy Bible, when a child is *born*, the focus is not, necessarily, placed on the child, as much as it is placed on the father or lineage of the child. The father is the source of the child's identity or surname, which has to do with the child's family ties and birthright.

In humanity's case, the physical source or lineage of EVERYONE is the first man, who was called Adam. As noted, *A-d-a-m* is both the name and the term that describes *the first one of a new kind*; and, as it relates to *destiny*, **whatever happened to [the] Adam happened to EVERYONE else of the same** *kind*.

Due to a disobedient or faithless act, Adam and Eve became stained with Sin *in* their flesh and, eventually, they grew distant from Jehovah-God. As a result, man*kind* became more carnally-minded or less spiritual—less heavenly minded.

Subsequently, EVERYONE is naturally born at a distance from, or lacking original relationship with, the Holy God, because of inherited Sin. And, because of that distance or separation, EVERYONE naturally begins life believing that physical things on Earth are the *primary* basis of ALL reality and truth.

What Did Jesus Say?

The following excerpt of Scripture is taken from a conversation between Jesus and a religious leader of the Jews, named Nicodemus:

> [Nicodemus said,] *"[Master], we know that You have come from God as a teacher; for no one can do these signs that You do unless God is with him."*

> *Jesus answered and said to him, "Truly, truly, I say to you, unless one is born <u>again</u>,[G509] he cannot see the kingdom of God."*
>
> *Nicodemus said to Him, "How can a man be born when he is old? He cannot enter a second time into his mother's womb and be born, can he?"*
>
> *Jesus answered, "Truly, truly, I say to you, unless one is born of water and the Spirit, he cannot enter into the kingdom of God."*
>
> *"That which is born of the flesh is flesh, and that which is born of the Spirit is spirit."*
>
> *John 3:2b-6*

In John 3:3, the Greek word for "again" is *anōthen*. Most versions of the Holy Bible traditionally translate Jesus' statement using the *common* definition "again," despite the fact that, in almost every *other* place in Scripture where the word G509 appears, it, more often than not, implies a *position, rank,* or *order*. For example: "**from the first**" or "**from above**" or "**from the top**."

Those definitions make up the Strong's Concordance's *root* and *common* definitions for the referenced Greek word. For example, following are three verses of Scripture, in the Holy Bible's New Testament, where *anōthen* or G509 is used and underlined:

> *[John speaking to his own disciples about Jesus,] "He who comes <u>from above</u> [out ranks us] all, [anyone else, myself included, who is born of man, is of the earth and is worldly; and, therefore, we tend to speak only of worldly things or concepts]. He who comes from heaven [out ranks us] all."*
>
> *John 3:31*
>
> *And the veil of the temple was torn in two <u>from top</u> to bottom.*
>
> *Mark 15:38*

> *But the wisdom <u>from above</u> is first pure, then peaceable, gentle, reasonable, full of mercy and good fruits, unwavering, without hypocrisy.*

James 3:17

Therefore, a more meaningful and descriptive translation of the phrase Jesus used in John 3:3 is: *unless one is born **from the first** or born **from above**…*, as in, **born *from the spiritual realm of Heaven***, which came *first* (as it relates to order) and is *above* or superior to the physical Earth (as it relates to rank).

As stated before, we ALL have a natural tendency to only accept the things we can physically sense (*e.g.*, see, hear, or touch). And, in some cases, we will even accept a thing (concept or principal) if we can logically understand it with our carnal mind, even if we can't see it, hear it, or touch it.

That's because, if a *thing* or an event can be **reduced** to a formula, calculation, or mathematical equation to **explain** why and how *it* exists, then that *thing* ceases to be as much of a mystery.

That's what Nicodemus wanted: to logically understand Godly or spiritual *things*, which he could not see, hear, or touch with his physical-self. But as Jesus pointed out, *unless people are born from above,* they will never truly *see* or recognize and accept such things.

Following is the *extended version* of what Jesus said in John 3:6:

> **Physical human birth begins a natural *kin*ship or family tie with this Sinful world. That *kind* of birth results in a Sin-consciousness and an overwhelming familiarity with misery and physical death. But, a supernatural faith-based birth from above begins a *kin*ship or family tie with the unseen God in Heaven; which means, this *kind* of birth results in a new and peaceful consciousness towards God. And, because of that, the Word and the Will of God *can* now truly reign in the hearts of men.**

That's what it means to be **born from above**. This new *birth* indicates a *new beginning*. But, in order for us to begin a new *kin*ship or family tie with God, **our old *kin*ship or family tie with this Sinful**

world has to end in death. And, the only way we can die and still have life in this physical world is to be baptized *in*to Christ.

Baptized *into* Christ: Going Down in the Water

When something is *baptized*[28] it is [over-] *whelmed* or made fully wet. The implication is to **make the thing fully wet by covering** or **submersing it in a liquid**, such as water.

In the past, my view of water baptism was as follows: people are first dipped or submerged in water and then they are raised up from the water. But contrary to such modern-day thinking, **baptism is *not* a two-part process**. If something is baptized in water, it is <u>submersed in water, period. End of process</u>.

A good example of water baptism is a *sunken* ship. The ship <u>*remains* covered by the water indefinitely</u>. **Raising the ship from the water is a different process** or a different course of action.

Baptizing a person in water, *in* the name of Jesus Christ, is a public ceremony, which expresses the person's heartfelt desire to be **identified *with* the physical Death of Jesus Christ**.

> *Or do you not know that all of us who have been baptized into Christ Jesus have been baptized into His death?*
>
> *Romans 6:3*

When we are baptized *in*to Christ, **spiritually**, we enter into His physical death and burial (Colossians 2:12a); because, **through faith**—obedient expectancy, or through confidence in God's Authority, **we have physically died with Him**. Remember, Sin can only be permanently removed or destroyed through death.

> *Knowing this, that our old self was crucified with [Christ, so] that our body of [Sin] might be done away with, [so] that we should no longer be slaves to [Sin];*

---

[28] Strong's Exhaustive Concordance Of the Bible, Greek reference # 907

For he who has died is freed [or justified] from [Sin].

Romans 6:6-7

If our bodies are dead, then Sin no longer has a home or base of operation in us. And if Sin has no place in us, then the guilt of Sin can, eventually, be removed or cleansed from our minds.

It takes mature-humbled-obedient-Christ-like-faith for people to truly *consider* themselves to be physically dead with Christ, and to truly *see* a new physical life, in this world: *justified* by faith.

Born of the Spirit: Coming Up Out of the Water

Spiritually, if we are convinced[G3982] and we are fully persuaded[G4102] of the gospel of Jesus [the] Christ, and then we are baptized, by being physically **submerged *in* water**, symbolically, WE BECOME ONE WITH *THE BODY OF CHRIST, AT THE POINT OF HIS DEATH*. And, **whatever happened to His Body, also happens to us**.

Since Christ was physically raised (up) from the dead in newness of life, **we are spiritually raised (up) *with* Him**, in newness of life, by the same Holy Spirit of God (Romans 8:10-11). That's good news!

Below is the continuation of Jesus' conversation with Nicodemus:

> *"Do not marvel that I said to you, 'You must be born [from above].'*
>
> *"The wind blows where it [wills or desires to] and you hear the sound of it, but do not know where it comes from and where it is going; so is everyone who is born of the Spirit."*
>
> *Nicodemus answered and said to Him, "[In what way is it possible for these things to happen]?"*
>
> *Jesus answered and said to him, "Are you the teacher of Israel, and do not understand these things?*
>
> *"Truly, truly, I say to you, we speak that which we know, and we bear witness of that which we have seen; and you do not receive our witness.*

> *"If I told you earthly things and you do not [believe], how shall you [believe] if I tell you heavenly things?"*

John 3:7-12

Naturally, the *wind* itself is invisible to our physical sight; but its affects and presence are **seen**, **felt**, and **heard** as it moves over the Earth, rustling leaves on trees or causing blades of grass in a field to sway back and forth. But even though the *wind* is a familiar part of Nature, Nicodemus could neither describe its appearance, nor could he explain *how* it moves or determine where it was going; except, of course, in general terms of direction and speed.

Yet, in his old age, Nicodemus knew, from personal experiences, *the wind is real*, even if he couldn't describe or explain it.

By the same token, even if he couldn't explain it, Nicodemus, who was a teacher of God's people, should have readily accepted the truth that **the Spirit of God does move upon men**, as the Law and the Prophets have already said (Exodus 31:3, 2 Samuel 23:2, Isaiah 42:1, 44:3 and Ezekiel 2:2). Unfortunately, he, most likely, never experienced the Holy Spirit, personally, due to stubborn disbelief. (As you may recall, he did say to Jesus, **we** *know you were sent from God, because of the [miraculous] things You do* (John 3:2b); so, apparently, they simply chose to **dis**believe Him.)

Here is the *extended paraphrased version* of what Jesus said to Nicodemus, as it relates to John 3:7-12:

> **Anyone who is truly born from above will more readily accept the truth that God's Spirit is very active in this world, strengthening and renewing the hearts or minds of His people. But neither you nor anyone else, who says they *know God*, should over analyze or question in *dis*belief *how* His Spirit moves upon people.**
>
> **Basically, as a teacher in Israel, you should have *already* known and believed, at least, some of what I was saying about the Holy Spirit changing people's lives. God has already said (through His Prophets *of old*) that the Holy Spirit would be poured out upon [flesh and blood] people**

(Ezekiel 36:25-27 & Joel 2:28-32), **in order for them to have new hearts, to go with a new Covenant** (Jeremiah 31:31-34).

Let's connect the pieces.

"And God raised Him up again, putting an end to the agony of death, since it was impossible for Him to be [held by death]."

Acts 2:24

Jesus was *not* born into the world as a Sin-stained person; and, He never committed a sin. Therefore, **He was not liable to the punishment of physical Death** the way EVERYONE else was and is. As such, Jesus was qualified to be God's unblemished or spotless sacrificial Lamb in the ultimate ceremony of Atonement *for the whole world*—everything that adorns or decorates the Earth.

By accepting that responsibility, **He chose to become the very image of Sin for our sake** (2 Corinthians 5:21).

As God's Lamb, Jesus allowed Himself to be slaughtered. That is to say, He allowed Himself to be beaten or punished and then crucified or put to death, in the same way a sinner or law-breaker would have been forcefully punished and executed back in that time period, over two-thousand years ago.

After He died, His **flesh and bone** body was buried in a tomb (Matthew 27:60). His body was *flesh and bone* because **His blood** (where**in** the oxygen, breath*, or **spirit of His physical life** flowed*) was spilled-out as He was being punished or beaten (John 19:1-3), and as He was *dying* on the cross.

But, three days after being placed in a tomb, Jesus' lifeless physical body received God's Breath or Spirit of Life, again. This was similar to the event, at the beginning of this world, when **the lifeless form or the body** of the first Adam received God's Breath of Life.

But this time, **Jesus did *NOT* remain or resume as *a living soul*.** That is to say, He was *not* just a breathing, **blood-flowing**, decaying life-form that is natural to, and limited by, this physical universe.

Jesus has a new *kind* of body. Yes, it is still a *flesh and bone* body (Luke 24:39), but it is much different than our current *physical* bodies. He has a glorified non-decaying flesh and bone body that is both natural AND *super*natural—beyond the limitations of this physical universe (Ref. Mark 16:19, Acts 1:9, & 9:3-6).

> *The last Adam became a [(re-) vitalizing or] life-giving spirit.*
>
> *1 Corinthians 15:45b*

The resurrected and, now, the supernatural Jesus is **another Adam:** He is the **FIRST ONE of a new *kind*** of life-form, from which comes *all* others of the same *kind* (Ref. Acts 26:23, 1 Corinthians 15:20-23, Colossians 1:18, and Revelation 1:5). Like the first, the last Adam, Jesus [the] Christ, also *had* three primary responsibilities:

1. To stand before God and receive the blessing (*i.e.,* verbal adoration) and God-given Authority for Himself and, subsequently, for His *kind*.

2. To set the tone or pattern of agreement with God's plan for Himself and for His *kind*.

3. To reproduce His own *kind* (*i.e.,* in His own likeness, after His image) and grow them up in unity, with access to the same Authority He received from God, so that they, too, will be victorious over Sin and Satan.

Jesus [the] Christ has become the glorious conclusion of BOTH spiritual and physical things—in Heaven *and* on Earth (Ephesians 1:10). Jesus' glorified body is still functional in *this* physical world (Luke 24:41-43) and it is very much at home in Heaven (Hebrews 1:3c), which is the spiritual realm of God.

Jesus Christ accurately reflects God's glorious intentions for us ALL (Hebrews 1:3). That makes Him a better *A-d-a-m* or a better source that *re*produces a more exact image and likeness of God in human form (Colossians 1:15). Meaning, unlike the first Adam, **He could recognize evil *like God*, but He preferred not to obey it**.

Consider the following key points very carefully:

   ☞ This physical universe was created *for* the first Adam; as such, the authority God gave him—to subdue and rule—WAS *LIMITED TO* THIS PHSYCAL UNIVERSE.

   ☞ As the last Adam **and** as the Word of God, Jesus transcends this physical existence; He is capable of influencing BOTH the physical and the spiritual universes (Ref. Luke 24:36-43).

   ☞ As the last Adam **and** as the Word of God, **ALL THINGS were created _by_ Him**. (Ref. Colossians 1:16-17, Matthew 11:27, 28:18, John 3:35, 5:22-23, 13:3, 17:1-3, Romans 14:9, 1 Corinthians 15:24-27, Ephesians 1:20-22, Philippians 2:9-10, Hebrews 1:2-3, 2:8, 12:2, 1 Peter 3:21c-22)

   ☞ As the last Adam **and** as the Word of God, Jesus Christ was given Authority over ALL THINGS, including powers, principalities, etc., IN THE HEAVENLIES, IN THE EARTH, AND UNDER THE EARTH.

   ☞ Since He is over **everything** (except over God Himself), and He has given us His Name, we can **proclaim the good news of salvation to all of creation**—not just to man*kind*..., and signs and wonders will follow those of us who have faith...; and, in His Name, we will [change things in both the physical and the spiritual realms]. (Ref. Mark 16:15-18, John 17:18)

   ☞ That's why Jesus said to us, regarding this connection between both realms of existence: ...*Whatsoever you shall bind* [knit, tie, or wind] *on earth, shall be bound in heaven; and whatsoever you loose* [break up, destroy, dissolve, melt, or put off] *on earth shall be loosed in heaven*. (Ref. Matthew 18:18)

The concept of **transferable authority** was touched on in the previous chapter and it will be expounded upon, now. As a reminder, certain principles and customs from the *past* have been either lost or diluted in the *present*.

When a trusted ambassador, a trusted messenger, or a trusted subordinate was sent out by a superior with authority, **he/she carried the same authority as the superior who sent him/her, in order to accomplish the assigned task**. At no time did the TRUSTED subordinate speak or act on his/her own behalf; because, **while in service to the superior**, the subordinate was not his/her own self: **his/her identity was replaced or upgraded**.

The servant only expressed the desires, in the same way or mannerisms, of the one who sent him/her. Therefore, it was, literally, like talking directly to the one in authority.

> *...He died for all, so that <u>they who live</u> might no longer <u>live</u> for themselves, but <u>for Him</u> who died and rose again on their behalf.*

> *2 Corinthians 5:15*

Concerning Himself and His service to God, Jesus said:

> *"I and the Father are one"* [—*we are in agreement, in unity—we are of the same Mind*].

> *John 10:30*

> *"For I did not speak on My own initiative, but the Father Himself who sent Me has given Me a commandment as to what to say and what to speak.*

> *"I know that His commandment is eternal life; therefore, the things I speak, I speak just as the Father has told Me."*

> *John 12:49-50*

And, when we are truly born from above, we are in service to, and we are in agreement with, God, through Christ.

Again, while praying to the Father for us, Jesus said:

> *"As You sent Me into the world, I also have sent them into the world.*

"For their sakes, I sanctify Myself, that they themselves also may be sanctified in truth [in Me].

"I do not ask on behalf of these alone, but for those also who believe in Me through their word;

"That they may all be one; even as You, Father, are in Me and I in You, that they also may be in Us, so that the world may believe that You sent Me."

John 17:18-21

The **Promise** of the gospel is **Righteousness**: *salvation from Sin.* The glorious **Purpose** of the gospel is **UNITY**—all of us being ONE with the Father, *so that God may be all in all.* (1 Corinthians 15:28c)

Therefore, we have been buried with Him through baptism into death, in order that as Christ was [awaken, roused or raised] from the dead through the glory of the Father, so we too might walk in newness of life.

Romans 6:4

And if Christ is in you, though the body is dead because of [Sin], yet the spirit is [life] because of righteousness.

But if the Spirit of [God] who raised Jesus from the dead dwells in you, [God] who raised Christ Jesus from the dead will also give life to your mortal bodies through His Spirit who indwells you.

Romans 8:10-11

Therefore, if any man is in Christ, he is a new [formation]; [old or primeval things have] passed away; behold, new things have come [to be].

2 Corinthians 5:17

Remember, baptism does *not* involve bringing up the thing that was submersed. **When we *remain in* Christ, He also *remains in* us.**

Spiritually, Christ, the Living Word of God, enters us in the same way that surrounding water rushes in and fills the inner chambers of a sinking ship; thereby, taking it deeper. Another example is the way color dye is absorbed *into* the threads of a piece of cloth that is submerged in it; thereby, forever changing its description.

> ***And just as we have*** *[naturally* ***put on, as clothing]*** ***the image of the earthy*** *[or the first Adam],* ***we shall*** ***also [wear] the image of the heavenly*** *[or of the spiritual Adam, Jesus Christ].*

> *1 Corinthians 15:49*

The Significance of *Water* Baptism

In a *physical* ceremony of water baptism, **two *spiritual* processes** are represented.

One: the actual baptism or submersion into Christ's physical Body—His Death, as illustrated by going underneath the water.

Two: the very separate and *necessary* process of being raised (up) in newness of life *with* Christ. This is illustrated by an emerging or coming up from the water in order to **start breathing again** or breathing anew. Of course, whether or not it is understood to be a separate process, a physical water baptism ceremony *must* end with the person coming up from the water: we ALL need air to breath.

But the thing we must learn to *see*, by **the eyes of our faith**—our obedient confidence in God's Authority—is: we are a new or different creation (*i.e.*, a new formation) when we emerge from the water. Spiritually, **we are still *in* Christ**, who was given new life by God and is, Himself, the *reason* for our new life.

(**The eyes of our faith** or our obedient confidence in God's Authority to save us **is not the same as merely exercising our imagination**, as if salvation is merely a matter of self-discipline and pretense and the spirit-world is a far off fantasy-land. Through signs and wonders, **the spirit-world must be more real to us than the things that are in this physical world**.)

...Baptism now saves you—not the removal of dirt from the flesh, but an appeal to God for a good [co-perception or moral consciousness]—through the resurrection of Jesus Christ,

1 Peter 3:21

Water baptism is also a form of washing. Washing is the middle-part of the *consecration* process.

To **consecrate something means to make it sacred or holy**. When something is consecrated it is, first, set apart or removed from common everyday use. It is then washed or cleansed. And finally, it is given a different or new identity and purpose other than what it was commonly known and used for before.

In these last days, God has chosen to consecrate the *minds* or hearts and bodies of man*kind*, through Christ:

1) **Removed from common use**: When people hear and then are convinced and truly believe in the saving work of Jesus Christ, they *begin to* transcend mere carnal-thinking that is common to this world. More accurately, they are *being* delivered from the mental captivity of carnal desires that are common to Sinful man*kind*.

2) **Cleansing or baptism**: Through baptism, the old *self* is covered or whelmed over *in* Christ. This means the mind is *being* cleansed from the guilt of Sin, as the Sin-stained body is *being* spiritually put to death, daily.

3) **New identity and life**: When people are born of water and the Spirit, they have a new identity in this world, and they have a new way of thinking about this world. These people are **new creations** or of a new formation.

That is restoration! *That* is what completes the process of reconciliation between us and God. Not only is our debt cancelled, through death, but even our *original* mandate or scope (*i.e.*, be fruitful and multiply) is increased, through new life. Because Sin longer reigns in our physical—mortal—bodies, we are more than conquerors, in Christ, by faith.

...In reference to your former manner of life, you lay aside the old self [the old man of flesh], which is being corrupted [ruined, shriveling or withering (away)] in accordance with the [delusional longings it has for things that are forbidden].

And that you be renewed [renovated] in the spirit [breath, life] of your mind [understanding or will],

And put on the new self, which, in the likeness of God, has been created in righteousness and holiness of the truth.

Ephesians 4:22-24

Those verses of Scripture speak to our part of the process: we must continue to *reverently work- or walk-out our own salvation*, so that we are like Christ in this world.

I have been crucified with Christ; and it is no longer I who live, but Christ lives in me; and the life which I now live in the flesh I live by faith in the Son of God, who loved me, and delivered Himself up for me.

Galatians 2:20

Happy Birthday?

"I tell you that..., there will be more joy in heaven over one sinner who repents...."

Luke 15:7a

In most modern societies, the birth of a child is a time or an event to celebrate. For the parents, it is a joyous occasion, followed by years of intense care-giving and nurturing. For the child, there is an overwhelming sense of the unknown; because, all things are new and are not yet understood or appreciated.

But scripturally, the real celebration or **the first** most noteworthy event actually occurred in a person's life around the age of two, when the child is *weaned* or transitions from breast milk to solid foods. At that point in time, **the child will be *treated differently*.** Physically, it is an indication that, mentally, **he or she can receive and understand** *basic* **verbal instructions.**

For example, take the accounts of Isaac and Samuel, two of the Holy Bible's most noteworthy men. Anyone who knows the story can imagine how happy Abraham was after his wife, Sarah, gave birth to *their* first long-awaited son, Isaac. But, as joyous an occasion as the birth of Isaac was, that was not when the *celebration* occurred. The Scripture states, Abraham made a great feast on the day Isaac was weaned or ripened—he became old enough to eat solid foods; meaning, he was no longer an infant (Genesis 21:8).

Many years later, an Israelite woman, named Hannah, desired to have children more than she desired anything else; but she was barren or infertile. One day, she vowed to God that if He gave her a son, she would lend or dedicate that child to Him, forever. God heard her prayers. When her first child, Samuel, was born, she waited until he was ripened or weaned before she presented him to the Lord, in order to serve in His House. Samuel grew to become one of God's greatest prophets. (Ref. 1 Samuel Chapters 1-3)

> *Therefore, putting aside all malice, and all guile and hypocrisy and envy and all slander,*
>
> *Like newborn babes, [intensely crave] the pure milk of the word, that by it you may grow [as it relates] to salvation,*
>
> *[If perhaps] you have tasted the kindness [graciousness or usefulness] of the Lord.*
>
> *1 Peter 2:1-3*

So, *when* we taste the kindness of God and we recognize His gift of salvation, and when we intensely crave and are nurtured—made strong—by the fundamental teachings of the Cross, then we, too, will grow up spiritually. Our relationship with God will mature into something *relational* and not just something *religious* or infantile.

Spiritually speaking, **we need to come of age more quickly, so that we can understand, recognize, receive, and fulfill His Will** for our lives. When that happens, we will stop allowing the storms of life to toss us—our thought life—around like unanchored ships.

Yes, I imagine there is rejoicing in Heaven *when one sinner repents* (Luke 15:7a). But, again, repenting is more than a onetime prayer in which we emotionally confess our sins.

As state previously, to **truly repent** means to start *thinking differently* [from a point in time, and then continuing to think differently from then on, and *not* just in the moment or on occasions].

In our case, repenting starts with a Quality Decision to drink in, so as to be nourished in our minds by, the sincere milk of the Word. But, as our minds are being renewed day-by-day, we must, eventually, be weaned *or we must mature beyond* the milk or the **fundamental teachings of the Cross** (*i.e.*, ever learning, but never understanding that we died to Sin with Christ). Because, only mature and obedient people *in* Christ are capable of chewing on, so as to fully digest and be nourished by, the solid meat of God's Word.

In his letter to the Jews, the Apostle Paul (whom most theologians believe penned the New Testament's Book of Hebrews) wrote:

> *For though by this time you ought to be teachers, you have need again for someone to teach you the elementary principles of the oracles of God, and you have come to need milk and not solid food.*
>
> *For everyone who partakes only of milk is not accustomed to the word of righteousness, for he is an infant [a immature Christian].*[G3516]
>
> *But solid food is for the mature, who because of practice have their senses [judgment or perception]*[G143] *trained to discern good and evil.*
>
> *Hebrews 5:11-14*

That means, **only the faithfully mature or obedient in Christ truly have a new life in this world**. A *new Christ-like* life means a *different kind* of life from what we have known. We have been repurposed for victorious thinking, now, in *this* life.

It is extremely important to understand the following:

> **If we say we have a new life *in* Christ, then the new life we live** (*i.e.*, what we think, what we say, and what we do on a regular basis) **is *not* our own**. If we are *still* living our *own* life—doing and thinking the same old way, then, most likely, we are still operating with our *old* Sin-consciousness, which is set or focused *only on* carnal things.

Since, by faith, we consider our body as being **spiritually crucified with Christ**, we are no longer *kin* to, or we are no longer in *kin*ship with, this Sinful world. Nevertheless, **we still live *in* this physical world, *in* a physical body**, which is still decaying or dying.

For now, that just means the following:

> When we are *in* Christ, or **as** we take on the Mind of Christ, it is as if a new mind is being poured inside of an *old* body: temporarily pouring new wine in an old wineskin.

Therefore, the evidence of our new spiritual life is <u>not a new body, yet</u>. For now, while we are in this world, <u>**the only evidence of a new spiritual life is our truly renewed Christ-like-faith-filled mind**</u> **that sees things more from God's spiritual perspective**, which, then, allows His Promises to remain in us, fully intact.

> *[Jesus said,] **"It is the Spirit who gives life;** [because, in this spiritual process,] **the flesh profits nothing** [or has no useful role in bringing about the required change]; **the words that I have spoken to you are spirit and are life."***

> *John 6:63*

Since the beginning of the world, *spirit* has always been a source of *inspiration* for the invisible mind. Spirit or breath can be produced by *exhaling*.

As noted, one of the few ways exhaling occurs is when a life-form (natural or supernatural) is **speaking or _breathing_ out words**. Christ is the physical manifestation of **God's spoken Word**, regarding our salvation from Sin and our new life.

As in the previous analogy of how water rushes in and fills every room of a sinking ship, when we are spiritually baptized or submerged _into_ Christ—God's Living Word, He also enters _in_ and _inspires_ every area of our mind, which is being renewed daily.

The Sanctuary of God

[Jesus said,] **"Come [forward, towards] Me, all who are [exhausted, fatigued or wearied** from being over burdened with mental anxieties] **and I will give you rest** {from the burdens of the Law}."

Matthew 11:27-28

In the past, a common Israelite—non-priest—could come into the Sanctuary to offer up sacrifices for the personal sins he/she committed. But, once they reached the altar, in the courtyard, they could go no further. Most likely, some of God's people desired to enter into His manifested glorious presence. But they could not.

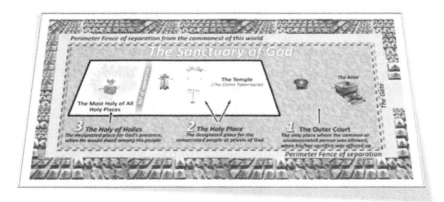

*Enter [through] **His gates with thanksgiving [adoration and worship], and** [into] **His courts with praise. Give thanks to Him; bless His name.***

*For the Lord is good; **His loving-kindness is everlasting, and His faithfulness** {extends} **to all….***

Psalms 100:4-5

Following is a comparison of what the spiritual process of salvation looks like for anyone who has been convinced^{G3982} after **seeing and repeatedly hearing** the good news of his/her salvation:

- **By Faith, We Enter the Gates of His Sanctuary** with a heart of adoration and worship, so that we will walk into His courtyard with praise for what He has done.

- **By Faith, We Approach the Altar as a living sacrifice** to God. Just to be clear: this is NOT a sacrifice FOR our sins, because Christ has already paid that debt in full for us; instead, this is a personal or self-sacrifice OF our will and old-self. Meaning, if we desire to draw any closer to God, then we must lay ourselves—common Sinful desires of the flesh—on the altar to be **progressively** slaughtered or put to death. Only then can a new spiritual creation or new life exist. (Many believers have yet to do this in a progressive and meaningful way.)

- **By Faith, We are Cleanse in the Laver** before entering the Temple, where God's presence is. At the Laver—large bowl, which is filled with living *water* or the Holy Spirit of God, we can wash our minds from the perverted and limited carnal thinking of the past, in order to be pronounced completely clean and consecrated to God.

- **By Mature Faith, We See Ourselves Being Presented to Christ, Our High Priest,** in order to attend to His earthly duties in the Temple or holy place. For us, today, the Temple is our new life—mind and body: it is where we live and work in a manner worthy of the Lord's Name, so as to please Him in all respects, while bearing fruits of righteousness and increasing in the knowledge of God.

- **By Mature Faith, We Draw Closer to the Holy Place** where the glorious manifested presence of God—the Holy Spirit—dwells. Today, that place is our renewed mind or innermost part.

> **Physically**, the holy of holies was a partitioned-off portion of the Temple, where the most sacred things of God (*e.g.*, the Ark and Mercy Seat) were kept. **Spiritually**, the holy of holies is the *eternally-aware* part of our mind; it is the God-consciousness portion that was closed off after Sin entered the world. But, when Christ died on the cross and the inner veil in the Temple was torn from top to bottom, the outer Tabernacle (the renewed mind) became one with the Most Holy of all holy places (the God-consciousness).

As such, when we progressively breakdown the barrier that separated us from a direct connection to eternal concepts from Heaven, our mind is, once again, flooded with, and is receptive to, eternal thoughts; because, our renewed mind is *ONE* with the active, or the once again living, spirit-part of God in us.

Again, the physical Temple was patterned after the true-spiritual Temple in Heaven. God had the physical one built because **He needed a consecrated or holy place on Earth** *where* **His glory could rest and dwell among His people** (Ref. Exodus 25:8-9).

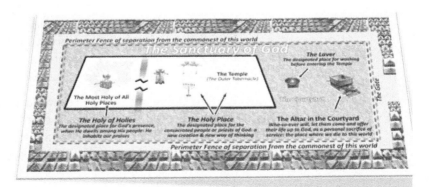

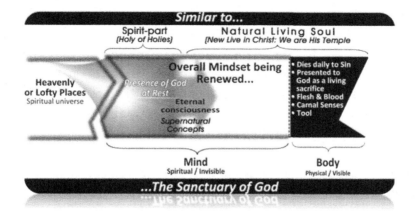

But, since EVERYONE was/is unholy by nature, **a *high priest* was set apart and appointed by God** to oversee and care for the Sanctuary. Actually, that person was required to perform the sacrifices ***FOR* all the people** individually, and he had to perform the annual Sacrifice of Atonement ***FOR* all the people** corporately.

Obviously, due to the large and ever-increasing number of Israelites, the high priest would have to sacrifice continuously for the people, not to mention having to perform the other ceremonies for their corporate worship. Literally, that's non-stop work for one man.

> *Then the Lord spoke to Moses, saying, "Bring the tribe of Levi near and set them before Aaron the priest, that they may [attend to or] serve him.*
>
> *"And they shall [hedge about, guard or protect the high priest's duties and the duties of the whole assembly] before the tent of meeting, to [work the works] of the tabernacle."*

Numbers 3:5-7

All of the Levites—one of the original twelve tribes—were **set aside FOR God** (Numbers 3:44-45 & 8:17-18). That meant **they were no longer counted *with* the other tribes or people,** nor would they have a portion of the land. They belonged to God and, as such, **they were to receive a sacred inheritance** or a consecrated portion **from Him** (Ref. Numbers 18:21 and Deuteronomy 10:9).

What is significant to note is: **God consecrated the Levites unto Himself, and then He GAVE them to the *high* priest**, in order for them to attend to *his* (Aaron's) duties AND attend to the duties of the *people*. The high priest's duties were to care for the House of God; and, the people's duties were to worship God in holiness.

The combined roles of the priests were to perform routine services, sacrifices, and worship to God in His Temple. That meant, **God saw the priests *as* a consecrated version *of* the people**.

In the same way that the Levites were consecrated unto God and then presented to Aaron, *their* high priest, **faith-filled** believers are set apart (from this Sinful world) unto God and are then presented to [the] Christ, *our* High Priest (Ref. John 17:6) **to <u>also</u> BE servants or priests *with* Him**.

> *"Truly, truly, I say to you, he who believes in Me, the works that I do, he will do also; and greater works than these he will do; because I go to the Father.*
>
> *"Whatever you ask in My name, that will I do, so that the Father may be glorified in the Son.*
>
> *"If you ask Me anything in My name, I will do it."*
>
> *John 14:12-14*

As a consecrated version of the people, **collectively**, we ALL are capable of doing more (*i.e.*, in number or quantity) miraculous works and labors of love than Christ, because He went to the Father after only two and a half years of ministry. However, at our current rate, we are off track and off course from where we should be, spiritually.

Corporately, many of us are like infants looking up to Heaven in desperation for health and financial assistance. **It is as if we still don't know who we really are, in Christ**.

Therefore, if anyone is in Christ, he is a new creature; the old things passed away; behold, new things have come.

Now all these things are from God, who reconciled us to Himself through Christ and gave us the ministry of reconciliation,

Namely, that God was in Christ reconciling the world to Himself, not counting their trespasses against them, and He has committed to us the word of reconciliation.

Therefore, we are ambassadors for Christ, as though God were making an appeal through us; we beg you on behalf of Christ, be reconciled to God.

He made Him who knew no sin to be sin on our behalf, so that we might become the righteousness of God in Him.

2 Corinthians 5:17-21

Under the new Covenant, *God still meets with, and dwells among, His people in earthly temples* or holy places. But, today, **those holy temples are not made with cloth or brick and mortar**. God does not prefer to meet with us only in our local church buildings, as we are inclined to think.

For we are the temple of the living God; just as God said, "I will dwell in them and walk among them; and I will be their God, and they shall be My people.

"Therefore, come out from [among the world] and be separate," says the Lord. "And do not [attach yourselves to] what is unclean; and I will [bring you into My favor].

"And I will be a father to you, and you shall be sons and daughters to Me," says the Lord Almighty.

2 Corinthians 6:16b-18

The Holy Spirit (the Divine inspiration) of God rests on *and* in us, according to our faith—confident and obedient expectation.

> *You also, as living stones, are being built up as a spiritual house [or dwelling] for a holy priesthood, to offer up spiritual sacrifices [well received or approved] to God through Jesus Christ.*

1 Peter 2:5

Here is one meaning of that verse:

- Spiritually, each believer is a stone

- Spiritually, each believer is a priest—consecrated servant

- **United together in worship, we *all* make up** ONE SPIRITUAL HOUSE or dwelling place—the Church.

From that ONE dwelling place we *all*, as priests, offer up spiritual sacrifices of praise that are acceptable to God, through Christ.

Chapter 17

THY KINGDOM COME

Seek first [the kingdom of God] and His righteousness;

Matthew 6:33a

As stated in Chapter 11, the word *kingdom* is made up of two words: **king**'s **dom**ain. Together, these words describe **the territory or place where a king reigns or has absolute authority**.

Today, there are very few *true* kingdoms left in the world. For that reason, most of the common definitions and ideas of a *kingdom* come from historical reference books, movies, and television programs.

The United States of America (USA) is *not* a kingdom. This country was purposely formed as a *democracy*. That means it has a *government by the people*—elected citizens, *for the people*—the peoples' representatives. A *true* kingdom is not a democracy; rather, it is a **mon**archy. That means *only one-person rules*; and, the privilege to rule is, usually, passed on through inheritance or, in some cases, through force.

In ancient times, the main reasons people *chose* to live within a king's domain or territory was to be protected by His army and have convenient access to common trade and resources. But rarely did the people have either a vote or a voice in the decisions affecting that kingdom.

The king decided. The people obeyed. That was the natural order of things in a *true* kingdom.

An honest and caring king made honest and caring decisions *for* his people. But even if the king's decisions were neither honest nor caring, the people did not have a legal basis on which to protest or challenge him.

They could, however, simply choose to leave the borders of his kingdom and try to survive on their own. In fact, those Colonials who were credited with forming this nation—the USA—were themselves fleeing from an abusive king (monarchy) and his unfair rulings.

Today, more people around the world are used to some form of democratic government where they, the people, have a voice (*e.g.*, elections, assemblies, representatives, etc.). Of course, that voice may be smaller or weaker in some countries, in comparison to others.

In places where the people have neither a voice nor a vote, there are, in some cases, organized protests or other forms of civil unrest, as the people struggle to have their *say* in the way things are done. At the very least, people want to have their opinions considered by those with decision making authority.

For those and other reasons, it is difficult for most people, today, to grasp the concept of totally submitting themselves to a king or a self-governing ruler. Especially a spiritual (unseen) King, such as Jehovah-God.

Quite often, the explanation of God's Kingdom is confusing. Perhaps, in part, because some people, understandably, apply the same definition to the *Kingdom of God* as they do to the *Kingdom of Heaven*. But there is a difference.

The Kingdom of God is any place *where Jehovah-God has absolute rule.* That simply means it is any place (*e.g.*, our hearts) where His Authority and Holy nature reigns: **Obedient-based faith**.

The Kingdom of Heaven is any place where the spiritual (*e.g.*, the supernatural or Higher) concepts and principles of Heaven reign. As it relates to us, that place is within any heart or mind that is (being) renewed to think higher than the carnal thoughts of this Sinful world: **Spiritual Awareness**.

And, although it is *not* impossible to do, **it is extremely difficult to establish the Kingdom of God without first establishing the Kingdom of Heaven**—signs and wonders. That was the first message from God to His people was to prepare them for spiritual things.

Now in those days John the Baptist came, preaching in the wilderness of Judea, saying,

"Repent, for the kingdom of heaven is at hand."

For this is the one referred to by Isaiah the prophet when he said, "The voice of one crying in the wilderness, 'Make ready the way of the Lord, Make His paths straight!'"

Matthew 3:1-3

John the Baptizer was a forerunner of Jesus. In other words, he was *a sign or a voice for what was to come*. His purpose was to prepare the people for the new way or the spiritual route that God would take to redeem the people, through Jesus [the] Christ, apart from the Law of Sin of Death.

John's message to the people was simple: begin to *rethink* how you envisioned salvation and God's righteousness, because unseen *spiritual things are about to impact your lives* for the better.

Then Jesus arrived from Galilee at the Jordan coming to John, to be baptized by him.

But John tried to prevent Him, saying, "I have need to be baptized by You, and do You come to me?"

But Jesus answering said to him, "Permit it at this time; for in this way it is fitting for us to fulfill all righteousness." Then he permitted Him.

After being baptized, Jesus came up immediately from the water; and behold, the heavens were opened, and he saw the Spirit of God descending as a dove and lighting on Him,

And behold, a voice out of the heavens said, "This is My beloved Son, in whom I am well-pleased."

Matthew 3:13-17

After being baptized by John (Ref. Leviticus 8:6), Jesus was led into the wilderness where He remained steadfast in His purpose to do God's Will, while being tempted by the devil. After that He went to Capernaum to begin His ministry. He began by also preparing the people for spiritual things, before He could set the groundwork for the kingdom of God.

> *From that time Jesus began to preach and say, "Repent, for the kingdom of heaven is [near]."*
>
> *Matthew 4:17*

The Kingdom of Heaven

As stated before, *the Kingdom of Heaven* refers to the reign and rule of **Godly spiritual principles**. For a while, such principles were hidden from the thoughts of the people; but, now, these principles are MORE accessible and *can* readily be seized or taken hold of by people of faith—confident obedience to God's Authority.

These eternal or spiritual principles are NOT for creating a perfect paradise on Earth. That's not what God intended the Israelites to do in Canaan, nor is it what He wants Christians to do, today. The reason being: **Sin is still in the world**.

The Kingdom of Heaven is a treasure that is to be sought after by people (Matthew 13:44); but it is also *alive* or living, so that it will also, itself, seek after precious possessions or people (13:45-46). The Kingdom of Heaven is a safe haven (13:31-31); it is compassion and righteous judgment (18:23-35); it is extremely influential (13:33); and, it crosses religious and social boundaries (22:2-10). The Kingdom of Heaven is a source of inspiration that people gather around; and, it is something that can easily captivate and gather people into itself (13:47).

That being said, more than one *kind* of person will be associated or identified with the Kingdom of Heaven or with spiritual concepts. Meaning, there are people who worship God in spirit and in truth, and there are also false worshippers. This fact is supported by **the overall meaning** of several parables Jesus spoke, regarding the Kingdom of Heaven.

Following is one of those parables in particular:

... "The kingdom of heaven may be compared to a man who sowed good [wheat] seed in his field.

"But while men were sleeping, his enemy came and sowed tares also among the wheat, and went away.

"But when the wheat sprang up and bore grain, then the tares became evident also [because they bore no grain].

"And the slaves of the landowner came and said to him, 'Sir, did you not sow good seed in your field? How then does it have tares?'

"And he said to them, 'An enemy has done this!' And the slaves said to him, 'Do you want us, then, to go and gather them up?'

"But he said, 'No; [if perhaps] while you are gathering up the tares, you may root up the wheat with them.

"Allow both to grow together until the harvest; and in the time of the harvest I will say to the reapers, 'First gather up the tares and bind them in bundles to burn them up; but gather the wheat into my barn.'"

Matthew 13:24-30

Jesus later explained the meaning of this parable to his disciples, when they were away from the general population:

"The one who sows the good seed is the Son of Man,

"And the field is the world; and as for the good seed, these are the sons of the kingdom; and the tares are the sons of the evil one,

"And the enemy who sowed them is the devil, and the harvest is the end of the age; and the reapers are angels.

> *"Therefore, just as the tares are gathered up and burned with fire, so shall it be at the end of the age.*
>
> *"The Son of Man will send forth His angels, and they will gather out of His kingdom all stumbling blocks, and those who commit lawlessness,*
>
> *"And will cast them into the furnace of fire; in that place there shall be weeping and gnashing of teeth."*

Matthew 13:37b-42

A *tare*[G2215] stalk looks very much like a wheat-stalk; but it does not produce grain (*i.e.*, fruit). As it relates to Jesus' parable, a tare is a person who only appears to be godly; but, in reality, he or she is not or, perhaps, is no longer godly. In fact, they make it difficult for others to be godly.

The term **tare** does **_not_** describe common sinners; because, common sinners do *not* intentionally look and, in this case, sound like the true worshippers of God. A tare or false worshipper is someone who has a type of faith,[G4102] but their faith is not or is no longer *in* God, as much as it is *in* and *for* him or her*self*.

So, what or who are tares?

In Matthew 13:41, Jesus identifies some of their characteristics: they are **stumbling blocks** or objects of offence that cause others to stumble and fall in their spiritual walk, and they are wicked or lawless. But again, this is not describing common sinners; rather, it is describing people in our churches or in other places of worship.

And, that description is not limited to regular folks sitting in the pews or the audience. Most sobering is the fact that Jesus assigned those same characteristics to some of the self-appointed religious leaders of His day: Scribes and Pharisees that belonged to rival religious schools of thought.

> *"Even so you... outwardly appear righteous to men, but inwardly you are full of [deceit] and lawlessness."*

Matthew 23:28

In the past, different schools of thought were formed for the same reason different denominations exist, today. God's Word, and various subject matters of life that may or may not be directly addressed in His Word, can be interpreted slightly different from one group to the next.

Like most religious movements, it is reasonable to assume that they (*i.e.*, the Scribes and the Pharisees) started out with good intentions: to teach and to lead people in the ways of God. But, perhaps, over time, those who found themselves in charge became too controlling; and, because God, at times, seem to be distant and/or absent, they began to use what influence they had over the people for selfish gain.

At some point, these leaders convinced themselves that it was okay to make their personal requirements equal to the religious requirements of a, seemingly, distant God. Apparently, it had gotten to the point where God's Will became secondary and their self-serving interpretations of, and their additions to, His Word became primary.

In other words, they elevated themselves and became self-appointed law-givers, instead of teachers of the Law:

> **Then Jesus spoke to the multitudes and to His disciples.**
>
> **Saying, "The scribes and the Pharisees have seated themselves in the chair of Moses;**
>
> **"Therefore, all that they tell you, do and observe, but do not do according to their deeds; for they say things and do not do them."** *{Basically, Jesus was saying: do as they say, not as they do; because, there will be some of God's original intention in what they say, even though they themselves do not do as He says.}*

Matthew 23:1-3

In time, the masses, or those people who wanted to know God's Will, quickly began to feel overwhelmed, as they tried to carry out the desires of God and the desires of self-appointed law-givers, too. Matthew Chapter 23 gives the full picture of what Jesus was saying; but the accusation can be summarized in verses 4-6.

> *"...They [bundle up a lot of oppressive religious rules], and lay them on men's shoulders; but they themselves are unwilling to [carry such a burdensome load, even for a moment].*
>
> *"[Everything they do, they do with the intention of being] noticed by [other people]; for they [will even try to exceed God's own recommendations, in order to appear more pious and committed to His House and to His work].*
>
> *"And they love the place of honor at banquets, and [they prefer] the [best] seats in the [church],"*

> *Matthew 23:4-6*

Today, as in Jesus' time, **tares look and sound like Godly people**, because they probably were, at one time, Godly people. But eventually, they deliberately conspired in their hearts to rule in the House of God, instead of serving in it.

> *"So then, you will know [or recognize] them by their fruits.*
>
> *"Not everyone who says to Me, 'Lord, Lord,' will enter the kingdom of heaven; but he who does the will of My Father, who is in heaven.*
>
> *"Many will say to Me on that day. 'Lord, Lord, did we not prophesy in Your name, and in Your name [did we not] cast out demons, and in Your name perform many miracles?*
>
> *"And then I will declare to them, I never knew you; depart from Me, you who practice lawlessness."*

Matthew 7:20-23

More than any spiritual fruit, **tares are devoid of humility and Godly love**. As a further example of what Jesus was saying, the Apostle Paul was indirectly describing tares, while he was making a point on the importance of LOVE, in 1 Corinthians 13:1-3, which has been enhanced:

- If I speak with the tongues of men and of angels, but do not have love, I have become a noisy gong or a clanging cymbal—I am a distraction to others.

- If I have the gift of prophecy, and know all mysteries and all knowledge; and if I have all faith, so as to remove mountains, but do not have love, I am nothing—I provided no lasting proof of God's love for the world.

- And if I give all my possessions to feed the poor, and if I surrender my body to be burned, but do not have love, it [does not benefit me in the end]—I will have my reward (*i.e.*, martyrdom and the gratification of men) in this life; but, I did not truly honor God, neither did I store up any treasure in Heaven, where it matters most.

The Kingdom of God

The Kingdom of God is *not* a religious fraternity or a special club that people are admitted into once they've recited *a verbal prayer of salvation*; nor is the Kingdom of God our local church body or assembly. Yes, God's kingdom is currently being established on Earth, but **He has no plans to force His Holy nature onto *this* Sinful world**.

Here's how Jesus described God's kingdom:

> *"The kingdom of God is not coming with [evidence visible for inspection with physical eyes];*
>
> *"Nor will they say, 'Look, here it is!' or, 'There it is!' For behold, the kingdom of God is [inside you]."*

Luke 17:20a-21

That, of course, is the same picture God used to describe His kingdom, too. After the Israelites were delivered out of Egypt, God instructed Moses to explain His reason for saving them.

> *'Now then, if <u>you</u> will indeed obey My voice and keep My covenant, then <u>you</u> shall be My own possession among all the people [in the world], for all the earth is Mine;*
>
> *'And <u>you</u> shall be to Me a [dominion or kingdom]^{H4467} of priests and a holy nation.'*
>
> *Exodus 19:5-6a*

God was saying the following:

> The **people**... *were set free from a life of inherited bondage... for the purpose of becoming* **His priests or consecrated servants**... *through their* **willing obedience to His Word**.

At that time, God was referring to the Israelites. But He implied that *His people are* **THOSE who have faith in**—obedience to—**the gospel they hear and cheerfully expect it to be fulfilled**.

Again, it is both necessary and beneficial to refer to God's past dealings with the Israelites as a point of reference. Through them, He established patterns and set plans into motion. And, once God begins a pattern or plan, He does *not* deviate from it (Ref. Malachi 3:6a).

God intended then, as He intends now, for *His Way*—holiness and righteousness—to rule and reign in the hearts or minds of His *people*. That meant, then, as it does, now, **the people themselves were/are to be God's** kingdom, not the land of Canaan or any other place on Earth.

God wanted then, as He wants today, for His kingdom—His people—to be *un*like any other kingdom on Earth. If time-travel was possible and we could go back and randomly examine many of the man-made kingdoms that existed in the past, I believe we would easily find people who did not totally agree with *every* decision their king made.

Just because people in a kingdom *physically* or outwardly obeyed the decrees of their king didn't mean they did so *willingly* or wholeheartedly. That's why it was important for the Israelites to, eventually, *love or prefer the Ways of God with their whole self*.

Again, **God is not self-conscience so as to command people to love Him**. Moses instructed the people to love God (Deuteronomy 6:4-6), because he recognized the truth: **when you truly love** someone in authority, you will wholeheartedly **honor and obey** him/her without fear or regret.

That's how God's kingdom or His people were and are to differ from any other kingdom or people on Earth: **LOVE and FAITH**— confident obedience from a willing heart or mind, **not out of forced servitude and fear**.

> There is no fear [terror] in love; but perfect [love or affection]^{G26} casts out fear, because fear involves punishment, and the one who fears is not perfected in love.

1 John 4:18

That same *kind* of love made David *a man after God's own heart* (1 Samuel 13:14 & Acts 13:22). David didn't just try to do what was right simply because the omnipotent or all-powerful God said so; although that *is* a good enough reason. David loved God and he loved His Ways; which meant, he loved *righteousness* and hated evil. That made it easier for him to do what was right.

And, when David did sin, his sorrow and grief were not based on fear or terror that God was going to punish him. He was deeply sorrowful, because **he knew his sins naturally separated him from God**, whom he loved.

Back then, if all the Israelites had a heart or **mind** like David, just imagine how wonderful things would have been for them. But, as is commonplace with a carnally-intoxicated humanity, the lust of the eyes and flesh, and the pride of life often prevails over a person's otherwise sober *intentions* to obey God's Word.

Fall on the Rock and Be Broken

[Jesus said,] *"From the days of John the Baptist until now the kingdom of heaven suffers violence [forces or presses itself into], and violent [energetic] men take [or seize upon] it by force."*

Matthew 11:12b

Due to the constant presence of Sin and its many familiar expressions (*e.g.*, death, sicknesses, diseases, perversions, confusion, adversity, etc.), the spiritual and eternal concepts of Heaven must be *pressed* into this darkened carnal world, in order to overcome ignorance about God and various religious strongholds. And, due to our inherently carnal mindset, people who desire to seize the spiritual and eternal concepts of Heaven must violently press or personally force these concepts into their thinking.

[An excerpt from Jesus' Sermon on the Mount], *"Enter through the narrow gate; for the gate is [wide, spread out and flat]*[G4116] *and the way is [spacious] that leads to destruction, and there are many who enter through it {because it is natural, convenient, and effortless—easy}.*

"For the gate is small and the way [has obstacles][G4728] *that leads to life, and there are few who find it" {because it requires greater effort}.*

Matthew 7:13-14

It is easy and quite natural to be *self-centered*: thinking about, and concerned only with, your own affairs. Left unchecked, self-centeredness can easily and naturally morph into *selfishness*: neglecting the needs of others. That is why it is often difficult to purposefully maintain a close long-term relationship with another person; because, even when two people are supposedly in agreement on reaching the same goal, often, there are varying viewpoints on how best to pursue and accomplish it.

That's why, corporately, it can be even more difficult to find true **solidarity in the absence of persecution,** due to our self-centered and selfish natures—our innate quest for personal convenience.

> ***Jesus said to** [the Chief Priests and religious leaders about their rebellion],* **"Did you never read in the Scriptures, 'The stone which the builders rejected, this became the chief corner stone; this came about from the Lord, and it is marvelous in our eyes'?**
>
> **Therefore, I say to you, the kingdom of God will be taken away from you and given to a people, producing the fruit of it.**
>
> **And he who falls on this stone will be broken to pieces; but on whomever it falls, it will scatter him like dust."**
>
> *Matthew 21:42-44*

In the best of circumstances, self-imposed humility—willingly falling on the Rock and breaking up/off one's prideful nature—is better than persecution, which is often a form of judgment befalling a disobedient person or nation. A vital part of being humble is to consciously seek to **honor God in spirit and in truth, first, before asking Him *for* things we need and think we want.**

If believers—from the pulpit to the pews—were completely honest, they would have to admit that **today's Church can, mostly, be identified by *our personal attempts to apply faith*[G3982] *for our needs*.** And, although we know that **unity** is something we should have in the Church, in these modern times of relative peace and safety, it does not seem to be as important to us as it is to the Father.

Yes! It is great when there is agreement within a small local assembly—church; but it is doubtful that such small pockets of unity are what Jesus had in mind when He prayed to the Father, on *all* of our behalf (Ref. John 17:20-26). When unity becomes as urgent to us as it is to the Father, there will be a spiritual burden and continual prayers from us all, for us all, to move beyond **the status quo,** wherein **it is acceptable to remain conveniently separated from other believers,** because we disagree on various points of salvation and on Who God IS and what He actually said and/or meant.

> *Seeing the people, He felt compassion for them, because they were distressed and [scattered about]^{G1590} like sheep without a shepherd.*
>
> *Then He said to His disciples, "The harvest is plentiful, but the [workers or teachers]^{G2040} are few.*
>
> *"Therefore, beseech the Lord of the harvest to send out workers into His harvest."*

Matthew 9:36-38

Someone who is truly sent from God will always seek to unite His people—*all* of them. That person is **spiritually aware** enough to know that he/she is just a laborer. That person is **spiritually aware** enough to know that he/she is not the head of the Church, not even of a local assembly of believers. That person is **spiritually aware** enough to know that he/she has been *entrusted* with God's sheep and, as such, he/she WILL give an account of his/her actions or care to the Head of the Church, Christ.

But there is not always a keen sense of spiritual awareness in our local churches, today, because there are little to no undeniable signs and wonders in the Church, as a whole. And, since we do not, yet, have a collective awareness of spiritual concepts, there is little to no unity within the Church, as a whole. And, since there is little to no unity among believers, there is little to no Christ-like compassion for the lost.

Case in point, most believers—from the pulpit to the pew—*seem* to be okay with people remaining *lost*: without a knowledge of both God and their salvation. For the most part, many believers are under the **erroneous impression that Sinful people are rejecting Christ,** because they do not want to *come into our churches to religiously worship Him with us.*

In truth, many unchurched people are not rejecting Him, **they are actually rejecting us**—His people. More accurately, they are rejecting our worldly divisiveness: our myriad of denominations, each claiming to be right or professing to hold the truth, while asserting *how* and *why* everyone else is wrong!

Yes; obviously, there are erroneous doctrines in the world, today, as there always have been and always will be. But, in reality, a lot of points of division exists, primarily, because of **a lack of true spiritual awareness**; and, the lack of true spiritual awareness exists, primarily, because there is **a lack of undeniable signs and wonders**; and, the lack of signs and wonders exists, primarily, **because we, ourselves, are scattered about**.

And, being scattered about is often a sign for premeditated *independence*, so that we can *have things our own way*. Basically, each person or group worshipping in a way that seems acceptable or right in their own eyes. To an outside observer, who was looking into the Church, **one might think there was no Head to unify the Body of Christ**.

Chapter 18

REPENT

From that time Jesus began to preach and say,
"Repent, for the kingdom of heaven is at hand."

Matthew 4:17

As previously defined, **repent**[G3340] (metanoeō) **means to** *think differently* or to *reconsider*. Based on the various Scripture passages in which this word appears, the implication is to **rethink or reconsider your current behavior or actions, based on new information or on an ultimatum you've just received**.

Repenting (rethinking) is also the beginning of *repentance*. Repentance[G3341] is *regret or reversal (of a decision)*. As implied, repentance means, *compunction* or *regret* [as a result of guilt for doing wrong, which causes a] *change of mind afterwards*.

> *For the sorrow [heaviness] that is according to the*
> *will of God produces a repentance, [which leads to*
> *the type of salvation that will not cause regret]; but*
> *the sorrow of the world produces death.*

2 Corinthians 7:10

Repenting is an enduring process that leads to a renewed mind. Scripturally, to renew[29] means to renovate, improve or *completely* change for the better. As our minds are being renewed, we will naturally **redefine life**—its meaning and importance, and the process of **salvation**.

---

[29] Strong's Exhaustive Concordance of the Bible, Greek reference # 342

Think Differently About Salvation

For the Israelites *of old*, the difficult starting point was to rethink the way or the process by which people are saved from Sin:

- Do people become consecrated unto God by placing their confidence in the Mosaic Law and keeping up with its many decrees and sacrifices?

- Do people become consecrated unto God by placing their faith or confidence in Jesus Christ—His Death and His resurrection, in accordance with the grace of God?

He came to His own, but those who were His [own possession] did not [associate with] Him.

John 1:11

In referring back to the analogy of the slave, the taskmaster, and the King, from Chapter 14, when the King spoke to the first debtor-slave, who represented the Israelites, **it was *not necessary* for the King to point out the presence and influence of the taskmaster**. The Israelites had the Law and, more than any other nation of people, they were already aware of man*kind*'s inherited Sinful nature. Therefore, when the King arrived on the scene, this slave was already **working *to* overcome his taskmaster of Sin**.

Unfortunately, this particular slave found it difficult to believe or trust in the King's Authority and graciousness to deliver him; so, he continued to *work* within the confines of the Law, instead of **working to receive God's free gift of salvation, by faith**.

As for the Gentiles or non-Israelites, our circumstances were slightly different. Still, as in the case of the Israelites, these differences are relevant to ALL man*kind*, today.

Let's now focus on the *other* debtor-slave that was traveling through the same desert. As indicated before, this slave also had a taskmaster of Sin riding on his back; and, he too was required to pay off the same amount of debt, which originated with the same forefather, Adam.

But *this* slave lived in darkness.

In Him was life, and the life was the light of men.

John 1:4

It was not a literal darkness, in that he could not see his surroundings; rather, it was a *spiritual* darkness or obscurity, in that this slave, who represents the Gentiles, knew neither God nor His Law. As a result, he was unaware of the taskmaster's spiritual presence and influence.

In his early years, this slave very often did things he sometimes did not want to do; but, without God's Law for guidance, he couldn't see or recognize *why* his actions were wrong. So, at some point in his life, he completely stopped considering his dormant God-consciousness, which he did not understand. Instead, he naturally surrenders to the perverted desires coming from his Sinful flesh.

The people who [reside or dwell] in darkness [shadiness or obscurity] will see a great light; those who live in a dark land, the light will shine on them.

Isaiah 9:2 & Matthew 4:15

And, just like He did with the Israelite slave, the King also approached the Gentile slave and made the same announcement:

"Although I am a King, I have agreed to be your substitute. I have already gone ahead to your final destination, and I have paid your debt in full. Therefore, it is no longer legal for this taskmaster to hold you accountable for what your forefather did long ago. Legally, he can no longer hinder your speech and influence your path in life, unless you still want him to continue to do so."

"What?"

And the light shines in darkness, and the darkness did not [(eagerly) seize, attain, comprehend (or understand)] it.

John 1:5

"You became my substitute, why?"

"How do *you* know where I am going, when I don't even know?"

"What debt?"

"Why do you refer to me as a slave? I serve no man."

When we Gentiles hear the gospel of Jesus Christ for the first time, our initial reaction is the same as that of the Jews, as described by Paul in Romans 7:7-25. Before hearing the message of salvation, we also thought we were *alive* or free to be *and* to do whatever we wanted; or, so it seemed.

But, as we are hearing the truth (*i.e.*, Sin is actually alive and free *in* us and we were are slaves obeying the hurtful demands of a cruel taskmaster), the light of God's salvation begins to shine through our ignorance.

> *"Therefore, having overlooked the times of ignorance, [when we did not know Him], God is now declaring to men that all everywhere should repent."*

> *Acts 17:30*

Ideally, we ALL must begin to *re*think our common worldly idea of life. Really, we must ALL rethink what we thought *life* was.

But then, once Sin and Satan are seen as being the true enemies of our soul, we can*not* begin to think or reason with a religious-only mindset to believe that God intended for us to save ourselves, in our own strength. Yes; we are to **work out our own salvation...** (Philippians 2:12c), but we are to work it out **in accordance to grace, by faith**—obedient expectation, and not merely with learned public behavior and disciplined speech modification techniques.

Today, since there are little to no godly signs and wonders following, **too many believers**[G4100] **are still carnally-minded**. As such, people *may believe* in spiritual things, but they do not fully understand or relate to spiritual principles; and, therefore, they do not give sufficient value or realistic weight to God's Authority *in* and *for* their lives.

Whether they've been going to church for twenty days or twenty years, many believers are consumed with, and overwhelmed by, the cares of *this* life (*i.e.*, careers, financial debt, houses, cars, clothes, material wealth, etc.). That means they barely have time to process necessary spiritual concepts (*e.g.*, being thankful in advance of receiving the things they're asking God for; being content and joyful when they don't have everything they want or think they deserve in life; helping others when they themselves need help, etc.).

Therefore, when it comes to unity—**the most important godly spiritual concept of all**, in many cases, there is little difference between the average churched person and the average non-churched person. To both persons, relationships are merely a matter of convenience.

But, why is that?

The answer is rooted in an issue that was touched on earlier, in Chapter 14: **the way mainstream Christianity tends to define salvation**. As previously indicated, for the most part, **today's Church** routinely teaches that people can *hear one or more emotionally charged and convincing sermons, then pray "a prayer of salvation" and be completely "saved". And, at that moment, they have access to all of Heaven's resources, including God Himself, in Jesus' name.*

The thing is, a lot of people only seek after God when they're desperate. Unfortunately, they're not nearly as desperate to be free from their spiritual bonds to Sin as much as they are desperate to be free from the bonds of financial lack, health problems, social wounds, etc. But, under *those kinds* of desperate conditions, **most people do not truly find God**, because their search is too narrow.

For example, sometimes when I'm looking for an item around the house, I often have to ask my wife for help. Very often, my problem is: I routinely place **mental limitations on my search**.

Meaning, I often start with a mental image of what I *think* the item *should* look like or what I remembered it looking like (e.g., color, size, shape, etc.). As a result, I'm only depending on, or trusting in, my own limited perception to find what I need or *want*.

But, by doing so, I sometimes would overlook or pass by the very item I was searching for, because of my narrow vision or thinking. My wife, on the other hand, simply looked for the item with no preconceived notions of what it *should* look like.

That being said, instead of looking for a love-based relationship with the true and living God, a lot of churched people are only looking for the fulfillment of the promises that church leadership made to them, on God's behalf: *God will solve their personal and financial problems*; *God will heal their bodies*; *God will make them happy in this life*; and so on. But, as real and as valid as these issues are, unfortunately, **most churched people are *not* thinking about their lives from a spiritual point of view**, which is necessary to endure *the spiritual race* and its many hurdles.

In most cases, when people are told they are completely "saved" and they now have access to God, because of a simple prayer, it all sounds more like religious pleasantries because, more often than not, they don't *feel* any different. But, just in case, many of them are desperate or eager enough to *try*out their naturally small faith by asking God for the stuff they've always wanted in life.

But, after asking for a while (*e.g.*, days, weeks, months, or years) without being granted their requests, most churched people stop praying or asking God for help; and, they simply return to pursuing their unfulfilled desires and goals on their own. As for God, well, He simply becomes *the token centerpiece of the religious part of their life*, which they display on holidays or special occasions.

There is "a disconnect" that must be recognized, first.

For example:

> If we read Psalms 37:4, which says, *"Delight yourself in the Lord; and He will give you the desires of your heart,"* then we must FIRST consider **the position we must be in for God to give us the desires of our hearts**. In this case, we must first be in the place where we *delight ourselves in Him*.

To "delight yourself" (H6026) means *to be soft, pliable,* or excessively *delicate* [in personality, as opposed to being stubborn or strong-willed]. The implication being: God can then shape or fashion us to His Will, first. Then, **we will desire the same things He desires**, because we will *be on the same page* as Him, using the same definition of life.

Repenting leads to mature faith;[G4102] because, mature faith *is* a renewed or renovated mind. Only a renewed mind can fully contain and support a vision of God's spiritual kingdom (or spiritual rule and reign) within.

Many churchgoers, today, define and measure their *salvation* according to how well they can discipline themselves in public, instead of how much they *willingly* pursue the heart of God and **prefer not to sin**, especially when there's no one else around.

But there is a reason for this: it is easier for church leaders to instruct people to change their behavior, especially in public, because that approach *seems* to produce more immediate results than attempting to change peoples' hearts, which takes time and patience. The problem is, people can change their public behavior patterns just as quickly as they change clothing; and, most of the times that's exactly the case, figuratively.

Unfortunately, our churches are full of **hypocrites**, from the pulpit (the leaders) to the pews (the masses). That statement is *not* as opinionated or mean-spirited or self-righteous as it may sound. A hypocrite is <u>not just</u> someone who says or teaches one thing but then doesn't hold him or herself to that same teaching.

Actually, the original meaning of the Greek word *hupokritēs* is not *as* negative or offensive as it has come to be, today. Originally, **a hypocrite**[G5273] **was defined as a stage performer**; more specifically, a hypocrite was *an actor or actress playing out a role.*

However, the root word, which is *hupokrinomai*, reference number G5371, is more negative. That word means *to decide* (speak out or act) *under a false part* or *to pretend.*

Based on Church history, it would seem, for decades, churchgoers often make certain proclamations or confessions while they are *in character* (*i.e.,* saying and doing religious things), *in* costume (*i.e.*, usually, dressed in nice clothes, with their hair perfectly styled, perhaps, in makeup), and on stage (*e.g.*, at church or another type of assembly, etc.); but, then, literally they have a change of heart once they've been removed from that **set**ting.

Like many other habits or patterns in life, **religious hypocrisy is *not* always intentional**, although it can become so if it continues to go unchecked. As indicated before, religious hypocrisy can be, and usually starts out as, **a learned behavior**.

I've heard church staff and leadership say something along these lines: *if the service—songs and sermon—didn't move the people, then it wasn't a good service*. In other words, one of the acceptable signs and goals of a "good" church service, these days, is when tears flow, especially at the altar.

For that and other reasons, many talented, book- or street-smart preachers often give sermons that stir up *guilt for bad behavior* when they want to *move* or emotionally *touch* the people. Of course, the more people there are in the audience, the better the chances of stirring up emotions of guilt, simply by calling out common sins.

Then, at the end of the sermon, like prosecuting attorneys giving their closing arguments, preachers will aggressively *try* and *convict*[G3982] the people of their sins, and then *convince*[G3982] them to either make a public commitment to "serve" Christ or to give a large financial gift, in order to ease the guilt of Sin. Usually, the people are convinced and have enough conviction to do both.

A lot of people, past and present, have heard many guilt-riddled sermons that present valid reasons for them not to commit sins. And yet, many of them still have a natural fondness to sin. But, as controversial as it may sound, ***the need to stop sinning* should <u>not</u> be the main focus of the gospel**, which means "good news." The focus or essence of **the gospel** is, *the holy and eternal **God of Love** can now dwell with or in us,* by faith.

If Sin and bad behavior remain the major talking points of the gospel, then people will naturally keep, and continue to develop, a guilty conscience, due to the various slip-ups we all *will make* in this world. Therefore, it is crucial that a guilty conscience NOT be the foundation on which an *im*perfect and Sin-filled humanity attempts to build a relationship with a Just and Holy God; under those circumstances, it will be almost impossible to renovate the mind.

Renovation takes time; and, at first, it can be **a messy process**, as old walls (*e.g.*, strongholds of fear, low/no self-esteem, pride, etc.) are being torn down, and old fixtures (*e.g.*, lying, deceit, various addictions, etc.) are being stripped away. That's why **a new spiritual life is *not* likely to be the immediate results of a one-time confession** or a one-time emotional experience of remorse; although, either one is *a good starting point*.

To verbally confess that Jesus Christ is Lord, and to believe[G4100] that God raised Him from the dead, does indicate that a person is starting to think beyond the confines of mere carnal or physical concepts. But it doesn't mean he or she now has, or will ever have, enough **spiritually-obedient Christ-like faith** to effectively *keep him or herself separated from this perverse generation* to live a victorious life over Sin (*i.e.*, being in the world, but not *of* it).

I am referring to, what seems to be, mainstream Christianity's common use of Romans 10:9-10, as the de facto standard for the Christian new birth experience. **Seldom are the full benefits of salvation *immediately* realized through a simple onetime verbal confession**, which is, usually, **emotionally-driven and is made in the absence of an undeniable manifestation**.

Yes, *a verbal confession of belief* that is based on Romans 10:9-10 can be a good *starting* point; after all, *starting* a right-relationship with God isn't too difficult. Typically, what is difficult is renewing our Sin-filled and carnally-based minds enough to truly believe that what we've confessed is true: it actually becomes the basis of our reality.

An Examination of Romans 10:9-10

...If you confess with your mouth Jesus as Lord, and believe in your heart that God raised Him from the dead, you shall be saved,

For with the heart man believes, resulting in righteousness, and with the mouth he confesses, resulting in salvation.

Romans 10:9-10

Since the 1940's or so, I would guesstimate that millions of people have been "saved", as characterized by various Christian denominations, because they have recited some version of "the Sinner's Prayer," **based on a stand-alone or isolated excerpt of Romans 10:9-10**. But I would also guesstimate, in most cases, an examination of their lives, long after they uttered that prayer, would reveal that many of them did not or have not, really, renovated their minds, so as to **truly see spiritual things in Heaven as being more real than the physical things of this world**.

As such, most of the people who have met the simple criteria of a verbal prayer will, probably, not show significant changes in the way they approach(ed) or live(d) their lives, in general. At best, many of them will try to attend church and try to modify their behavior.

Before continuing any further, let me make the following two points about this examination of Romans Chapter 10:9-10:

1. The purpose is not to identify who gets into Heaven and who doesn't get in. No one, except God, can say *exactly* who will be in Heaven and *exactly* what it took for them to get there. On a personal note, I believe a lot more people will be in Heaven than some contemporary Christian denominations teach. But, in the grand scheme of things, Heaven should not be the main goal of the believer's life, because it is not the main focus of the gospel. The main goal and focus are: **love and unity with God and one another**, through freedom from Sin.

2. The purpose is not to contradict the requirement of confessing the Lordship of Jesus Christ. As Paul pointed out, certain people, eventually, need(ed) to do that.

But, in Romans 10:9-10, the Apostle Paul was *not* revealing an all-inclusive quick-n-easy formula or prayer for EVERYONE to *obtain* the complete package of salvation. <u>When isolated</u>, **Romans 10:9-10 and similar passages can easily be misinterpreted.**

For example, let's examine a similar type of passage, before continuing with Romans 10:9-10:

> *Therefore, I make known to you that no one speaking by the Spirit of God says, "Jesus is accursed;" and no one can say, "Jesus is Lord," except by the Holy Spirit.*

> *1 Corinthians 12:3*

Is the second half of that passage saying that God's Holy Spirit is in and with *anyone* who speaks out the words, "Jesus is Lord"?

If so, would it, then, be completely **im**possible for a deranged serial killer, who may have read a Bible in his or her past, to say those exact words before, during, or after killing someone?

No!

It would *not* be impossible.

Anyone capable of speech can utter the words, "Jesus is Lord," regardless of what he or she was doing or was about to do.

There is a deeper meaning. In order to understand what the Apostle Paul was saying is to consider the subject matters prior to and after verse 3.

In 1 Corinthians 12:1, Paul had just introduced the topic of **spiritual gifts**, as it relates to **corporate edification or growth.** The context of that topic, and surrounding ones, is **unity** or oneness.

As background, Paul was writing that particular letter to people— the church at Corinth—to whom he had already taught the elementary message of the cross. And, like Moses, Paul wanted them to be unified in their faith, despite any physical, cultural or economic differences; because, unification was the only way they could collectively reproduce the SAME love of God.

After some deliberate meditation or thoughtful consideration on surrounding passages, in Chapter 12, it should become clear that Paul was saying the following:

God is not divided and neither should His people be. There are many members of His Body (or there are many people within the Church at Large); and, as such, there are different expressions or manifestations of the Holy Spirit at work among them all. But... **and this is the point of verse 3** ...there is ONLY ONE HOLY SPIRIT or Mind of God, just as there *should* only ONE BODY of CHRIST or Church.

In the context of spiritual gifts and unification, it becomes clear that, in verse 3, **Paul meant the following**:

There will NEVER be two people [perhaps a Jew and a Gentile], who have the SAME Holy Spirit or Mind of God, saying two different things. The Holy Spirit will not use one person to [erroneously] say, "Jesus is accursed—banned or excommunicated by God;" and then, at some other time, use another person to [rightly] say, "Jesus is Lord."

In that same way, Romans 10:9-10 must also be placed into proper context. Yes, it says that a person's confession results in their salvation. But **IT WAS NOT INSTRUCTING A PERSON TO SIMPLY RECITE OR DECLARE SOMETHING, IN ORDER TO BE SAVED**; rather, it was describing what a person says as a result of giving eternal life to what he/she truly believes in his/her heart.

Upon closer examination, we see that even though that letter—the entire book of Romans—was and is, conceivably, meant for all Christians, including us today, **Paul's overall intention was to compare the Jews' and the Gentiles' response to God's grace**.

More specifically, Paul was pointing out how the Gentiles of his day, typically, could accept God's gift of salvation without having to deal with religious baggage, while many of the Jews, for whom God's gracious gift of new life was intended, had major difficulties embracing it. In part, it was due to their familiarity with the [Mosaic] Law of Sin and Death and, in part, it was their inherent stubbornness.

At any other time, stubbornness would have been the right tool to use, or the right mindset to have, in order to resist carnal desires or temptations that opposed God's Law. But, in this case, they were actually resisting God's grace or kindness and freedom from the Law.

As background, the Apostle Paul started the letter—the book of Romans—by promoting **the gospel or person of Jesus Christ as the means to salvation** for everyone who fully believes in Him. And, although that good news was meant for everyone, it was, naturally, intended for the Israelites/Jews, first. But, to Paul's dismay, history was repeating itself: God's people were, again, committing idolatry.

> *For even though they knew God [through His Law], they did not honor Him as God, or give thanks; but they became futile in their [discussions, debates, reasoning, and thoughts], and their foolish heart was darkened.*
>
> *Professing to be wise, they became fools*
>
> *And exchanged the glory of the incorruptible God for an image in the form of corruptible man and of birds and four-footed animals and crawling creatures.*
>
> *Therefore, God gave them over in the lusts of their hearts to impurity, that their bodies might be dishonored among them.*
>
> *For they exchanged the truth of God for a lie, and worshiped and served the creature rather than the Creator, who is blessed forever.*
>
> *Romans 1:21-25*

The above passages were *not* describing humanity's religious decline after the creation of the world; these were describing the, overall, history of the Israelites. The very picture Paul paints in Romans 1:21-32 can be seen in the OT's book of 2 Kings 17:7-23 and in other passages describing the times when the Israelites *of old* turned their backs to God—His Law—to please their flesh.

Fast forward to Paul's day when many of the Jewish teachers and students of the Law were opposing the gospel of Jesus Christ for, basically, the same reason as in their past: idolatry. But **this time it was religious idolatry**: they chose to worship the Law and the

Covenant more than the Covenant Maker, God. So, even though they knew about God's far-reaching Promise of a new and better Covenant, they conveniently refused to let go of the old one.

In Romans Chapters 2-8, Paul laid out a comprehensive comparison between the abilities of the Law and the abilities of God's grace to save people. He described how God's initial work of salvation was to fulfill the Law of Sin and Death through faith in the cross or the death of Christ. Most importantly, he revealed how God can provide *new life* in this world, through His Holy Spirit; something the Law could never do.

But, despite the fact that **God foreknew the Jews through His covenant with them**, and despite the fact **He that predestined them** to be the first to be made righteous by faith, they were missing out.

Therefore, in the proper context, **Romans Chapter 10 was about the Israelites/Jews.** In verses 6-10, Paul was actually repeating something Moses had said to them in the OT's book of Deuteronomy 30:11-14. In the chapters before and after Deuteronomy Chapter 30, Moses was establishing the terms of the Covenant God made with the His people. Among other things, Moses gave them specific instructions; he gave them warnings; and, he gave them a road map to get back to the place of God's Promise.

Moses was letting them know: **obedience** to God's Law **would keep** them *free* and *safe* in the Promised Land. But Moses knew they were disobedient by nature; which is why he talked about **restoring them back** to the Promised Land, even **before they ever entered into it**.

To paraphrase, Moses told the Israelites the following:

> **When** you disobey [in the future] and are taken captive by other nations [because of your disobedience], you do *not* need to beg or bargain with God, in order to be made free; the solution to your problem [of captivity] is *not* a big mystery that requires deep meditation or great intelligence to solve; nor is the solution too far out of your reach, so don't look up to Heaven or beyond the sea for it.

Meaning, God's Word (at that time, the Law) had the power or ability to save them (Ref. Deuteronomy 30:12-13). The only thing necessary for them to do was collectively *turn their hearts back* to obeying the Word, which God had already given to them, and they would be saved (again) from the captivity and bondage of their oppressors (Deuteronomy 30:1-3).

In Romans Chapter 10, Paul was continuing, from Chapter 9, to express anguish over his Jewish brethren, who were stumbling over and rejecting the *gospel of Jesus Christ*, which *is itself the power or ability [of God] to rescue [individuals* from this Sinful world], **especially the Jews** (Romans 1:16). But the Jews were rejecting the good news, because they did not recognize God's *type* of salvation.

As God had previously done with the Israelites, through Moses and the prophets, He was again doing, through Paul and the other Apostles. He was telling them that the answer to their salvation from captivity was already *with* them. But, this time, things were different; there was a deeper spiritual plan in motion:

- The answer to their salvation did *not* require a physical response (*e.g.*, observing more ceremonies, meals, and festivals, or making more animal sacrifices); instead, it required a spiritual or mental response of repenting (rethinking) that leads to faith; and, as a result...

- This God-*kind* of salvation would bring about spiritual awareness and mental rest, which, when you truly believe, it will be more beneficial than physical rest.

Unfortunately, similar to their ancestors, the Jews of Paul's day were narrow-mindedly looking for **physical relief**, in the form of salvation and rest from their Roman oppressors. But Paul and the other Apostles were, directly and indirectly, saying: God, through Jesus, wanted to spiritually save them from Sin; and then, most importantly, they would have a new or better life of righteousness, regardless of whether they were oppressed by the Romans or not.

In Romans Chapter 10, Paul was doing a comparison between *the righteousness of God*, which was, at one time, based on the Law, and the righteousness of God, which is, now, based on faith. In verses 9 and 10, **Paul was NOT revealing a quick-n-easy narration to get the complete package of salvation**; instead, **he was revealing a very deliberate sequence of events necessary for his religious-minded <u>JEWISH</u> brethren to be** *converted* **to a salvation based solely on the grace of God and faith** (Romans 10:1-4).

As for the Law, it is true that all instructions from God should be obeyed, to the letter; but, some instructions from God were meant to be temporary, until something more perfect or complete is ready to be implemented. And, as important and influential as the Mosaic Law was, it was only meant to be temporary; because, the Covenant for which the Law was established, was only meant to be temporary.

The Law of Sin and Death was fulfilled or fully satisfied with something greater: Christ Jesus, the Living Word of God, Who was the personification of His grace. But, since the Jews did not recognize the time of transitioning—from one covenant to the next, they were overlooking the very thing they wanted to find: God's presence.

So, while it is *not* recorded in Scripture, I can picture the following:

> When Jesus died on the cross and the veil in the Temple was torn, by God, from top to bottom (Matthew 27:50-51), most likely, the religious leaders immediately *re*paired the veil.

> Meaning, even though the Holy Spirit was indicating that the separation between God and His consecrated servants was finally removed, the self-appointed law-givers or religious leaders took it upon themselves to intentionally or unintentionally hide what God did, so as not to disrupt the religious status quo they'd established (Ref. Matthew 23:13).

The Jews' position on Jesus Christ's work of salvation was *not* one of ignorance. For the most part, the religious leaders knew the essence of the gospel of Jesus Christ; many of them simply *rejected* it. But Paul sincerely wanted any Jew that had a true zeal for righteousness to look beyond the Law and see God's grace—His free gift of salvation—and His provision for a new life.

> *...If you confess [or acknowledge] with your mouth Jesus as Lord, and* <u>*believe*</u>*[G4100] {or have a faithful response} in your heart* <u>*that God raised Him from the dead,*</u> *you shall be saved,*

Romans 10:9

Again, Paul wasn't trying to get the Jews to make a quick-n-easy confession, so that they could then be labeled *Christians*. No, the kind of life-changing confession he sought was *not*, necessarily, indicating the start of the renewal process; rather, **it was a sign that change had <u>already</u> taken place.**

> *...For with the heart man beliefs,[G4100] resulting in [justification], and with the mouth he [acknowledges his covenant or gives thanks], resulting in salvation [rescue or safety].*

Romans 10:10

The framework of Romans 10:9-10 is the same spiritual principle Jesus used when He taught the masses and His disciples:

> *"The good man out of the good [deposit or wealth] of his heart [speaks] forth what is good; and the evil man out of the [hurt, malice, or disease] in his heart [speaks] forth what is evil; for his mouth speaks [according to] that which [is super abundantly present in] his heart."*

Luke 6:45

God looks at the contents of the heart or mind.

Attentiveness and *thoughtful consideration* (or obedient-and-Christ-like-faith) to what God has said and Promised requires a renewal of the heart or mind. That's the reason God instructed the Israelites to [continually] meditate, which means *to ponder, mutter or speak*, on His Word day and night (Joshua 1:8).

A self-serving religious person will outwardly obey God's Law, because he or she knows that their disciplined behavior will naturally result in respect and praise from undisciplined people. But the person that actually finds heartfelt delight in God's Word is inwardly blessed (happy) and righteous (justified) in the sight of God, where it matters the most. (Ref. Psalms 1)

The point being: the content and makeup of a person's heart/mindset are **revealed** by the words he or she **routinely and sincerely speaks** (Ref. Luke 6:39-44). Therefore, if a Jew chose to confess that Jesus is [the] Messiah, in essence, he/she would be acknowledging Him as the Lamb of God; and, as such, he/she would be acknowledging His Authority to atone or cover over Sin, once and for all.

That, of course, meant **the Law**—something Orthodox Jews studied all their lives—**would become obsolete**. THAT WAS/IS AN EXTREMELY *BIG DEAL*; a concept we Gentiles can't grasp.

And, the following is worth repeating: *not only would the Israelite who confessed Jesus have a new spiritual life, but he or she would also be saved or freed from the numerous ceremonies and burdensome sacrifices of the Law.* That, too, was a big deal; it is also a type of freedom we Gentiles cannot fully appreciate.

Considering the overall context prior to Chapter 10, Romans 10:9-10 is an indication that a traditional Jew has repented or has turned away from following the Mosaic Law (as the *only* means of obtaining righteousness with God), and he/she now believes that Jesus Christ is the Living Word of God, whereby people are saved from this Sinful world. Along those same lines, Romans 10:9-10 was also necessary for the Jew who believed in Christ, but, as described in the NT's book of John 12:42, he/she did not publicly confess their belief for fear of losing their rank or position.

Yes, if taken at face value, one can easily see why Romans 10:9-10 is considered to be a good *starting point for anyone* who hears the message of God's grace and then desires to begin the process of rethinking the meaning of life. On face value alone, I can see why we have, traditionally, taken a verbal confession of Jesus Christ and connected it *with* the spiritual new-birth process.

That kind of a confession was, indeed, meant to announce a radical change. Still, a verbal acknowledgement of Jesus Christ from someone who is *only* hearing the gospel audibly—absent of an undeniable manifestation from Heaven—can*not* be considered an accurate measurement to determine a truly **repentant** heart.

On the one hand, it is possible and very common for people to verbally acknowledge Jesus Christ without ever forcing their way into the Kingdom of Heaven—into spiritual and eternal principles. As a result, these people will have difficulty making Jesus Christ the true *Lord* or Administrator of their lives; and, they will have difficulty establishing God's kingdom—His rule—and Law of *love* within.

On the other hand, it is nearly *im*possible for people to have a mature persuasion[G4102] of Christ, but never verbally confess Him as the Way to God and His righteousness. It is attentive listening and persuasion of the heart that causes the mind to be renewed and causes the mouth to speak out, in accordance with God's Word.

Think Differently About Sin

Generally speaking, people routinely look at the outward appearances and actions of others; then, based on their own mental prejudices and preferences, they will form opinions *for* or *against* others. But, just because certain people (on the basis of race, gender, age, generation, etc.) *look like* they are capable of behaving in a certain way—good or bad—doesn't mean they *are* that way.

And, even if some people act exactly how they look, they may be acting (*e.g.*, badly) out of hurt or immaturity. Or, they may be, at the time, only acting (*e.g.*, politely) in accordance with their family or professional training, instead of from the core of their heart.

The Scripture bears out and is clear on the following principle: **the condition or character of the heart—the non-physical self—**is more important to God than outward physical *appearances* (1-Samuel 16:7). God judges [for or against] a person with *His* heart, based on **the overall condition or content of *their* heart—mind**.

Here are a few supporting passages:

Then the Lord saw that the wickedness of man was great on the earth, and that <u>every intent</u> of the thoughts of his heart was only evil continually.

And the Lord was sorry that He had made man on the earth, and He was grieved in His heart.

Genesis 6:5-6

Then God said to him in the dream, "Yes, I know that in the integrity of your heart you have done this, and I also kept you from sinning against Me; therefore, I did not let you touch her."

Genesis 20:6

"But from there you will seek the Lord your God, and you will find Him if you search for Him <u>with all</u> your heart and all your soul."

Deuteronomy 4:29

"And you shall love the Lord your God <u>with all</u> your heart and with all your soul and with all your might.

"And these words, which I command you today, shall be on your heart;"

Deuteronomy 6:5-6

"Blessed are the pure in heart, for they shall see God."

Matthew 5:8

Since **the spiritual or non-physical God** in Heaven looks at man*kind*'s spiritual or non-physical self, **mature <u>consecrated servants</u> know to pattern the character and content of their own hearts** after the known character and content of His Heart.

But **believers who are still carnally-minded** will, typically, gauge their spiritual relationship with the unseen spiritual God in Heaven according to how well they can control their speech and physical actions. In reality, <u>they're more conscientious or mindful of pleasing other people than they are of pleasing the unseen God in Heaven</u>. As such, **they consider their spiritual or unseen thought-life to be off-the-record or private, and of little to no real consequences**.

For example, most believers can proudly say, *they have never murdered someone with whom they disagree*. But, as moral and as disciplined as that may sound, physically murdering someone is not the only sin of disagreement.

Also, today, at a time when the world is cheerfully promoting more extreme forms of social freedoms (*e.g.*, identity or gender preference, and sexual promiscuity), a married believer, who has *never physically "slept" or carried out sensual acts with a person other than their spouse*, would feel righteous in saying, *I have never committed **adultery***. Of course, **physical contact** being the most common definition for adultery among most people, even believers.

But whereas <u>the Mosaic Law increased the reach and awareness of Sin</u>, by listing **forbidden physical acts** *for God's people*, so they would be **holy** or **different from other nations**, <u>Christ increased the reach and awareness of being holy</u>, by increasing the distance that separates God's consecrate servants from the world.

God's people or believers *should*, progressively, desire to have a different mindset or a new heart; so that, in time, not only will they live (*i.e.*, act and do things) differently from the world, more importantly, they will **BE completely different** (*i.e.*, they will **naturally think** and, therefore, **naturally speak** differently).

> *For it is written, "You shall be holy for I am holy"*
> {says the Lord}.

> *1 Peter 1:16*

The goal is for **God's people to become His consecrated servants**, in this world. As such, they can willingly and more successfully resist the devil and keep their minds free of carnal-only thinking, which is common to those *of* this world.

To elaborate on the previous two examples, on several occasions, while teaching people who were still under the Old Covenant, Jesus quoted familiar moral codes or principles from the Mosaic Law. But He then elevated those moral codes of the Law to higher moral codes of the heart—spiritually.

> *"You have heard that [your forefathers] were told, 'You shall not commit murder' and 'Whoever commits murder shall be liable to the court.'*
>
> *"But I say to you that everyone who is [enraged] with his brother shall be guilty before the court; and <u>whoever shall say</u> to his brother, 'Raca' [or worthless (as a term of utter criticism)] shall be guilty before the supreme court; and <u>whoever shall say</u>, 'You fool' [dull or stupid (as if to say, 'shut up and wither away')], shall be guilty enough to go into the fiery hell."*

> *Matthew 5:21-22*

> *"You have heard that it was said [in the Law], 'You shall not commit adultery';*
>
> *"But I say to you, that everyone who looks on a woman [other than his wife] to lust [or long] for her <u>has committed</u> adultery with her already <u>in his heart</u>."*

> *Matthew 5:27-28*

Carnally-minded believers will naturally have difficulties with spiritually-based laws and concepts for two main reasons: ① they have never experienced an undeniable manifestation from Heaven and, therefore, when they hear about spiritual laws and concepts, they have no point of reference from which they can begin to understand such things; and, ② like Nicodemus (referred to in Chapter 16, under the section titled, *What Did Jesus Say?*), they remain blinded by the religious status quo, which makes it difficult for them to see the truth, even when it is right in front of them.

There is a common drawback in our churches. Although people are taught *what a spiritual Christian life looks and sounds like* (*e.g.*, how to act and what say), they have little to no true spiritual encounters. As such, **the average believer can only imitate a spiritual Christian life** using the most common and convenient method: *muscle memory*—repeatedly doing and saying the same things over and over until, hopefully, those actions and words become *second nature*.

But, without an undeniable spiritual manifestation from Heaven, **it is unlikely that the average churched person will be made to fully understand and appreciate spiritual things**, overall. They may know about spiritual principles from reading the Bible and/or listening to a variety of sermons, but they do not fully respect and adhere to such principles.

Too **many believers have had their faith established solely on the persuasive and/or enticing words of men**. That means, their **belief in spiritual principles** is built primarily on, and is, therefore, **limited to, the words of men's wisdom and not in demonstration of the Spirit and of [God's] power** (1 Corinthians 2:4-5). That is why many of them still struggle to fully forgive others; and, they struggle to find hope and/or meaning in life; and, even more importantly, they struggle to trust God, Whom they know *of*, but do not, necessarily, *know*.

So, when it comes to spiritual moral codes of the heart, inwardly, these believers will always ask, *where is the harm in only thinking about hurting someone or only thinking about being intimate with someone other than [their] spouse? After all, nothing actually happened, because there was no physical contact.*

But, to the mature-obedient-Christ-like consecrated servants of God, *who have been enlightened and have tasted of the heavenly gift and have been made partakers of the Holy Spirit, and have tasted the good Word of God and the powers of the age to come* (Hebrews 6:4b-5), the truth of the matter is obvious. Even though there would be no physical witnesses and there would be no physical evidence for a crime scene investigation (CSI) unit to gather up and use against us in a court of law, were we on trial for repeated mental murders, **we still missed the mark of unity—to love one another**.

And, even though there would be no chance of catching a sexually transmitted disease (STD) or having to deal with an unwanted pregnancy after repeatedly committing adultery in our heart or mind, **we still missed the mark of faithfulness:** we are guilty of **infidelity**.

Physically?

No!

But <u>we</u> are still guilty.

How?

To *see* the answer, let's go back to the beginning.

Remember, Adam's physical body, which the non-physical or spiritual God formed, was lifeless until *God breathed Himself or Mind and spirit (life breath) into it*. As indicated in Chapter One, the body is, basically, a vessel or a covering for the invisible or spiritual mind to operate and function in this physical world.

So, to repeat what I hope is abundantly clear by now: **the lives of God's consecrated servants are so much more than a physical existence** or reality.

- Our mindset—how and what we CONTINUALLY think— defines our identity, individuality, or self; therefore...

- Our current state of mind determines our boundaries— what we are capable of thinking, saying, and doing— good or bad; as such...

- Our mindset has more impact on our circumstances than our actions; because...

- Our physical actions are expressions of how and what we think is true, glorious, valuable, profitable, meaningful, comforting, convenient, etc.

Therefore, just because we didn't use our physical bodies to carry out a burning ungodly desire of our heart, it doesn't mean we are innocent **in the sight of God**—spiritually. If we passionately hate someone, yes, that person is still physically alive; but, **to us, that person might as well be dead,** because we will see him/her as being **worthless**: having no value or potential. If that is the case, then we are not a vessel that contains God's unconditional LOVE.

In the matter of adultery, the other person may be clueless as to our longing for him/her. But, in our heart or mind, we have already **been unfaithful** to our spouse. If that is the case, then we are not a vessel that contains God's type of *faithfulness*.

Yes, physical actions do matter in this physical universe. But, remember, the invisible spiritual universe is more real and relevant than this physical one; because, the invisible spiritual God made this physical universe, and we were made in His image. Our physical actions are a direct result of our spiritual-self—thought-life or mindset, good or bad: whether through premeditation or an emotional outburst; whether in courage or in fear; whether clean (sane) or insane (unclean), etc.

THAT'S WHY GOD FIRST LOOKS AT THE THOUGHTS AND INTENTIONS OF THE HEART—AT OUR TRUE SELVES—AND NOT JUST AT WHAT WE PUBLICLY SAY AND DO, good or bad.

Chapter 19

THE CHURCH OF GOD?

...In Christ Jesus the blessing of Abraham might come to the Gentiles, so that we might receive the promise of the Spirit through faith.

Galatians 3:14

Today, ALL believers can have the *blessing* of Abraham.

That's good news!

That's good preaching!

But in many cases, the above Scripture excerpt and other similar Biblical passages about the "blessing of Abraham" are often taken out of context, in order to lure people into church buildings. Unfortunately, in many cases, this is not, primarily, being done for the sake of the people, but for the purpose of enlarging a ministry's financial base.

Whether intentional or unintentional, the term "blessing of Abraham" has often been **mis**interpreted by some Church leaders to mean worldly possessions or *material wealth*. Although Abraham had material wealth and he received even more from God, the "blessing of Abraham" was *not* about material wealth; and, as the rest of that opening passage says, its purpose or outcome is that *WE receive the Spirit of God, through faith.*

The word *blessing[30]*, in both the Hebrew and Greek languages, refers to a *benediction, eulogy, fine speaking or (verbal) adoration* of someone. **God spoke well of Abraham by calling him *"righteous," because of his faith*** (Genesis 15:6, Romans 4:3-8, 4:20-22, Galatians 3:6). And, because of that, **God** also **called Abraham His friend** (Ref. Isaiah 41:8b and James 2:23).

---

[30] Strong's Exhaustive Concordance Of the Bible, Hebrew reference # 1288, Greek reference # 2129

In truth, **such verbal adoration or blessing was and is the very foundation and fulfillment of God's Promise to Abraham and to all of us**. To paraphrase, God said, *in Abraham's seed*, which is to say, in Christ, *all nations or ethnic groups of the Earth can receive the same adoration or verbal approval of righteousness, based on their faith* (Ref. Genesis 18:18, 22:18 and Galatians 3:6-9, 14 & 16).

I don't know about anyone else, but that's the best *blessing* I can think of: **for God Himself to *call* me a righteous and faithful *friend*.** And, because of that, **He can entrust His Holy Spirit to me**.

Now, *that's* good news!

Talk about having friends in *high* places.

You can't go any higher in rank than God's Throne. How could we not prosper spiritually *and* materially from that *kind* of a relationship with God?

Yes, **material wealth *can* come *with* that blessing**; but, let's be perfectly clear: God *never* promised to give the land and all of its wealth to those of us, who are *now* under a spiritually-based Covenant; at least, not in the same way He promised those who *were* under the Law. Churched people only think He did, because some Church leaders routinely take the best physical perks from the Old Covenant God made with the Israelites and attach those to the new spiritual covenant He made with us, through Christ.

They do so because **the Promise of material wealth, more so, conveniently addresses the needs and desires of people.** Such an enticing promise speaks to their physical issues more directly than a eulogy from an unseen-spiritual God.

It would be a pity if God's people were so carnally-minded that the most vital spiritual experiences (*i.e.*, God's presence, His verdict of righteousness, and His friendship) are devalued or even despised, in comparison to the desire for material wealth. But, in the absence of frequent undeniable manifestations from Heaven, that's the very attitude many churchgoers *seem* to have, today.

The pendulum of mainstream Christian doctrine has nearly gone full-swing: from the old-school religion-based *hell-fire and brimstone* sermons, which scared people into the Church, to the contemporary *get it quick and easy* sermons, which lure people in by suggesting **God is obligated** *to do everything we want, as long as we have enough faith-muscle* (*i.e.*, the knowledge) to make it happen.

The hell-fire and brimstone approach produced fear-filled believers, who, in many ways, were blind to God's unconditional love. The problem with that is, when God's love is hidden from His people, the real meaning of His glory is also hidden; because, "God is Love" (Ref. 1 John 4:16). As a result of such messages, our churches were and, to a certain extent, are still full of religious people who gage their personal relationship with God on the self-approval they *feel* when they successfully maintain an *outward* appearance of holiness—controlled actions and speech.

The quick and easy approach is, even now, producing churches full of people who are *not* so much interested in getting to know God and His Ways, as much as they are interested in getting Him to give them whatever they need and want. Consequently, many people that attend church **do not honor God**, wholeheartedly.

Just like the average *"get rich quick"* TV Infomercial, the average *"get it quick and easy"* sermon routinely suggests that God will fix peoples' financial problems in little to no time at all. But, too often, such sermons tend to ignore or downplay the fact that many of the financial problems people face are caused by poor spending habits, which are, usually, a result of never having been properly taught how to manage money (*e.g.*, prioritize spending, saving, investing, so as to leave an inheritance, etc.).

Many people, today, are under social pressure to be *successful* or, at least, have an appearance of success, as defined by worldly standards. As such, they continue to spend money they don't actually have; which is typical in a credit-based financial system.

It is seldom true when a TV Infomercial claims that *little to none of your time or effort is required to go from rags to riches*. And, it is seldom true when a church sermon claims that *little to no work* (**respons**ibility of change) *is required on your part to be debt-free*.

At this point, let me clearly state the following:

> This clarification of *Abraham's blessing* is in **NO** way meant to suggest that believers should be satisfied with, or settle for, a life of poverty; nor is it meant to contradict anyone's dreams of having a profitable job or business, or receiving an inheritance, or even winning the lottery.

There is nothing wrong, at all, with having money and lots of it. As the OT's book of Ecclesiastes says, *money can answer or respond to a lot of problems [in this world]* (10:19b). And, in the hands of trustworthy people, money will also help spread the gospel.

That's why the Apostle John wrote what he did in his letter to Gaius, a trustworthy believer: *[I would, I wish, or I pray]*[G2172] *above all else that you prosper and be in good health*, even as your [soul or life] prospers or *succeeds in reaching* {the desires of you heart}. Based on 3 John 1-8, the implication was: *I pray that you prosper and remain safe and sound, so that you can continue to finance and physically help with doing the Lord's work, as you have been.*

Yes; within a mature Body of Christ, 3 John 2 would be a blanketed prayer for *all* believers. But, contrary to most popular sermons on that verse, **John's desire or prayer for prosperity and sound health was targeted**. Specifically, his prayer was for Gaius and, presumably, anyone like him, who was or is, 1) **an active and trustworthy servant of God** and 2) **a faithful supporter of other creditable servants of God**, because he and others were capable and willing to remain true to His calling. When it comes to serving God (*i.e.*, His people) in a financial and/or physical manner, some believers are physical and/or financially *capable*, but they are not *willing*; and, others are *willing*, but they are not *capable*.

As with anything, **money is a matter of the heart**.

To most people, the evidence of money's impact and influence is extremely overwhelming, and many have strayed from the faith pursuing it. Money is not evil; but, **the love of money** [more than the love of God and His people] **is the root** of all kinds of evil or ills (1 Timothy 6:10a).

It is not uncommon for some believers to put on hold their hunger and thirst to *know* God and to serve His people, until after they have achieved a reasonable measure of worldly success. And, while doing so, many believers have taken a convenient and systematic hands-off approach, regarding *their own testimony of faith*: they have, all but, entrusted the study of God's Word and serving His people to *their fellow believers*, who are paid to do *the work of the church*. Yet, they still consider themselves to be sufficiently involved in the process of ministry—service, because of their generic prayer support and well-wishing.

But, as sad a commentary as that is, the situation is more grievous: People are *giving what they can spare financially*. But, in many cases, their giving is not for the sake of being compassionate for others or for the sake of honoring God. In most case, they are giving for the primary and/or sole purpose of *receiving* something in return. More unfortunately is the fact that such reasoning is being promoted by those in Church leadership in order to get people to give, usually, to meet the financial needs of the local church.

Yes, there *can be* an expectancy to receive at an appointed time when we give; but **there is a difference** between cheerfully giving to a good work with a heart of compassion and in having the mindset of giving something to receive something in return. The former *is* done with honor and respect *for* the things of God, while the latter is, typically, done to *expect* something *from* God.

Regardless of how much we give, **our giving should be unconditional**; because, we know that our TRUE reward come, later.

Workers Are Sent into His Harvest

And [when Jesus saw the multitudes or masses], He felt compassion for them, because they were distressed and [disorganized or scattered] like sheep without a shepherd.

Then He said to His disciples, "The harvest is plentiful, but the workers are few.

> *"Therefore [beg] the Lord of the harvest to send out worker [toilers, teachers] into His harvest."*

> *Matthew 9:36-38*

"The harvest" or "the masses" are people, in general: Jews and Gentiles, men and women, rich and poor alike that are weary, spiritually malnourished, weak, and scattered. It is fitting that there was no indication given as to the exact number of people Jesus saw when He made the above statement; because, spiritually, He was seeing or referring to people of every nation, ethnic group, and culture of the world. And, as He indicated, **the harvest belongs to God**—the Lord of the harvest, Who is responsible for sending out workers to help nourish, strengthen, and bring unity to His people.

In several of his letters to the churches and to his co-laborers, the Apostle **Paul made clear distinctions between** *the masses* (the harvest or the people) **AND** individual *workers* (laborers or teachers), **like himself**. These were and are the workers Jesus spoke about to His disciples. These were and are the individuals (Apostles, Prophets, Evangelists, Pastors, and Teachers) called or hired by God (the land owner) and are sent out to cultivate (*care for* and grow up) the harvest (the masses) in His field (the world). Not everyone is *cut out* and prepared by God for this *kind* of work.

> *For, I think, God has [shown] us [the apostles or the ones whom He has sent, to be lowest] of all, as men condemned to death; because we have become a spectacle to the world both to angels and to men.*

> *We [workers] are fools for Christ's sake, [so that you (the masses) can be wise] in Christ; we are weak, but you are strong; you are [honored or glorious], but we are [less honored or glorious].*

> *1 Corinthians 4:9-10*

Paul did NOT have low self-worth, so as to suggest that it's okay for Apostles and other ministers (servants) of the gospel to be hungry and *homeless* vagabonds, as he seemed to describe in 1

Corinthians 4:11. He was NOT suggesting that servants, such as himself, be viewed by God's people as the *scum of the world* (4:13).

Even though social and economic conditions were much different in Paul's day, the overall implication he made is the same for us, today:

> There should always be a sincere spirit (mindset) of humility (lowliness) in Church or religious leadership; because, **the harvest** (the masses *for* whom the workers were hired to care for) **should be viewed as being more valuable or important**.

Does that analogy describe the mainstream Church, today?
No!

Actually, from the Scripture and from religious-world history, it is likely that the Church, as a whole, hasn't been that way since around the time of Acts 4:31-37. Even now, due to the rock star status that some ministers have obtained and many others long for, it's probably the exact opposite viewpoint from what Paul presented.

To repeat, Scripturally, there isn't anything wrong with a pastor or minister of the gospel having a lot of money; nor is there anything wrong with a minister owning a nice home or two, or having multiple cars or even a private plane and yacht. The difficulty or the snare lies within our innate human nature: ① the lust of the eyes, ② the lust of the flesh, and ③ the pride of life.

Unfortunately, many religious leaders, past and present, have conveniently chosen to identify themselves with material wealth. Some, supposedly, do so in order to be an image of *success* and, thus, to *inspire* the masses and other co-laborers to have greater faith in God *for* the same amount of wealth. But **that kind of success and that kind of inspiration are,** more times than not, **rooted in fulfilling inherent worldly (carnal) desires and are often a substitute for the lack of spiritual prosperity**.

Also, some religious leaders admittedly identify themselves with wealth because **they are convinced that God is rewarding them now,** based on their faithful and tireless service to Him and to His people. While that may or may not be the case, there is a difference in being *supported* by the gospel (*as a soldier in a war would be*), and in assuming *compensation, based on the amount of visibility or popularity achieved with the masses* in the same way that a secular entertainer or celebrity would demand from the world.

Again, **it always comes down to the condition of a person's heart**. In this case, is the worker truly satisfied knowing that he or she *will* receive praises from God, later, in the afterlife; or, does he or she receive a greater, **more realistic**, satisfaction in gaining material wealth, now, in this life?

The answer to *that* question may be found in the answer to another question: **who originally *called* or hired the individual into ministry or servitude?**

Some people were and are placed into Church leadership roles based on committee selections; some are placed in leadership roles based on a family name alone. Some people have set out on their own after attending seminary or another religious education program, based on what seemed like a *good idea* to serve God and pastor (shepherd) His people; and, the list goes on.

Of course, just because God did *not*, necessarily, call or place a person in a Church leadership role doesn't mean the person has or will ever have wrong motives. Along the same lines, just because God *did* call and place a person in leadership doesn't mean the person will not develop wrong motives, later.

To repeat, for those ministers or servants who were and are called into Church leadership by God, **both Jesus and the Apostles, taught and/or suggested that the servant's TRUE rest and reward comes later**, after all the work is done—*after* they've shown themselves to be faithful and obedient servants **unto the end**.

The Apostle Paul advised Timothy, a fellow leader or co-laborer in Christ, not to focus on material wealth. Paul went on to remind Timothy of other co-laborers who actually started out with good intentions, but then got off track because they loved material wealth more than they loved God.

Paul wrote to Timothy:

> *But those who [are bent on getting] rich fall into temptation and a snare and many foolish and harmful desires which plunge men into ruin and destruction.*
>
> *For the love of money is a root of all sorts of evil, and some by longing for it have wandered away from the faith, and pierce themselves with many pangs.*
>
> *But flee from these things, you man of God; and pursue righteousness, godliness, faith, love, perseverance and gentleness.*
>
> *Fight the good fight of faith; take hold of eternal life to which you were called, and you made the good confession in the presence of many witnesses.*

1Timothy 6:9-12

Today, many of the people in Church still love and/or trust money more than God, because there are some leaders in our churches who love and/or trust money more. So, instead of making disciples who truly have the Mind of Christ, many Church leaders are making *disciples of worldly success*, supposedly, in the name of God. That means, when it comes to living a truly Christ-like or Spirit-led life, churched people differ very little from people *in the world*: they are more carnally-minded than spiritually-minded.

The following is a well-known, and often misused, OT Scripture that is routinely read or quoted before tithes and offerings are collected, in order to get people either to give or to give *more*:

> *"You are cursed with a curse, for you are robbing [God], the whole nation of you!*
>
> *"Bring the whole tithe into the storehouse, so that there may be food in My house, and test Me now in this," says the Lord of hosts, "if I will not open for*

> *you the windows of heaven, and pour out for you a*
> *blessing until it overflows."*

> *Malachi 3:9-10*

In that familiar OT passage, **the "tithe" itself was not the main focus** of what God was saying to the Israelites; just like, in other such passages of OT Scripture, the Sabbath, Fasting, or any other ceremony mentioned were not the main focus for other harsh rebukes—tongue lashings, which the people received from God. It was **the condition of their hearts** while they were *doing* or not doing those required acts.

So, in order to fully understand *why God was being robbed* by the whole nation, you must start at the beginning of *that* book.

> *"'A son honors his father, and a servant his master.*
> *Then if I am a father, where is My honor? And if I*
> *am a master, where is My respect?' says the Lord*
> *of hosts to you, <u>O priests</u>..."*

> *Malachi 1:6a*

The first one and a half chapters of Malachi were directed at the priests (*i.e.*, religious leaders). **The priests** can, and usually do, directly or indirectly **influence the people's tone and *behavior of worship***. During the time of the prophet Malachi, the priests were disgraceful: they despised the repetitiveness of the sacrificial ceremonies; and, as an immediate reward for their duties, they kept for themselves the best of what the people were offering up to God.

The example of dishonoring God was established: the people decided to keep more for themselves, too (Ref. Malachi Chapter 3). As a result of the priests' abuse and self-serving attitude towards the (holy) things of God, the people had all but stopped honoring God by *returning* the tithe—the tenth of the harvest and the livestock—to the priest, in His stead.

The shortcomings of the priest and the people were the same: **the natural desire to please one*self* will often outweigh any religious-only desire to honor and respect *unseen*-spiritual things**.

That was then.

But, is that same scenario playing out, now?

Yes!

Due to a lack of genuine spiritual manifestations, many in church leadership, eventually, grow weary of the never-ending self-sacrificing work of serving people; so, they begin to *despise the work of the church*. And, as an immediate reward, they often begin to hold back for themselves the best of the financial gifts the people give *for* the Lord's work.

Therefore, some in leadership have set a dishonorable tone: the people are keeping more for themselves, too. People have become both weary and leery of giving to support the servants' extravagant lifestyle, while they themselves are often in need.

> *[Again, the Lord is talking to the priests]* "*...For those who honor Me I will honor, and those who despise [disesteem or distain] Me will be lightly esteemed [despised or made small]"*

> *1 Samuel 2:30c*

Instead of choosing to seek and to set a spiritual and sincere tone of honoring God, many in church leadership have decided to make convenient secular adjustments for both theirs and the people's shortcomings. They have customized and repackaged the Old Testament's concept of *seedtime* (sowing) *and harvest* (reaping) to target people's natural desire for wealth.

There is an abundance of enticing prosperity-driven sermons that contain a lot of generous promises made on God's behalf. As such, an intentional strategy has been established: many churched people have come to **view their *charitable* giving** (tithes, offerings, and miscellaneous labor) **as *an investment* from which they expect or, in many cases, they insist on receiving dividends or interest and payouts in a timely manner.**

So, *that which is supposed to be* a sincere act of *giving **as unto the Lord*** has become, more or less, *an eagerness to **receive from the***

Lord to meet our own needs. Unfortunately, most churched people, including leadership, still struggle with giving to the unseen God and with receiving from Him, because they do not yet have a genuine spiritual experience from which to begin to understand such things.

> But, where there is an understanding of spiritual things, due to signs and wonders, the people are NOT taught to give based on their wants and needs; because, their own needs will be met in accordance with their mature faith (Ref. Mark 11:24). Instead, they are taught to *give* because they love and honor God, they love and honor His people, and they desire to advance His kingdom.

Yes! When we freely and cheerfully give, we will freely receive some form of gratitude, in this life, from believers and non-believers.

But our mindset should be:

- Even if I never receive a material return in this life for my giving, I know that I will hear the Lord say, *"Come, you who are blessed of My Father, inherit the kingdom prepared for you from the foundation of the world."* (Ref. Matthew 25:34b)
- Even if all I get from my giving is an assurance that God loves me, it is enough, because *[He] loves a cheerful giver* (Ref. 2 Corinthians 9:7c).

Store Up Treasure in Heaven

"Do not store up [or amass] for yourselves treasure [wealth] on earth, where moth and rust destroy, and where thieves break in and steal.

"But store up for yourselves treasure in heaven, where neither moth nor rust destroys, and where thieves do not break in and steal;"

Matthew 6:19-20

In Matthew Chapter 19, beginning with verse 16, a young rich man asked Jesus a question: *what [one] good thing can I do, in order to have **eternal life**?*

Jesus began to answer that question by listing off some basic, but important, commandments from the Mosaic Law, which the man—an Israelite—needed to obey, in order to *live a long life* on Earth. The man proudly, responded by saying, *he had obeyed those commandments for most of his [natural] life.*

Sensing that the man wanted to be praised for dutifully obeying the Law, Jesus then took the conversation to the next level, spiritually. He told the man EXACTLY what he needed to do, in order to *start* living or to *begin* the process of recognizing *eternal life*, while still here on earth:

> If you [really] want to be complete [meaning, spiritually mature and satisfied] in this world, start by selling your possessions and giving to the poor, and you will have treasure in Heaven; then come, follow Me.

By telling the man to *sell all that he had and give to the poor*, **Jesus was NOT trying to incite or force a gesture of good religious-behavior; NOR was He teaching a doctrine of *humility through poverty*.** There was more depth to what Jesus said; because, although **the man** may have been dutifully *keeping* the Law, he **was not perfecting its true spiritual meaning**: to love and honor the Lord God, first, with all of his heart; and, to love his neighbor as much as he loved himself (Ref. Matthew 22:36-40).

> **"For where** [or whichever place: on earth or in Heaven] **your treasure** [or the thing in which you place the greatest value] **is, there your heart** [the mind—thoughts, feelings, etc.] **is also."**

> *Matthew 6:21*

First, he needed to truly honor God.

Meaning, even though the desire to accumulate wealth did not go against God's Law, this man, obviously, respected the power or ability of wealth, which he could physically see, more than he respected God, whom he could not see. Second, if he truly honored God in his heart, then he could, more accurately, love his fellowman.

God had already instructed His people to remember the poor (Leviticus 19:10, Deuteronomy 15:4 & 15:7). And, although the man probably did give to the poor as part of his religious duties, he instinctively saw his wealth as being for himself—for his own security and peace of mind.

Most likely, he was so carnally-minded or focused only on the realities of this physical world that he could never considered or see any spiritual benefits—treasure in Heaven—that come from **carefree or unconditional giving** in the sight of God, where it mattered most. Finally, if the man truly wanted to be pleasing to God, then it would have been in his best interest to *follow Jesus*, in order to learn how to worship God in spirit and in truth, and learn how to love his fellowman, unconditionally.

But, based on the man's response to Jesus' life changing invitation, he did not have the right heart to follow or travel the same route as Jesus, even though he, probably, would admit that Jesus was someone sent from God, just like Nicodemus and others had come to see (Ref. John 3:2b). Instead, he went away distressed or heavy-hearted at the thought of giving up all he had gained.

Jesus made this same point, in other passages of Scripture:

> You can't place your confidence or trust in two masters at the same time; eventually, you will cling to, trust in, and prefer one more than the other; therefore, you cannot serve {the invisible or spiritual} God and {physical} wealth (Ref. Matthew 6:24 and Luke 16:13). *{The implication being: carnally-minded people will instinctively trust and value physical wealth more.}*

Again, this has nothing to do with a pro-poverty religious mentality, as if to suggest God wants us to be poor by avoiding worldly wealth. There is **nothing** in the Holy Scriptures to suggest God wanted this man and, subsequently, every believer to be humbled through poverty.

As indicated before: **it is always a matter of the heart**. What is most abundantly present in the heart—the subject-matter that consumes our mind or thought-life the most—will naturally be expressed in our outward actions and words.

The rich young ruler, who asked Jesus the question, had a choice in the matter. Jesus did NOT tell him that *God needed to take his wealth away, in order to get him back on track.* It is always more beneficial for a person to willingly humble him or herself inwardly, through heart-felt agreement with God, than to be humiliated, through the shame or guilt of judgement. *Fall willingly on the rock and be humbled, or else be crushed when the rock (i.e., judgment) falls on you* (Ref. Luke 20:18).

> *...Wisdom is protection [shade or defense] just as money is protection; but [you can profit from knowing this one thing, wisdom can preserve, revive, save, or make whole the lives of those who master it.]*

> *Ecclesiastes 7:12*

The implication of that passage is as follows: no doubt, money can solve a lot of problems and make a lot of things right; but wisdom, when mastered, can lead to [long and eternal] life, whereas money will not. The reason being: money, usually, becomes the master over people, instead of being mastered *by* people. That's why some people have come to **mis**-quote 1 Timothy 6:10a, believing it to read, *money is the root [cause] of all evil.*

But again, it is *not money itself* that is the root cause of all kinds of evil—worthlessness, depravity or pain; rather, as that verse of Scripture more accurately says, *it is **the LOVE or preference of money [over everything else,** including God] that is the root of all kinds of evil.*

Have the Mind of Christ: Pursue the Heart of God

> *Then Jesus said to His disciples, "If anyone wishes to [travel on the same road and in the same direction I'm traveling in, he or she must deny or*

forsake their own worldly ambitions and plans to win or conquer the world—gain its wealth; instead he or she must take up the cross of sacrifice, exposing themselves to death and ridicule by the world, the way I am doing].

"For whoever wishes to save [or preserve his or her life for the purpose of gaining this Sinful world], shall lose their life: but whoever loses [or destroys his or her ties with this world, on account of Me, will find new life and purpose in this world].

"For what [benefit is there for a person if he or she gains this whole Sinful world, but then he/she is condemned to Death because of Sin? At that point, what, then, can that person give to God in order to escape Death in the end?]"

Matthew 16:24-26

The implied answer to the question, in the last Scripture verse, is "nothing". There is no amount of money or anything on Earth that a person can give, in order to escape the judgment of physical Death, which has been decided against the world, because of Sin. Like Christ, believers need to pursue the Mind or the spiritual *ways* of God, and not just settle for having a book-smart knowledge of Him.

There is a difference:

On the one hand, yes, typically, a person who has only *an intellectual knowledge of God* has an interest in, and a fascination with, knowing what He has said and done in the past, and knowing what He has Promised to do in the future. But that knowledge is often used to try and *work the system* (*i.e.*, attempting to hold God accountable to fulfill His Promises of good towards us, while conveniently neglecting his/her responsibility of loyalty to conviction and a renewed mind).

On the other hand, a person who desires to *know the Mind, the Heart, and the spiritual ways of God,* **in the same way Christ did,** also has a sincere interest in, and a fascination with, knowing what God has said and done in the past, and what He has Promised to do in the future. But this person then rightly uses his/her **renewed mind** to understand "the why" or the meaning of what God has said and done, so as to more accurately respond to everyday situation in a wise or Christ-like manner—in words and in actions.

This kind of understanding is dynamic or full of eternal life. Again, it allows us to *catch a glimpse* of the true mannerisms, customs, and Will of God (Romans 12:2). That is to say, as much as it is possible for us to see into the spiritual realm of God, as our minds are being renewed day by day.

> *For who among men knows the thoughts of a man except the spirit [or mind] of the man which is in him? Even the thoughts of God no one knows except the Spirit of God.*
>
> *Now we have [not received the spirit or mind of this Sinful world, again, but we have received the spirit or Mind who is from God], so that we may know the things [that are freely] given to us by God,*
>
> *Which things we also speak, not in words taught by human wisdom, but in [words] taught by the Spirit, combining spiritual thoughts with spiritual words [or judging one thing in connection with another].*
>
> *1 Corinthians 2:11-13*

This kind of knowledge is more intimate and deliberate. Glimpsing and gaining this kind of knowledge about God is much easier **if we desire to honor Him**—have a great deal of admiration or respect for Him; and, if we have made a quality decision. Add to this the fact that **God actually wants us to know Him** by or through the Holy Spirit.

> *"...The Son can do nothing of Himself, unless it is something He sees the Father doing; for whatever the Father does, these things the Son also does in like manner.*

"The Father loves the Son and shows Him all things He is doing;"

John 5:19-20a

Obviously, someone who is committed to pursuing and *glimpsing* the Mind of God, through Christ Jesus, obeys His commandments. But again, the added value and dynamics are as follows: the more we know about God's mannerisms and His Will—how He sees us and what He wants for us—the more God-like (meaningful) decisions we will make when faced with *everyday* choices or circumstances (*e.g.*, things the Bible may not specifically address).

Yes, it does come down to the once-popular slogan, "what would Jesus do" (WWJD). But, unless a person is a true disciple (self-disciplined learner) of Christ, and not just familiar with popular Bible verses, the slogan WWJD will be lifeless or meaningless, just as *belief without faith is dead* and *faith without works is dead*.

We need to grow up or mature spiritually, so as to know what God requires of us, first. Only then can we accurately handle the things He has prepared for us.

Now I say, as long as the heir is [still] a child, he does not differ at all from a slave, although he is owner of everything,

But he is under guardians and managers until the date set by the father.

Galatians 4:1-2

Although that excerpt of Scripture was referring to the Jews being kept under the guidance of the Law until God's true (spiritual) plan of redemption—grace—was revealed, it still makes the point: just because we are predestined by God to be co-heirs or co-possessors of <u>His glory</u> together with Christ that does *not* mean we are instantly ready to handle deep spiritual stuffs, concerning eternal glories, the moment we are first convinced[G3982] or give mental assent that God exists.

Godly wisdom must precede the use of Godly Authority and Power. Unfortunately, in church buildings and in personal prayer closets all over the world, there are still un-weaned spiritual infants—young and old immature believers—who are repeatedly trying to access spiritual gifts and use spiritual Authority and Power they're not mentally prepared to receive and maintain.

Physically speaking, a responsible father would burden neither his *infant nor his adolescent child* with the weight of being the vice-president of the family business, regardless of how much he loves the child and wants the child to inherit all things. Along the same lines, no responsible father would give his *immature* child a shiny new (real) sports car, no matter how much the child begs for it. In that moment, the father is showing just how much he loves the child by denying the request, *for the time being.*

In that same way, but spiritually speaking, **we believers, also, need to mature and grow up in spiritual wisdom and in Godly understanding**. Again, this is different than naturally aging or simply growing older into adulthood; because, spiritual and even mental growth does not, necessarily, keep in step with one's physical age.

> ***And [Christ made] some [believers to be] apostles, and some [to be] prophets, and some [to be] evangelists, and some [to be] pastors and teachers,***
>
> *Ephesians 4:11*

Why did God, through Christ, call or *spiritually hire workers* to help grow up (cultivate or care for) the masses (His harvest) in this world (His field)?

> ***[To equip] the saints [with everything they need] for the work of service, [and to follow His blueprints for] the building up of the body of Christ,***
>
> *Ephesians 4:12*

How long should the hired laborers work or how long should they serve the masses?

Until we all [are unified in] the faith and [unified in our recognition or acknowledgement] of the Son of God, [at which time we will, collectively, become the fully matured image and likeness of Christ on earth].

Ephesians 4:13

Why do we all need to have the Mind of Christ?

[Then], we [will] no longer [be as infants, allowing ourselves to be carried] here and there by [every wind of teaching devised by men who use slight-of-hand and knowingly speak lies with a straight face, because they have strayed from the faith];

But [love compels us to speak the truth, as such we] grow up in all aspects into Him, who is the head, even Christ,

Ephesians 4:14-15

As a result, we all are mature enough to take on our full inheritance and become the servants, the stewards, and the rulers God intended for us to be **on Earth**. But, before that can ever happen, we must allow God to change us—bring us up to a higher spiritual meaning of life, instead of us trying, in vain, to change Him: begging Him to aid us in successfully obtaining the mere carnal desires and meaning of life.

Above anything else, we MUST be in the perfect Will of God.

The PERFECT WILL of God

As I hope is evident, by now, anyone, at any time, can be in the PERFECT WILL of God. Anyone, at any time, can know exactly what God wants for them; because, His Will is the same for everyone.

Knowing God's PERFECT WILL for our *new* and consecrated life is not complicated. It is not a big mystery that must be revealed with hours of prayer and fasting; nor is it so spiritual that we need to have someone prophesy and then interpret it to us.

God's PERFECT Will for us ALL is that we LOVE—have affection and compassion for—one another, so that ❶ we *all* may be ONE (God in Christ—His Word, and Christ or His Word in us); and thereby, ❷ we can show or present tangible proof to the world that His Word is TRUE: **God is LOVE. LOVE is the most complete or PERFECT Law**; and, that law will NEVER pass away or be improved upon in this life or in the one to come (Ref. 1 Corinthians 13:8).

> *[Dear ones], let us love [or have social and moral compassion for] one another, for love [compassion] is from God; and everyone who loves [or has social and moral compassion] is born of God and knows [perceives or understands] God.*

> *The one who does not love [or the one who has no compassion, for whatever reason] does not know God, for God is love [compassion].*

> *[Here is the proof of God's compassion and the best example of what love is:] … God sent His only begotten Son into the world so that we might live through Him.*

> *[By that act of kindness, the essence of love was made apparent or was revealed—not our love [affection] for Him, but His love [affection] for us, in that He sent His Son to cover over our Sins.]*

> *[Dear ones], if God so [generously] loved us, we also ought to love one another.*

> *[There is a whole lot of information we don't know about God, but Love is the one thing we have clearly seen of Him]; if we love one another, God abides [dwells, is present, or remains] in us, and His love is [accomplished or fulfilled] in us.*

> *[If His love is accomplished or fulfilled within us, then that is proof or evidence that we are in Him and that He is in us], because He has given us His Spirit [or Mind].*

John 4:7-13

If someone says, "I love God," and hates [detests (to the point of persecuting] his brother, he is a liar; for the one who does not love his brother whom he has seen [with his physical eyes] **cannot** [possibly] **love God whom he has not seen.**

And this [is the greatest and the most important] **commandment we have from Him, ...the one who loves God should love his brother also.**

John 4:20-21

Regardless of how passionate and sincere our words and good deeds are, these alone will never be enough to effectively convince people to seek after God, wholeheartedly. The **primary proof** that allows people to truly see and understand Jehovah-God **is our unconditional love for one another** (Ref. John 17:20-26).

Love is patient, love [does useful things], [love] is not [insanely jealous]; love does not brag and is not arrogant,

[Love] does not act unbecomingly; it does not [plot against others to get its own way], [love] is not [easily provoked], [love] does not take [inventory of the wrongs it] suffered,

[Love] does not [cheer] unrighteousness, but [applauds] the truth;

[Love silently covers over all wrongs], [it never stops believing (for good) regardless of what happens], [it never stops expecting (good) regardless of what it sees], [regardless of the situation, love will always endure].

[There will always be a need for love];

1 Corinthians 13:4-8a

Glory to God, for evermore!

Peace be to the brethren, and love with faith, from God the Father and the Lord Jesus Christ.

Grace be with all those who love our Lord Jesus Christ with [an unending love].

Ephesians 6:23-24

HIAWATHA BOOKS
Durham, NC

Genesis

At the beginning of this physical universe, **Jehovah** (the Self-Existing) **God** created **space**, which the Holy Scripture refers to as the **heavens**. Albert Einstein, a renowned physicist (1879 – 1956), theorized that space is like a stretched-tight fabric, similar to that of a trampoline.

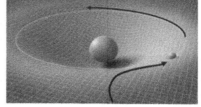

Gravitational pulls or paths are formed as a result of large objects on the fabric of space, as is the case when something heavy is placed on the surface of a trampoline. According to the Holy Scripture, that actually sounds like the very thing God did, in the beginning.

> ***Thus, says God the Lord, who created the heavens and stretched them out….***
>
> *Isaiah 42:5a*

> *… [Thus, says the Lord,] "**I stretched out the heavens with My hands….**"*
>
> *Isaiah 45:12a*

God then created the Earth. **Darkness** [mystery or obscurity] was everywhere; because, at that point, His creative work had no apparent purpose (Ref. Genesis 1:1-2).

God then called for **Light**[H216] [illumination or clarity]; and, when He did, His own glorious nature shined forth to brighten, nurture, and warm this planet; The Light also began to push away the Darkness or the mystery surrounding His creation.

God then separated or distinguished the Light, which He called **Day**, from the Darkness, which He called **Night** (Ref. Genesis 1:3-5), by setting the Earth in motion, spinning on its axis.

And, as the Earth spun, a basis for **time** was established. From a fixed point on the Earth, time measures the distance from the beginning of light to the beginning of Darkness to the beginning of Light, again; or, from dawn to dusk to dawn, again.

Eternity can be described as timelessness. One version of eternity is *a Day without end* or, really, endless Light (Ref. Revelation 21:23-25). God is Eternal; God is Light and in Him there is no Darkness at all (Ref. 1-John 1:5). Of course, another version of eternity is a *Night without end* or endless Darkness or, worse, a place where God's presence is absent.

On the one hand, it is likely that the creative events, specifically those that occurred during the **first three days**, were near-instantaneous. That is to say, those were exponentially accelerated celestial and terrestrial evolutionary events, which, from our perspective and limited scientific assessments, only appear to have taken billions of years.

On the other hand, it is also possible that those first creative works took tens of millions of *hours* to occur, and those millions of hours can still, literally, be defined as "three days."

Shortly, I will elaborate on the latter scenario; but, for now, keep the following two points in mind:

1. At the very beginning of Creation, the Earth was the only object in space; meaning, there were no other gravitational pulls to affect it.

2. At the very beginning of Creation, the term "Day" did *not* refer to sunlight; nor did "Night" refer to the absence of sunlight. "Day" was a time or interval of God's *Light or illumination* and *warmth*; and, Darkness was an interval of obscurity or mystery [and, presumably cold].

Moving on to the Fourth Day.

***Then God said, "Let there be lights**^H3974^ [a luminous

body, (the element of light), brightness, cheerfulness] *in the expanse of the heavens to separate the day from the night, and let them be for signs, and for seasons, and for days* [to be hot or warm] *and years* [a revolution of time]*;*

"And let them be for lights [H3974] *in the expanse of the heavens to give light* [H215] [luminous, kindle, set on fire, shine] *on the earth;" and it was so.*

Genesis 1:14-15

During the Fourth Day of Creation, other planetary bodies were called forth and, eventually, the Earth began a fixed orbit around our **sun**. At that point, the sun took over and began to govern the "day" with **natural light**, in order to contrast the natural darkness (Ref. Genesis 1:14-18).

Earth's orbit around the sun and the moon's orbit around the Earth set the current rotational speed for measuring **natural time**.

A *day* has come to be defined as the length of time in which natural sunlight is present at a fixed point on Earth. And, at some point in human history, people began to measure **days and nights** by hours, and measure hours by minutes, and measure minutes by seconds, in order to more closely monitor time and measure shorter occurrences in Nature. They also began to group days and nights into larger periods, called weeks; and group weeks into months, in order to measure longer events, such as seasons.

Eventually, people began to group the seasons together, referring to each complete cycle as a *year*. Of course, we have since learned that is the length of time it takes the Earth to orbit around the sun; roughly, 365 days and nights.

Here's the overall point: prior to the Fourth Day—before our sun and other planetary bodies were created, we can only speculate as to how fast the Earth was spinning on its axis. That means we don't really know how long *days* One, Two, and Three lasted, or how many hours it took to go from dawn to dusk and back to dawn, again, at a fixed point on Earth.

Based on our modern-day system of using time to measure natural and solar events, consider this: prior to the Fourth Day, the distance, in time, from dawn to dusk to dawn again—one Day, could have easily exceeded 8,760,000 hours, or what we would *now* calculate as one day-and-night-cycle lasting 1,000 years, instead of lasting a mere 24 hours.

The 1,000-year timeframe is used in consideration of several passages of Scripture (*e.g.*, Psalms 90:4 and 2 Peter 3:8) that suggests *a day* or an age-of-time *with the Lord is as 1,000 years and 1,000 years is as a day*. In fact, the duration could just as easily have been the equivalent of 10,000, 100,000, or 1,000,000 years, since God does not exist *in time*.

This is just something for us to keep in mind as we think or talk about the many wonders and mysteries of Creation, which the scientific community was meant to validate, not denounce.

Footnote References

Definitions: The main source for Hebrew and Greek word definitions was "The Exhaustive Concordance of the Bible: Showing every word of the text of the common English version of the Canonical Books, and every occurrence of each word in regular order; together with Dictionaries of the Hebrew and Greek Words of the original, with reference to the English words: By James Strong, S.T.D., LL.D. Hendrickson Publishers, Peabody, Massachusetts 01961-3473."

Sample Contents from the Strong's Exhaustive Concordance

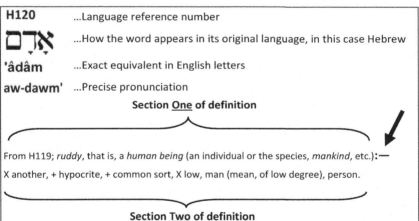

H120	...Language reference number
אָדָם	...How the word appears in its original language, in this case Hebrew
'âdâm	...Exact equivalent in English letters
aw-dawm'	...Precise pronunciation

Section <u>One</u> of definition

From H119; *ruddy*, that is, a *human being* (an individual or the species, *mankind*, etc.):—

X another, + hypocrite, + common sort, X low, man (mean, of low degree), person.

Section <u>Two</u> of definition

Section One: Before the following punctuation marks ":—", the history of the word is given (appearing as a number reference (*e.g.*, "From H119"), followed by a radical or root meaning.

Section Two: After the punctuation marks, the different renderings or interpretations of the word are given, arranged in the alphabetical order of the leading terms.

1   **H120, אָדָם** 'âdâm, *aw-dawm'*

From H119; *ruddy*, that is, a *human being* (an individual or the species, *mankind*, etc.): - X another, + hypocrite, + common sort, X low, man (mean, of low degree), person.

2   **H7307, רוּחַ, rûach, *roo'-akh***

From H7306; *wind*; by resemblance *breath*, that is, a sensible (or even violent) exhalation; figuratively *life, anger, unsubstantiality*; by extension a *region* of the sky; by resemblance *spirit*, but only of a rational being (including its expression and functions): - air, anger, blast, breath, X cool, courage, mind, X quarter, X side, spirit ([-ual]), tempest, X vain, ([whirl-]) wind (-y).

G4151, πνεῦμα, pneuma, *pnyoo'-mah*

From G4154; a *current* of air, that is, *breath* (*blast*) or a *breeze*; by analogy or figuratively a *spirit*, that is, (human) the rational *soul*, (by implication) *vital principle*, mental *disposition*, etc., or (superhuman) an *angel, daemon*, or (divine) God, Christ's *spirit*, the Holy *spirit*: - ghost, life, spirit (-ual, -ually), mind.

3   **H6754, צֶלֶם, tselem, *tseh'-lem***

From an unused root meaning to *shade*; a *phantom*, that is, (figuratively) *illusion, resemblance*; hence a representative *figure*, especially an *idol*: - image, vain shew.

4   **H1823, דְּמוּת, demûth, *dem-ooth'***

From H1819; *resemblance*; concretely *model, shape*; adverbially *like*: - fashion, like (-ness, as), manner, similitude.

5   **H5397, נְשָׁמָה, neshâmâh, *nesh-aw-maw'***

From H5395; a *puff*, that is, *wind*, angry or vital *breath*, divine *inspiration, intellect* or (concretely) an *animal*: - blast, (that) breath (-eth), inspiration, soul, spirit.

6   **H3533,** כבש, kâbash, *kaw-bash'*

A primitive root; to *tread* down; hence negatively to *disregard*; positively to *conquer, subjugate, violate:* - bring into bondage, force, keep under, subdue, bring into subjection.

7   **H7287** רדה, râdâh, *raw-daw'*

A primitive root; to *tread* down, that is, *subjugate*; specifically to *crumble* off: - (come to, make to) have dominion, prevail against, reign, (bear, make to) rule, (-r, over), take.

8   **H7854,** שטן, śâṭân, *saw-tawn'*

From H7853; an *opponent*; especially (with the article prefixed) *Satan*, the arch enemy of good: - adversary, Satan, withstand.

9   **H1966** הילל, hêylêl, *hay-lale'*

From H1984 (in the sense of *brightness*); the *morning star:* - lucifer.

10   **H2530,** חמד, châmad, *khaw-mad'*

A primitive root; to *delight* in: - beauty, greatly beloved, covet, delectable thing, (X great) delight, desire, goodly, lust, (be) pleasant (thing), precious (thing).

H8378, תאוה, ta'ăvâh, *tah-av-aw'*

From H183 (abbreviated); a *longing*; by implication a *delight* (subjectively *satisfaction*, objectively a *charm*): - dainty, desire, X exceedingly, X greedily, lust (ing), pleasant. See also H6914.

G1937, ἐπιθυμέω, epithumeō, *ep-ee-thoo-meh'-o*

From G1909 and G2372; to set the *heart upon*, that is, *long* for (rightfully or otherwise): - covet, desire, would fain, lust (after).

11   **H2403,** חטאה חטאת, chaṭṭâ'âh chaṭṭâ'th, *khat-taw-aw', khat-tawth'*

From H2398; an *offence* (sometimes habitual *sinfulness*), and its penalty, occasion, sacrifice, or expiation; also (concretely) an *offender:* - punishment (of sin), purifying (-fication for sin), sin (-ner, offering).

G266, ἁμαρτία, hamartia, *ham-ar-tee'-ah*

From G264; *sin* (properly abstract): - offence, sin (-ful).

12 **H2398**, חָטָא, châțâ', *khaw-taw'*

A primitive root; properly to *miss*; hence (figuratively and generally) to *sin*; by inference to *forfeit, lack, expiate, repent,* (causatively) *lead astray, condemn:* - bear the blame, cleanse, commit [sin], by fault, harm he hath done, loss, miss, (make) offend (-er), offer for sin, purge, purify (self), make reconciliation, (cause, make) sin (-ful, -ness), trespassive.

G264, ἁμαρτάνω, hamartanō, *ham-ar-tan'-o*

Perhaps from G1 (as a negative particle) and the base of G3313; properly to *miss* the mark (and so *not share* in the prize), that is, (figuratively) to *err*, especially (morally) to *sin:* - for your faults, offend, sin, trespass.

13 **H7561**, רָשַׁע, râsha', *raw-shah'*

A primitive root; to *be* (causatively *do* or *declare*) *wrong*; by implication to *disturb, violate:* - condemn, make trouble, vex, be (commit, deal, depart, do) wicked (-ly, -ness).

14 **H5117**, נוּחַ, nûach, *noo'-akh*

A primitive root; to *rest*, that is, *settle* down; used in a great variety of applications, literally and figuratively, intransitively, transitively and causatively (to *dwell, stay, let fall, place, let alone, withdraw, give comfort,* etc.): - cease, be confederate, lay, let down, (be) quiet, remain, (cause to, be at, give, have, make to) rest, set down.

15 **H3478**, יִשְׂרָאֵל, yiśrâ'êl, *yis-raw-ale'*

From H8280 and H410; *he will rule* as *God; Jisrael,* a symbolical name of Jacob; also (typically) of his posterity: - Israel.

16   **H6299**, פָּדָה, pâdâh, *paw-daw'*

A primitive root; to *sever*, that is, *ransom*; generally to *release*, *preserve:* - X at all, deliver, X by any means, ransom, (that are to be, let be) redeem (-ed), rescue, X surely.

17   **G3807**, παιδαγωγός, paidagōgos, *pahee-dag-o-gos'*

From G3816 and a reduplication form of G71; a *boy leader*, that is, a servant whose office it was to take the children to school; (by implication [figuratively] a *tutor* ["paedagogue"]): - instructor, schoolmaster.

18   **H1471**, גּוֹי גּוֹי, gôy gôy, *go'ee, go'-ee*

Apparently from the same root as H1465 (in the sense of *massing*); a foreign *nation*; hence a *Gentile*; also (figuratively) a *troop* of animals, or a *flight* of locusts: - Gentile, heathen, nation, people.

19   **G5480**, χάραγμα, charagma, *khar'-ag-mah*

From the same as G5482; a *scratch* or *etching*, that is, *stamp* (as a *badge* of servitude), or *sculptured* figure (*statue*): - graven, mark.

20   **G932**, βασιλεία, basileia, *bas-il-i'-ah*

From G935; properly *royalty*, that is, (abstractly) *rule*, or (concretely) a *realm* (literally or figuratively): - kingdom, + reign.

G935, βασιλεύς, basileus, *bas-il-yooce'*

Probably from G939 (through the notion of a *foundation* of power); a *sovereign* (abstractly, relatively or figuratively): - king.

21   **G2644**, καταλλάσσω, katallassō, *kat-al-las'-so*

From G2596 and G236; to *change mutually*, that is, (figuratively) to *compound* a difference: - reconcile.

22   **H3722**, כָּפַר, kâphar, *kaw-far'*

A primitive root; to *cover* (specifically with bitumen);

figuratively to *expiate* or *condone*, to *placate* or *cancel:* - appease, make (an) atonement, cleanse, disannul, forgive, be merciful, pacify, pardon, to pitch, purge (away), put off, (make) reconcile (-liation).

23   **H3725** כפר, kippûr, *kip-poor'*

From H3722; *expiation* (only in plural): - atonement.

24   **G5483**, χαρίζομαι, charizomai, *khar-id'-zom-ahee*

Middle voice from G5485; to grant as a *favor*, that is, gratuitously, in kindness, pardon or rescue: - deliver, (frankly) forgive, (freely) give, grant.

25   **G3056**, λόγος, logos, *log'-os*

From G3004; something *said* (including the *thought*); by implication a *topic* (subject of discourse), also *reasoning* (the mental faculty) or *motive*; by extension a *computation*; specifically (with the article in John) the Divine *Expression* (that is, *Christ*): - account, cause, communication, X concerning, doctrine, fame, X have to do, intent, matter, mouth, preaching, question, reason, + reckon, remove, say (-ing), shew, X speaker, speech, talk, thing, + none of these things move me, tidings, treatise, utterance, word, work.

26   **H7716**, שה שׂי, śeh śêy, *seh, say*

Probably from H7582 through the idea of *pushing* out to graze; a member of a flock, that is, a *sheep* or *goat:* - (lesser, small) cattle, ewe, lamb, sheep.

H8163, שעיר שׂער, śâ'îyr śâ'ir, *saw-eer', saw-eer'*

From H8175; *shaggy;* as noun, a *he goat;* by analogy a *faun:* - devil, goat, hairy, kid, rough, satyr.

27   **G286**, ἀμνός, amnos, *am-nos'*

Apparently a primary word; a *lamb:* - lamb.

28 **G907**, βαπτίζω,, baptizō, *bap-tid'-zo*

From a derivative of G911; to *make whelmed* (that is, *fully wet*); used only (in the New Testament) of ceremonial *ablution*, especially (technically) of the ordinance of Christian *baptism:* - baptist, baptize, wash.

29 **H3423**, ירשׁ   ירשׁ, yârash yârêsh, *yaw-rash', yaw-raysh'*

A primitive root; to *occupy* (be *driving* out previous tenants, and *possessing* in their place); by implication to *seize*, to *rob*, to *inherit*; also to *expel*, to *impoverish*, to *ruin:* - cast out, consume, destroy, disinherit, dispossess, drive (-ing) out, enjoy, expel, X without fail, (give to, leave for) inherit (-ance, -or), + magistrate, be (make) poor, come to poverty, (give to, make to) possess, get (have) in (take) possession, seize upon, succeed, X utterly.

30 **G342**, ἀνακαίνωσις, anakainōsis, *an-ak-ah'ee-no-sis*

From G341; *renovation:* - renewing.

31 **G1288**, δεασπάω, deaspaō, *dee-as-pah'-o*

From G1223 and G4685; to *draw apart*, that is, *sever* or *dismember:* - pluck asunder, pull in pieces.

G2129, εὐλογία, eulogia, *yoo-log-ee'-ah*

From the same as G2127; *fine speaking*, that is, *elegance of language*; *commendation* ("eulogy"), that is, (reverentially) *adoration*; religiously, *benediction*; by implication *consecration*; by extension *benefit* or *largess:* - blessing (a matter of) bounty (X -tifully), fair speech.

Notes

Made in the USA
Monee, IL
04 February 2020